Praise for Susan Shumsky:

· "Shumsky has been there. That's what makes her a great teacher."
—Larry Dossey, MD,
best-selling author of *Healing Worlds*

"What I enjoy most about Susan is her ability to write and speak about practical spiritual matters that mean the most to people in a way that is simple and easy to understand."
—Ellen Davis, minister,
Unity Church of New Hope, Denton, Texas

"She knows her subject and uses personal sharing to illustrate application of spiritual teachings with humor and clarity. I recommend her."
—John Butler, spiritual director, Unity of Corvallis, Oregon

"Dr. Susan's message is so important—we all need this teaching!"
—Rev. Christy L. Hancock, Unity Center of Practical
Christianity, Long Beach, Mississippi

Susan Shumsky, DD

ASCENSION

Connecting With the Immortal Masters and Beings of Light

New Page Books
A Division of The Career Press, Inc.
Pompton Plains, NJ

ASCENSION
EDITED AND TYPESET BY KARA KUMPEL
Cover design by Dutton & Sherman Design
Printed in the U.S.A.
Unless otherwise credited, all illustrations are by the author.

To order this title, please call toll-free 1-800-CAREER-1 (NJ and Canada: 201-848-0310) to order using VISA or MasterCard, or for further information on books from Career Press.

Divine Revelation is a service mark registered with the United Stated Patent Office.

Ascension can familiarize readers with the highly specialized, complex subjects of meditation and ascension, but in no way claims to fully teach the techniques described. Therefore, personal instruction is recommended.

Ascension is not an independent guide for self-healing. Susan Shumsky is not a medical doctor, psychiatrist, or psychologist, and she does not diagnose diseases or prescribe treatments. No medical claims or cures are implied in this book, even if specific "benefits" or "healing" are mentioned. Readers are advised to practice the methods in this book only under guidance and supervision of a qualified medical doctor or psychiatrist, and to use these methods at their own risk.

Susan Shumsky, Divine Revelation®, Teaching of Intuitional Metaphysics, New Page Books, and any other affiliate, agent, assign, licensee, and authorized representatives make no claim or obligation and take no legal responsibility for the effectiveness, results, or benefits of reading this book or of using the suggested methods; deny all liability for any injuries or damages that readers may incur; and are to be held harmless against any claim, liability, loss or damage caused by or arising from following any suggestions made in this book or from contacting anyone listed in this book or at *www.divinerevelation.org*.

The Career Press, Inc., 220 West Parkway, Unit 12
Pompton Plains, NJ 07444
www.careerpress.com
www.newpagebooks.com

Library of Congress Cataloging-in-Publication Data

Shumsky, Susan G.
  Ascension : connecting with the immortal masters and beings of light / by Susan Shumsky.
    p. cm.
  Includes bibliographical references and index.
  ISBN 978-1-60163-092-6
    1. Divine Revelation (Organization) 2. Spiritual life. 3. Spirituality. 4. Ascended masters. I. Title.

BP605.D59S57 2010
299'.93--dc22
                                                                              2009045347

This book is written with great love for those who possess the extraordinary faith required to achieve the precious gift of eternal union with God. It is especially dedicated to those who accept that they can walk beyond death, and will settle for nothing less than physical immortality.

Preface to Milton: A Poem
by William Blake

And did those feet in ancient time,
Walk upon Englands mountains green:
And was the holy Lamb of God,
On Englands pleasant pastures seen!

And did the Countenance Divine,
Shine forth upon our clouded hills?
And was Jerusalem builded here,
Among these dark Satanic Mills?

Bring me my Bow of burning gold;
Bring me my Arrows of desire:
Bring me my Spear: O clouds unfold:
Bring me my Chariot of fire!

I will not cease from Mental Fight,
Nor shall my Sword sleep in my hand:
Till we have built Jerusalem,
In Englands green & pleasant Land.

Would to God that all the Lords people were Prophets.
— Numbers XI Chapter 29

Acknowledgments

Many people have generously contributed to this project. With their help, creating this book has been a joyous experience. Thank you to all the staff at New Page books, especially Michael Pye, for encouraging me to finally publish this book. I am grateful to Kara Kumpel, Kirsten Dalley, Diana Ghazzawi, and Laurie Kelly-Pye, who have added their expertise to this project.

I am grateful to Joanna Cherry, Libby Maxey, Sharula Dux, the real "Joseph," Sean David Morton, Andrew Blagg, and so many others who offered their beautiful stories and experiences. I thank Rian Leichter and P.J. Worley for continuing to support and promote our beautiful teachings.

I acknowledge our dear departed ones Dr. Peter Meyer, founder of Teaching of Intuitional Metaphysics; Rich Bell; and Maharishi Mahesh Yogi; my beloved mentors, who taught me how to experience God and to contact the beings of light. I give gratitude to all of my divine spiritual mentors, the beautiful divine beings, for guiding me and creating miracles throughout this project.

Thank you to all of my students, who make my efforts worthwhile. I give thanks to all those who participate in my educational programs.

I am especially grateful to Jeff and Deborah Herman. Thank you for your consistent faith, enthusiasm, support, friendship, and loyalty. Thank you for continuing to believe in me, through thick, thin, and otherwise.

Contents

Part III: Mystical Encounters

Part IV: Building Your Light Body

Part V: How to Ascend Now

Part VI: Greeting Your Inner Teachers

Foreword

For eons, humanity has experienced—and fully believed—a reality of limitation: we are small, powerless in the face of life's difficulties of lack, ill health, aging, death, war, and natural catastrophe.

We made up death long ago, when we lost our knowing that we are one with God. Believing death to be the end of soul and spirit has caused endless grief. Illness came directly out of warped thought and emotion to affect the body. Lack came from believing that physical reality is the only reality.

Now, for the first time in a very long time, humanity as a whole is lifting out of these beliefs. Yes, there is still ignorance and darkness, but the truth of divinity at the center of each person's consciousness can no longer be held back. It is bursting out, a blazing light, to shine through everything we know—and change it, every bit of it.

We are unlimited. Knowing that Goddess/God is the infinite and constant source of all good replaces the experience of lack with that of abundance of every kind of good. There is no need—and, in spite of all appearance, no natural course—for the body to age or die. If the spirit of a loved one leaves its body, knowing that life goes on—and on—afterward, soothes grief. If war or natural catastrophe is about to happen, our divinity can direct us out of harm's way.

A mind and heart fully united with its spirit may live in a body of perfect health, beauty, and eternal life. Completing one's purpose on the earth plane, a person may raise the frequencies of the body and step through into a lighter realm, leaving no form behind. Knowing we are one not only with divinity, but with all of life, ends dissonance between people, ends war, and returns us to our natural stewardship of Earth. The same knowing prompts us to serve as best we may, listening always, guided always, by our divinity.

This book explores our unlimited possibility as a divine human being in the world. It is a facet in the gem of expanding enlightenment upon our planet, and a true gift to the reader.

—Joanna Cherry, DD
Author of *Ascension for You and Me*, *Living Mastery*, and *Self-Initiations*
Founder, Ascension Mastery International
www.ascensionmastery.com

Part I

Opening Your Pathway to Ascension

Chapter 1

You Are Immortal

If you look in deep water only, you will find the pearl.
If you keep to the shore, you will find broken shells only.
—Sri Swami Sivananda

You will never die.

You are an immortal being of light, and you live forever in a body of light. This physical body that you temporarily inhabit is not your true home. You reside in a beauteous, radiant body of luminous spheres in multiple dimensions. You have never been born and you never die. You are ageless, without beginning or end.

Until now, you have probably identified yourself as your physical body, perishable and fleeting, subject to birth, survival, growth, change, decay, and death. Without a vision of immortality, you see only the shell. Without recognizing the underlying permanence of your being, you perceive only the chains of mortal life.

Beyond the mortal boundaries of your physical form, you embody luminous vibratory bodies in multiple dimensions. This claim might seem fantastic, but it concurs with the latest developments in theoretical physics. Superstring theory envisions a 10-dimensional or 11-dimensional space-time in which elementary particles are like musical notes played on a violin—"excitation modes" of inconceivably tiny elementary strings.

In other words, everything in the universe is made of vibration and light in manifold dimensions—including you. Infinitesimal elementary particles are swirling, shifting waves of colliding vibrations. These subtle elements, when broken down into their primary components, are simply pure energy. There is nothing in this cosmos with any solidity or substance whatsoever.

This book will open your eyes to these dimensions beyond mortal boundaries. You will begin a journey of awakening to your immortal self, which is who you really are. This light being of divine radiance and glory is your true nature, beyond the physical realm of death. You are not this body. You are not this mind. You are a magnificent being of brilliant, beauteous light—a being that never dies.

You Are the Source of Wisdom

Deep within your soul is a wise sage, the source of all wisdom. This "in-house counselor" is hidden deep in the recesses of your heart. Like a treasure buried at the bottom of the sea, it can only be used when brought to the surface. You have the capacity to dive deep within, recover this treasure, and open it. Only it takes faith in yourself and trust in a higher power.

This book guides you into the profound depths of that ocean to reclaim the "pearl of great price."[1] It is said that this cannot be gained by gold, silver, onyx, sapphire, coral, or pearls, for "the price of wisdom is above rubies."[2] Where is such wisdom found? Where is the treasure more precious than any cargo from the seven seas? It is the chamber of jewels within your own heart.

You are that treasure.

You are not alone and never have been. From your very first breath, a divine, immortal being of great light and beauty stood at the bedside of your mother, breathing vital energy into your being, kindling the very spark of life. And, when it comes time to leave this world, this radiant, eternal light-being will guide you home again.

This luminous inner divine being is all-powerful. It loves you unconditionally and is with you always. It will never leave you. This divine radiance within your soul is your own inner counselor, whom you might call your guardian angel, inner guru, higher self, divine being, inner divinity, or master-teacher within.

Nothing happens without your inner teacher's guidance. With every step you take, every decision, every move, your resplendent inner guru is always within you, guiding you, comforting you, and bringing you peace—even when you are not consciously aware of it.

Now is the time to realize your radiant, beloved inner guru. Now is the time to open to the divine effulgence within yourself. Now is the time to wake up and realize who you truly are—an everlasting, powerful, vast, glorious being.

You have picked up this book today because you seek inner wisdom. Perhaps you have already awakened to profound inner realities. Or maybe you think you have not. In either case, this book can help you develop a deep understanding of the immortal nature of your being.

How can I say this with such confidence? Because the wisdom and methods in this book have already helped tens of thousands of people realize their own eternal nature for themselves.

What You Will Learn Here

Many psychic mediums say they "channel" so-called higher beings. They consider these "spirit guides" to be external entities, disconnected from the soul of the "channeler." But in this book you will learn who the real divine beings are and where they truly live. You will discover the wise, all-powerful, all-loving, undying nature of your own eternal higher self and the loving teachers who guide you on your pathway.

Here you will meet many divine beings on this journey to self-discovery. Some of them are traditional deities, archangels, ascended beings, and masters from worldwide cultures and traditions. Others are personal to you. All of them are eager to meet you and communicate with you.

In this book you will explore:

- Who are the ascended masters and divine beings and how to meet them.
- Stories, beautiful paintings, and drawings of these immortal beings of light.
- What it means to experience ascension and walk beyond death.
- How to begin your own ascension process.
- Stories about miraculous encounters with ascended masters.
- Stories of some ascended master messengers.

- Stories of people living today who might be ascended masters.
- How to meet your own inner divine teachers and discover their names.
- How to hear, see, feel, and get "signals" from your inner teachers.
- Messages from the divine beings and masters of immortality.

FAQs About Ascension

Let us begin now by answering some of the questions you might have about ascension, masters of immortality, and what is covered in this book:

Q: What is immortality?

A: Immortality is eternal life. It means living beyond death. You have an immortal spirit, an eternal soul that never dies, even when your physical body dies. You live forever in that body of light, no matter what physical bodies you inhabit during your cycles of incarnation.

Q: What is ascension?

A: Ascension means consciously living forever in your body of light. After you attain ascension, you no longer need to experience birth or death in a human body. You can appear whenever, wherever, and in any form, according to your will.

Q: Who are the inner teachers?

A: They are radiant, wise masters of light within you: beautiful, divine, radiant light-beings dwelling in your own heart and soul. They may be deities, angels, archangels, ascended masters, divine beings, or aspects of your own higher self, such as your "I AM" self or soul self. You will discover them as you read this book.

Q: What is an ascended master?

A: Ascended masters are enlightened humans who have attained physical immortality by transforming their physical bodies into more refined, luminous, subtle material. In this book, you will read about many of them and see how some of them have appeared.

Q: Can ordinary people attain ascension?

A: Anyone with a sincere heart can aspire to this lofty pinnacle of human expression in divine form. Few have achieved this goal, but it is open to all. In this book you will learn more about walking beyond death and attaining physical immortality.

Q: How can I communicate with ascended masters and spiritual beings?

A: The entire secret to receiving messages from these divine beings is to ask for it. Anyone with earnest desire can receive divine revelations within their own heart through subtle sight, sound, and sensing. Through this book you will begin to do that.

Q: Are the methods in this book difficult to practice?

A: This book is easy to understand, logical, and practical, with simple-to-learn methods requiring no previous experience, background, training, or knowledge.

Q: Is this yet another ascended master cult, with strict rules and regulations?

A: This is not a cult. The universal techniques offered here impose no restrictions and are compatible with other religious philosophies, lifestyles, and personal beliefs.

Q: What if I do not agree with what is proposed here?

A: You may not agree with the concept of physical immortality. You may think that death cannot be overcome. However, if you have an open mind and are willing to participate in the experiment, this book can awaken you to the possibility of eternal life, beyond mortal limitations.

Eternal Life Is Yours

Eternity is your own nature. It is not something far away, impossible to attain, or reserved only for prophets who lived thousands of years ago. You were born to live immortal life and walk beyond death now. You have within your own soul a resplendent being of light that never dies. That is who you really are. Trust in that and place your life in the hands of that divine master of immortality. That inner guru will guide you home again to the place of perfect peace and eternal life—your true abode.

You are blessed and beloved of God, and your immortal self is one with God. When you find that buried treasure, never will you be alone again. This book will open your mind and heart to the abundant riches of that treasure chest within. You will discover and meet the immortal masters of light. You will develop your own awareness of eternal life within you. Your heart and soul will open to new vistas of consciousness not yet awakened within you. You will sail into an ocean of eternal life on waves of bliss.

Let us begin our inner journey to immortal life now.

Chapter 2

Who Are the Immortal Masters?

The best argument I know for an immortal life is
the existence of a man who deserves one.
—William James

Ascension is a state of eternal life, attained when an individual bypasses death and continues to live indefinitely. Does this sound far-fetched? For sure. But let us explore this seemingly unbelievable possibility now. Although all humans are born of a human womb, and are therefore programmed for death with every breath, I believe that some rare beings have managed to walk beyond death. So let us open our minds to the prospect that perpetual life does exist.

If you only believe what your senses say, immortal beings cannot and do not exist. All you see around you is the cycle of life and death. All living things are born, grow, age, and die—whether plant, animal, or human. Therefore the idea that a human or any other being could live indefinitely would certainly warp anyone's sense of reality.

We will begin our exploration of eternal life with the study of immortal masters. Then, later in this book, after you have seen that such beings might possibly exist, you will make a new leap of faith, to see how you might possibly aspire to ascension yourself.

Immortal Masters

Who are the masters of immortality? It is said they are immortal beings whose sole concern is for the preservation and welfare of this planet and its evolution. Ascended masters have attained the supreme state of spiritual enlightenment and have passed beyond the physical plane to dwell in the realm of supernal radiant light, each one serving God in his or her own unique way.

During their earthly life, these loving, compassionate beings apparently transformed their physical bodies into the finest physical material—*akasha*, a Sanskrit word meaning the element of ether or space. (The other four elements are earth, water, fire, and air.) They further de-densified their bodies, until they experienced that the primary building blocks of bodily elements are ultimately light and sound, with no gross material substance whatsoever. In this way, they mastered their material bodies and walked beyond death. *Soruba samadhi* (physical immortality) is the Sanskrit name for this exalted state.

In theory, this state is possible for every living human to attain. The status of ascended master is achieved through intense devotion to and identification with God. Ascended masters have surrendered to God to such a profound extent that they experience oneness with God continually. They fully identify themselves as God, and therefore as unlimited, acting from the level of infinite possibilities. They know themselves as immortal, perfect, and whole, because, in reality, everyone is already immortal, perfect, and whole.

Ascended masters have merged the physical body with the spiritual body, the body of God within, because, in reality, there is no difference between the human body and God's body. We are already fully merged and unified with God. The only difference between ordinary humans and ascended beings is they have fully realized their immortal nature—not only their immortal soul, but also on the level of their gross, material, physical body.

Ascension and Descension

An ascended state of mind and body apparently manifests under two rare circumstances: First, through a human transforming the physical body into light—"ascension." Or secondly, through a deity precipitating a physical body—"descension."

Ascension

A human being who has attained the status of immortality is an "ascended master." Out of the innumerable possible bodies where a soul may take incarnation, a human body is a rare, fortunate occurrence. That is because the human is the only species with the capacity to achieve the highest state of spiritual liberation. Not even angels and deities can attain the supreme state, called *Brahman* consciousness.

Ascended masters begin life in the ordinary fashion—born into a womb. However, they perfected themselves through lifetimes of spiritual practices. They completed their need for worldly desires and overcame all limitations. They burnt all "seeds of karma" or "seeds of desire" (*samskaras* in Sanskrit), which propel ordinary humans to incarnate into physical form repeatedly. Therefore, they no longer need to reincarnate. They have realized the full bloom of supreme spiritual enlightenment, called *moksha* in Sanskrit, meaning "liberation."

However, these amazing attainments are only the first baby steps toward ascension. In addition to their state of higher consciousness of supreme knowledge and liberation, ascended masters have also achieved the blessed state of physical immortality. Their body has transformed into a body of light. They do not and cannot die.

Their body is infused with an intense spiritual vibration and divine grace. A fragrance of holy sanctity and blessings wafts from their being. They live forever, coming and going at will, appearing and disappearing as needed. Their only desires are to serve, to lift all creatures into a higher spiritual vibration, and to heal all those who ask for healing.

Descension

In contrast to an ascended master, an *avatar* is a descension, or a deity taking embodiment in physical form. The Sanskrit root *ava* means "revealing" and *avataran* means "descending, coming down." *Avatar* means God revealed in an embodied state—that is, an incarnation of God. A full avatar is a full divine incarnation in a physical body, with full omniscience, complete control over all the elements of nature and over all the senses and sense objects.

Avatars are said to be of divine origin and birth and do not need a womb or a gestation period. They can simply appear, self-generating a body, possessing no human limitations. An avatar comes for a specific purpose when the Earth needs divine intervention. Ancient scriptures from India count 10 full avatars of the supreme Lord Vishnu, and many Indians believe Lord Krishna was the last full avatar. He lived about 3000 BC. However, many people think that Jesus was also a full avatar.

White Brotherhood

In the late 18th century, author of *The Cloud Upon the Sanctuary*, Karl von Eckartshausen may be the first in the West to write of a secret organization of enlightened mystics that live in ascended bodies after physical death. Eckartshausen called this organization, which guides the spiritual development of humanity, the "Council of Light." Later, H.P. Blavatsky called these beings "Masters of the Hidden Brotherhood" or the *Mahatmas* ("great souls").

The "Great White Lodge" of ascended masters, whose worldly headquarters is said to be the Himalayas, is a group of immortal beings whose sole desire is for the benefit of humanity and welfare of the Earth. These untiring disciples of God are working continually to preserve this planet's integrity, promote world peace, and guide humanity. Many people have had visitations from masters of the White Lodge, or have been initiated into its school or fraternity, the "White Brotherhood," or "White Sisterhood," themselves.

Just to clarify, the White Lodge is a group of divine beings of every race and nationality. The name has nothing to do with the color of skin, but with the purity of soul and the bright light emanating from the subtle body.

It is believed that the masters of the Great White Lodge often gather in their ascended master retreats, where they are ever vigilant to maintain the equilibrium of the Earth. Wherever there is strife or dissension, they can be called upon to correct the situation and perform their harmonizing work. Their work is aided by humans. Only at the call of humanity do they intercede. They never interfere with human affairs unless bidden.

In order to receive their intervention or blessings, all you need do is ask. In fact, the entire premise of this book is *Ask, and it shall be given you.*[1] You may call on these divine beings at any time to assist you. Ask often, for they do not come uninvited, unless there is a dire emergency.

In this book you will meet divine beings, ascended masters, avatars, and deities from several cultures. This book is in no way complete. It introduces you to a mere sampling of the many immortal masters throughout the world.

Ascended Master Retreats

Rev. Dr. Joanna Cherry, who is, in my opinion, one of the foremost authorities on ascension, has generously contributed to this book with the following description of ascended master retreats:

Figure 2a. The "Beautiful Many": The assembly of divine beings, angels, archangels, and deities is available to you at any moment. All you have to do is ask. Etching by Gustav Doré.

Ascended masters are people, just like you and me, who have identified with their own divinity to such a degree that death is no longer necessary. When such people complete earthly life and are ready for a lighter realm, they quicken the frequencies of their body and simply step into the new dimension, leaving no physical form behind. Then the focus is service to humanity and Earth, and in this work a physical body may again be resumed, at least temporarily.

Ascended masters live and work in retreats, usually on lighter dimensions, which are scattered throughout the world. In the United States, both Mount Shasta in far Northern California and Mount Moran of the Grand Teton mountains are known to be homes of ascended masters.

Ascended master retreats emanate such spiritual power that people are often drawn to them. When we desire to experience the greatness of our being, and to realize that we are, as it says in the Bible, the very likeness and image of God, being near one of these retreats can be helpful. We may communicate inwardly with the masters, whether we are near a retreat or not, and, in a lighter consciousness, we may even visit a retreat and experience wonderful gifts and blessings.

For many years, I have personally visited and served in these retreats. Here is a description of some of them:

Mount Shasta has a great golden hall for large gatherings of service or celebration. Most retreats have a similar hall. There are many smaller meeting rooms as well, and private rooms. Beautiful music often comes from both visible and invisible sources.

There is a "cleansing pool," as I call it—a beautiful round pool filled with sparkling golden liquid. Jumping into that pool cleanses not only your body, but also your emotions, your thoughts, your past—everything. And you do not even have to get wet.

Terraced gardens and fountains are covered with a sky like ours. You can walk through a forest of magnificent trees where nothing has been cut down, and visit a high waterfall. In a hall of records, histories are kept, including records of ascended masters. When you visit, you can be shown past lives that are important for you to know about.

Another thing others and I have experienced quite powerfully is a great crystalline pyramid that pulses in glowing colors of gold, pink, light blue, silver, aqua, and lavender. The inside of this pyramid is hollow, and people are invited inside for a spiritual initiation, or a healing, or to have uplifting crystals implanted into their subtle, etheric body. Usually at least four masters participate in a ceremony of this kind.

One of the experiences I love best is to breathe the air of an ascended retreat. It is entirely different from the air of this dimension, even air as pure as Mount Shasta's, where I live. Retreat air is incredibly alive and loving. It has everything needed to sustain you, though most masters do eat and drink.

In the Grand Tetons ascended master retreat, there is a section for inventions. When people are ready for a helpful new invention, a master creates it, and at the right moment, he or she releases it into the thought stream of humanity. I believe this is the reason so many

Nobel prizes have been awarded to two different scientists for discovering the same thing at exactly the same time.

One of the most amazing devices in both Mount Shasta and the Tetons is the acceleration chair, which greatly speeds the frequencies of the body. Guy Ballard's books, *The Saint Germain Series,* tell of an old man who sits in this chair and is completely rejuvenated in minutes.

The ascended masters feel a deep desire to help humanity realize what they have realized. If you find yourself in this realm, you will be assisted to choose where and how you wish to serve. You may find yourself on a committee (they have many!) or even more than one, to serve a particular purpose such as the ending of hunger, peace in the Middle East, or the encouragement of freedom. Much communication is done telepathically, but there are also frequent meetings to share what has been done and contemplate the next steps of that project.

There are many different levels of mastery within the retreats. But all who dwell there are living in service, love, and joy, surrounded by beauty. Highly skilled masters may manifest things from the ethers for loving use. They can travel by thought, within moments, anywhere on Earth or in the universe. Their bodies are eternally youthful and beautiful. They desire that what they do and how they live will benefit everyone, and they are available to assist anyone at any time. Simply call upon them and ask. *Ask, and it will be given you.*

Part II

Meeting the Masters of Light

Chapter 3

The Ancient of Days

I am the resurrection, and the life...whosoever liveth and believeth in me shall never die. Believest thou this?
—Jesus Christ

This section of the book is devoted to recounting both the history and legend of several ascended masters, avatars, and other divine beings. Many immortal masters are living on Earth now and have done so for thousands of years, serving untiringly, lifting humanity out of ignorance into the light.

These divine beings never interfere with human affairs unless called upon. That is the divine law. You can ask them for help in times of need, and rejoice with them in times of joy. To get started, make simple requests such as, "I call upon [name of divine being] for [purpose] now."

In this section, you will get to know these divine beings. Then you can decide which beings to call upon, contact, or communicate with, and for what purpose. This chapter contains descriptions and stories about some ascended masters associated with the Judeo-Christian religion.

Jesus the Christ

The many miracles performed by Jesus are widely known, including instantaneous healing and resurrection of the dead. His life was the exemplar of ascension for all people. He demonstrated the conscious

35

mastery and dominion that every human being can attain. In fact, he declared that it is possible for anyone to perform miracles even greater than his.

When the stone was rolled away from the sepulcher of Jesus three days after his death, his body had mysteriously vanished, despite guards having watched the tomb day and night. He had transformed his body and lifted it to a higher vibration of divine radiance with a flash of light. Thus a mysterious photographic impression was imprinted on the relic believed to be his shroud, housed at St. John's Cathedral in Turin until 1988, when it was bequeathed to the Vatican.

A total of 17 appearances of Jesus after his resurrection are recorded in the Bible. The first was just outside the sepulcher, where Jesus appeared to Mary Magdalene, saying, "I ascend unto my Father, and your Father; and to my God and your God."[1] Later he visited his disciples, eating food to prove his body was still physical. He was not a spirit or ghost, but a flesh-and-blood human.

After these visitations, Jesus brought his disciples to the hill of Bethany, "And it came to pass, while he blessed them, he was parted from them, and carried up into heaven."[2] Easter is the holiday commemorating this event.

Figure 3a. Jesus the Christ: "I AM the light of the world: he that followeth ME shall not walk in darkness, but shall have the light of life."—John 8:12. Out of respect and adoration, Jesus of Nazareth was given the title "Christ," from the Greek word *christos*, meaning "anointed." Every individual has a "Christ self," an "anointed" higher self, an enlightened inner being. Jesus exemplifies the qualities of the Christ and can help you realize the Christ within you.

Saint Issa and Konar

A Russian physician, Nicolas Notovitch published *The Unknown Life of Christ* in 1894. During his extensive travels, he visited a Buddhist convent in Himis, near Leh, capital of Ladakh, India. There he found two ancient volumes, containing more than 200 verses, titled "The Life of St. Issa," which describe the travels of Jesus during his "lost years," between ages 13 and 29. This was later confirmed by both Swami Abhedananda and Nicholas Roerich, who independently traveled to Himis and found the same text.

According to the text, Issa spent six years in Varanasi, Rajagriha, the temple of Jagganath in Orissa, and other holy cities, where he studied the Vedas. Then he traveled into Nepal, Tibet, and Persia, teaching monism and denouncing idolatry. He returned to Jerusalem at age 29. Fascinating details of his life and teachings, missing from the Bible, are described in this ancient text.

During his travels to Persia, it is believed that Jesus studied with a powerful ascended master named Konar. His specialty is strength and self-empowerment, and he often appears carrying a sword.

Figure 3b. **Konar:** A Persian saint believed to be one of Jesus' teachers, Konar is known for enormous power and strength.

India's influence on Jesus pervades the New Testament. One example is the Gospel of John, which opens with, "In the beginning was the Word, and the Word was with God and the Word was God."[3] This is a direct quotation from *Krishna Yajurveda* and other Vedic scriptures: "In the beginning was Prajapati [God the Creator], with Him was the Word, and the Word was truly the Supreme Brahman."[4]

Figure 3c. **Mother Mary:** "And the angel came in unto her, and said, Hail thou that art highly favoured, the Lord is with thee: blessed art thou among women...and blessed is the fruit of thy womb." —Luke 1:28, 42.

Mother Mary

Many people believe that Mary, mother of Jesus, was lifted into heaven by a host of angels who carried her into glory out of her tomb. This event, called the "Assumption of Mary," became an article of faith in the Catholic Church in 1950 and is celebrated August 15 every year. It is believed that after her death she disappeared from her casket, raised from the dead by Jesus, leaving behind only a bed of roses. Thus, "assumption" is a word that Catholics use to describe the ascension process.

Saint John the Apostle

Members of The Church of Jesus Christ of Latter-Day Saints believe that Saint John the Apostle did not die; instead, his body was translated (ascended) so he could remain on Earth until the Second Coming. This belief is based on three passages; one is in the New Testament: "He shall not die; but, If I will that he tarry till I come, what is that to thee?"[5]

Another is in the *Book of Mormon*: "Therefore, more blessed are ye, for ye shall never taste of death; but ye shall live to behold all the doings of the Father unto the children of men, even until...I shall come in my glory with the powers of heaven."[6]

The last is in the Mormon *Doctrine and Covenants*: "Verily, verily, I say unto thee, because thou desirest this thou shalt tarry until I come in my glory, and shalt prophesy before nations, kindreds, tongues and people."[7]

Saint Francis of Assisi

Saint Francis (1182–1226), a monk from Assisi, Italy, stated, "My life is the Gospel of the Lord." He is known as a "mirror of Christ." As a youngster, on his way to Puglia to be armed as a knight, Francis saw a vision of God, who instructed him to return home.

Francis's life was transformed one day when he descended from his horse and placed money into a leper's hand and embraced him. Whereas he previously disdained lepers, now he visited their homes, gave them alms, and lovingly kissed their faces and hands.

Francis received a glimpse of his divine mission while praying in the dilapidated chapel of San Damiano: "With his eyes filled with tears he was gazing at the figure of the Crucified. He heard a voice coming from the Cross: 'Francis, go and repair my church which, as you see, is falling down.'"[8]

Francis interpreted this to mean that he should repair the chapel of San Damiano, so he took a horse and a bolt of expensive cloth from his father's shop and sold them in the marketplace to donate money to the church. When his father furiously denounced him publicly before the bishop of Assisi, Francis disinherited his family and stripped off his clothing. He returned everything to his father, even his clothes.

Figure 3d. **St. Francis of Assisi:** St. Francis knelt in the small, decrepit chapel of San Damiano when he received his first vision of God.

His divine mission to "repair my church" had larger scope than Francis first imagined. He taught that it is not enough to study the gospels; one must live them. He founded a brotherhood of monks who possessed nothing and dressed in simple tunics. Their lives embodied discipleship, brotherly love, faith, compassion, healing, and surrender to God. Francis often said, "My brothers should always take Christ as their model."

In 1209, Francis journeyed to Rome with his 11 disciples to receive official approval from Pope Innocent III, who was too busy to see them. One night the Pope had a dream that the Lateran (cathedral church of the city of Rome) was falling down and being supported on the shoulders of this poor monk from Assisi. The next day he sent for Francis and approved the rule of his order of monks.

Francis was the first known stigmatic, received in September 1224 on Mount Laverna. Brother Leo, one of his disciples, visited Francis on Mount Laverna and often saw him in such rapture that Francis lifted off the earth in levitation, surrounded with light and splendor. See his "Simple Prayer" on page 225.

Figure 3e. **God Took Enoch:** "And it came to pass after this that my spirit was translated And it ascended into the heavens: And I saw the holy sons of God. They were stepping on flames of fire: Their garments were white [and their raiment], And their faces shone like snow."—Book of Enoch, 71:1. Image courtesy of History of Science Collections, University of Oklahoma Libraries.

Enoch

Enoch (also Hanoch) is one of the few biblical prophets who "translated" (ascended). In the Bible, not much is said about Enoch, except that he lived for 365 years, and at age 65 he fathered Methuselah.

The book of Genesis states, "Enoch walked with God: and he was not; for God took him."[9] The book of Hebrews says, "By faith Enoch was translated that he should not see death; and was not found, because God had translated him: for before his translation he had this testimony, that he pleased God."[10]

The book of Enoch, also known as 1 Enoch, is one of the most important apocryphal works, and influenced early Christian and Gnostic beliefs. The Ethiopian Orthodox Church regards it as canonical. The Book of Enoch is quoted in the Bible in Jude 14–15.

Describing Enoch's visions of heavenly and hellish realms, the book portrays archangels, fallen angels, the Messiah, resurrection, final judgment, and a heavenly kingdom on earth. Interspersed with this material are calendar systems, geography, cosmology, astronomy, and meteorology.

Melchizedek

An *avatar* (divine incarnation) named Melchizedek (also Melchisedec), king of Salem, is mentioned in the Bible. He is an immortal being—unborn and undying, with no beginning or end, no mother or father.

Melchizedek is called a "priest of the most high God,"[11] and he gave Abraham his blessing, after which Abraham tithed to Melchizedek the spoils of battle. Soon after this, God made a covenant with Abraham that his seed would be as numberless as the stars in heaven and that his descendents would extend from the Nile River to the Euphrates.

In Psalms, King David mentions the "order of Melchizedek"—a priestly office: "The Lord hath sworn, and will not repent, Thou

Figure 3f. **Melchizedek and Abraham:** "Melchizedek king of Salem brought forth bread and wine: and he was the priest of the most high God." —Genesis 14:18. Image courtesy of History of Science Collections, University of Oklahoma Libraries.

art a priest for ever after the order of Melchizedek."[12] In Hebrews 7, Saint Paul interprets that this psalm refers to Jesus, as Messiah and high priest, sitting at the right hand of God, and that the priesthood of Jesus "in the order of Melchisedek" is undying—abiding forevermore.

Moses

Lawgiver of the Israelites, and author of the Torah (the first five books of the Bible), Moses was born in Egypt about 1391 BC into the tribe of Levi. He freed the Hebrews from Egyptian slavery, and, for 40 years, led them through the wilderness of Sinai to Canaan. Many miracles occurred, including the parting of the Red Sea, through which the Hebrews passed when pursued by the Egyptians. Also, Moses ascended Mount Sinai and received the Ten Commandments. He received instructions through the Ark of the Covenant, a mystical palanquin over which God appeared in a cloud. Manna (spiritual nourishment) rained from heaven to sustain the Hebrews when supplies ran low. When water was needed, Moses used his staff to locate it.

Figure 3g. **Moses:** "The Lord bless thee, and keep thee. The Lord make his face shine upon thee, and be gracious unto thee. The Lord lift up his countenance upon thee, and give thee peace." —Numbers 6:23–26. Moses led his people out of the bondage of Egypt (meaning "darkness") into the freedom of Canaan, the "promised land" of milk and honey. This journey symbolizes the path of the soul from the bondage of darkest ignorance to the freedom of enlightenment.

Although Moses led his people to the border of the "the land of milk and honey," he was not allowed to enter the Promised Land, because he had disobeyed God. At age 120 Moses died in Moab. The New Testament states that Jesus took his disciples Peter, James, and John to a high mountain and became transfigured into a light being, while Moses and Elijah appeared in their ascended forms (Matthew 17:1–9).

King David

David, second King of the Israelites, born circa 1037 BC, was a great warrior, poet, and musician. All the future kings of Judah sprang from his bloodline. Egypt and Assyria were both in decline when David ascended the throne. Thus he overcame the Philistines and conquered Jerusalem.

David purchased the land on Mount Moriah, where the Islamic Dome of the Rock stands now. Under this dome, the exposed bedrock of Mount Moriah is known as the "drinking stone" or "water of life." According to Judaism, the world is spiritually nourished from this stone—the metaphysical center of the universe—where God's presence is felt more intensely than anywhere else. This is where David established a permanent home for the Tabernacle and the Ark of the Covenant.

Figure 3h. **King David:** "It is a good thing to give thanks unto the Lord, and to sing praises unto thy name, O most High...upon an instrument of ten strings, and upon the psaltery; upon the harp with a solemn sound. For thou, Lord, hast made me glad through thy work: I will triumph in the works of thy hands." —Psalm 92:1–4. A fierce warrior and powerful King, David was also a divinely inspired poet. He played the psaltery, the instrument of the day, on which he sang through the Psalms of the Bible, which are divine songs cognized from Spirit. The Star of David represents Spirit and Matter in eternal union. The triangle pointing upward represents heaven and the one pointing downward represents earth. Together these create wholeness greater than the sum of the parts.

However, David was not allowed to build his Temple on Mount Moriah, because of the blood on his hands from slaughtering nations of enemies of Israel. His son Solomon was given the honor of building the Temple.

Elijah the Prophet

Elijah (also Elias), one of the greatest saints of the Bible, performed many miracles, including raising the dead and manifesting food endlessly. When Elijah knew God was about to take him into heaven, he traveled to Jericho with his disciple Elisha. As they stood on the banks of the Jordan River, "Elijah took his mantle, wrapped it together, and smote the waters."[13] The river divided, and Elijah and Elisha walked to the other side on dry land.

Elijah asked his disciple Elisha if he had a final request before God would take him away. Here is what transpired: "And Elisha said, I pray thee, let a double portion of thy spirit be upon me. And [Elijah] said, Thou hast asked a hard thing: nevertheless, if thou see me when I am taken from thee, it shall be so unto thee; but if not, it shall not be so. And it came to pass, as they still went on, and talked, that, behold, there appeared a chariot of fire, and horses of fire, and parted them both asunder: and Elijah went up by a whirlwind into heaven."[14]

After this event, Elisha took Elijah's mantle, smote the waters, and asked, "Where is the Lord God of Elijah?"[15] The waters parted and Elisha crossed over the Jordan again. Then the sons of the prophets in Jericho, who came to meet Elisha said, "The spirit of Elijah doth rest on Elisha,"[16] and they bowed on the ground before him.

Afterward, Elisha began performing miracles, making the Jordan River potable and riverbanks fertile. Thus, a transference of energy, called a "walk-in" or *parkaya pradesh* (Sankrit for "transmigration of the soul"), occurred. Elijah's spirit entered into his disciple Elisha.

In the Jewish religion, *Pesach* (Passover) is celebrated every spring with a meal called the *Seder.* One place-setting is designated for Elijah, with a glass of wine to welcome the guest. The door to the family home is left ajar so he may partake in the meal. At Jewish circumcision ceremonies, a chair is saved for Elijah, who is required to witness all circumcisions when the "sign of the covenant" is placed upon the child. Thus, Judaism acknowledges Elijah's immortality.

Christians believe the immortal Elijah appeared at the Transfiguration of Jesus. Mormons believe Elijah returned in 1836 to visit Joseph Smith, and the Baha'i faith says that Elijah returned in 1844 in Shiraz, Iran, as the Bab.

Metatron

In the Jewish Rabbinic tradition, Metatron is considered the crown in the Tree of Life—the highest in the hierarchy of archangels. He is mentioned in the Talmud and other medieval mystical texts as the heavenly scribe. In the Kabbalist Zohar, Metatron is a heavenly priest and also the angel that led the Israelites through the wilderness in Exodus:

Figure 3i. **Elijah the Prophet:** The ascension of Elijah, a Jewish prophet considered to be immortal. While his disciple Elisha watched from the bank of the Jordan River, Elijah was taken up into heaven in a chariot of fire.

"Behold, I send an Angel before thee, to keep thee in the way, and to bring thee into the place which I have prepared. Beware of him, and obey his voice, provoke him not; for he will not pardon your transgressions: for my name [is] in him."[17]

In the apocryphal The Third Book of Enoch, Enoch is transformed into Metatron: "I asked Metatron and said to him: 'Why art thou called by the name of thy Creator, by seventy names? Thou art greater than all the princes, higher than all the Angels, beloved more than all the servants, honored above all the mighty ones in kingship, greatness and glory: why do they call thee Youth in the high heavens?' He answered and said to me: 'Because I am Enoch, the son of Jared.'"[18]

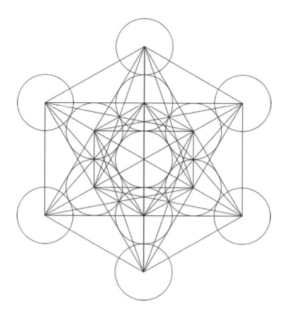

Figure 3j. **Metatron's Cube:** This is a holy symbol, drawn around an object or person to ward off demonic energies. In Kabbalist texts, Metatron forms the cube from his soul. Containing all five Platonic Solids, the Fruit of Life, and Star of David, the holy cube was used as a containment circle or creation circle in alchemy.

Holy Spirit

The Holy Spirit is traditionally one of the aspects of the Holy Trinity. It is the Spirit of God within every living thing, and the Spirit of wholeness within you. God is present everywhere and within everything. God lives, breathes, moves, and has its being in you, through you, and around you. There is nowhere that God is not. God is in every fiber of your being. That indwelling Spirit, God in you, is the Holy Spirit. (See Figure 3k on page 47.)

The Holy Spirit has both male and female aspects that you might contact and communicate with. The female aspect of the Holy Spirit is called AAA, which is pronounced Ah-ay-uh. The term AAA represents the Holy Trinity. That is because "A," the first word of the alphabet, is number "one," and oneness three times, AAA, is the Trinity. AAA is one of the main divine beings with which I regularly communicate.

But the Comforter, which is the Holy Ghost, whom the Father
will send in my name, he shall teach you all things,
and bring all things to your remembrance,
whatsoever I have said unto you.
—John 14:26

IAGA and IAGIM

The term *IAGA* is an acronym for the words "I AM God Almighty." Therefore, this divine inner teacher, which identifies itself as IAGA, might be the name of your own God self, the devotional aspect of God within you.

IAGIM is an acronym for "I AM God in Mankind." This is another inner teacher with which you might contact and communicate. It represents God within all human beings on Earth.

The Elohim

In the Torah (The Old Testament), *Elohim* is the name of God as creator and judge of the universe. It is one of three names attributed to God as creator in the book of Genesis. The Hebrew word *Elohim* is the plural form of *El,* the Canaanite word for God, but with a curious added vowel. God as plural might reveal that God is creator as God/Goddess or a pair of twin flames. (See my book *Exploring Chakras* for more information about how the universe is created by the God/Goddess.)

Figure 3k. **The Holy Spirit:** This divine being is traditionally depicted as a dove shining rays onto the Earth. Here, a female figure represents the feminine aspect of God. She stands on the sun of the omnipresent eternal Godhead. She is shown in white, representing absolute purity, radiating unconditional love.

Figure 3l. Twin Flames: The soul selves of twin flames hold hands within a diamond. The diamond represents their eternal union, beyond time and space. The bright sun of God shines upon their eternal love. The entire creation is made manifest through the union of male/female or yin/yang. Without duality, there can be no visible universe.

Many scholars believe the root of *Elohim* means "power" or "majesty." So Elohim might be the powers, majesties, or multiplied might that God uses as creator of the universe. Some metaphysicians believe the Elohim are highly advanced extraterrestrial beings that visit Earth when humans need help with planetary evolution. They are said to have propagated the human species: "That the sons of the Elohim saw the daughters of men that they were fair; and they took them wives of all which they chose."[19]

In the ascended master teachings, beginning with H.P. Blavatsky and Theosophy, the Elohim are hosts of spiritual beings called "Lords of Meditation" *(dhyani chohan)*. The "Seven Mighty Elohim" are equated with the "Seven Spirits Before the Throne" in the biblical Book of Revelation. They are said to be the cosmic creators of this system of worlds, the "Seven Builders Around the Throne" of ancient Sumeria, Gods of the seven pole-stars, whose seats were in the never-setting stars around the throne of Anu.

Archangels and Elohim of the Seven Rays

The archangels are seven beings of light that protect and assist humans in their spiritual evolution. Each of them represents one of the seven rays of God—seven unique emanations of God's holy light and love. Every individual is said to belong to one of these seven rays.

Figure 3m. **The Seven Archangels:** These supreme angels are radiating from the white Central God-Sun. Each of the seven is assigned to a particular ray of light (counter clockwise). **Michael** is pictured at the top in blue ray with a flaming blue sword. **Jophiel** is shown with a golden book in gold ray. **Chamuel** is seen with a pink heart, seated in pink ray. **Gabriel** is portrayed with a lily and pyramid in white ray. **Raphael** is in green ray with a green lantern and the serpent of healing. **Uriel** is in red ray with an open hand holding a flame. **Zadkiel** is in violet ray with his symbol, the transmuting violet flame.

The seven Elohim, which bestow and direct the seven flames that make up the sevenfold flame of the sacred fire, are associated with the seven rays and seven archangels of the rays of the Christ.

The chart in Figure 3n on the following page lists the qualities of the seven rays and equates the rays with specific colors and divine beings. The names of the archangels and Elohim are mentioned, along with their consorts or counterparts, known as their twin flames. Every archangel has an archeia, and every Elohim has a twin flame. Their retreats, or sacred places on Earth where they are said to reside, are delineated.

The chart is based upon a general consensus of ascended master teachings currently recognized. However, I would suggest you make your own determination by meditating with these divine beings and receiving direct messages from them. You can use the meditation on page 256 of this book.

Archangels and Elohim

No.	Ray	Color	Archangel	Archeia	Archangel Retreat	Elohim	Twin Flame	Elohim Retreat
1	Illumined Faith, Strength, Will, Divine Protection	Blue	Michael: "One who is as God."	Faith	Canadian Rockies, near Lake Louise, Canada	Hercules	Amazonia	Half Dome, Yosemite Valley, California
2	Wisdom, Illumination, Constancy, Understanding	Yellow	Jophiel: "Beauty of God"	Christine	South of Great Wall near Lanchow, China	Helios (Apollo)	Lumina	Lower Saxony, Germany
3	Love, Compassion	Pink	Chamuel: "Seeker of God"	Charity	St. Louis, Missouri	Heros	Amora	Lake Winnipeg, Manitoba, Canada
4	Purity, Poise Harmony, Resurrection, Ascension	White	Gabriel: "Strong man of God"	Hope	Between Sacramento and Mount Shasta, California	Purity	Astrea	Gulf of Archangel White Sea, Russia
5	Science, Truth, Precipitation, Healing	Green	Raphael: "God Who Heals"	Mother Mary	Fatima, Portugal	Cyclopea	Virginia	Altai Range, where China, Siberia, and Mongolia Meet
6	Grace, Peace, Service, Brotherhood, Ministration	Purple/ Gold, Ruby	Uriel: "Fire or Light of God"	Aurora	Tatra Mountains South of Krakow, Poland	Peace	Aloha	Hawaiian Islands
7	Freedom, Mercy, Transmutation, Ritual, Invocation, Transcendence	Violet	Zadkiel: "Righteousness of God"	Amethyst	Cuba	Arcturus	Victoria (Victory)	Near Luanda, Angola, Africa

Figure 3n.

Chapter 4

Divine Beings of the West

The stars shall fade away, the sun himself grow dim with age,
and nature sink in years, but thou shalt flourish in immortal
youth, unhurt amidst the wars of elements, the wrecks of
matter, and the crush of worlds.
—Joseph Addison

Hundreds of divine beings and masters are mentioned in various ascended master teachings—too many to cover in this book. However, in this chapter, we will meet a few known in Western mysticism, in the ancient classical world, and in Native American cultures. A more complete list can be found by visiting the Websites listed on page 119 of this book.

Saint Germain

The Comte de Saint Germain was an enigmatic character that charmed European diplomatic circles in the 18th century. His origin, real name, and so-called death remain a mystery. His whereabouts at any given moment was an enigma. Historians consider him an inscrutable personage.

Many writers believe he was the son of Prince Rakoczy Ferenz, Franz Rakoczy II (1676–1735), prince of Transylvania, national hero of Hungary. Saint Germain was said to be the wealthy heir to the house of Rakoczy.

He is described as a man of small height and slight build with dark complexion and black hair, usually powdered and tied back with a black ribbon. He dressed in well-tailored black velvet and satin clothes. He had a mania for diamonds, wearing them on his rings, watch, snuff box, sword, and on his buckles, estimated by jewelers to be worth 200,000 francs. He had no wrinkles and always looked youthful. He consumed no meat or wine and always dined alone.

Saint Germain was the foremost scholar and linguist of his day and excelled in history, chemistry, alchemy, poetry, art, music, and swordsmanship. He spoke French, German, English, Italian, Portuguese, Spanish, Greek, Latin, Sanskrit, Arabic, and Chinese so fluently that natives did not consider him foreign.

He played several musical instruments and composed music and an opera. His expertise was the violin and viola, with technique equal to Paganini. He painted portraits showing sparkling gemstones that matched the brilliance of the original stones. He was consulted about the authenticity of paintings by great masters. He introduced new methods of tanning and dyeing into the court.

Saint Germain removed flaws from diamonds and transformed them into perfect stones for Louis XV. He transformed an ordinary 12-sol piece into gold for Casanova. Marquis de Valbelle watched him transmute a silver 6-franc piece into gold in his alchemical furnace. Saint Germain claimed he learned these secrets in India.

Figure 4a. **Saint Germain:** The "man who never dies" was instrumental in the birth of many teachings. He is depicted in his ascended form, immersed in the Violet Flame of transmutation, purification, and healing.

A letter dated October 23, 1778, from Mr. Dresser to Baron Uffel, judge of the Court of Appeal in Celle, stated that Saint Germain was 182 years old but looked 40. Dresser said Saint Germain possessed certain liquid drops by which he achieved all his results, including the transmutation of metals, leathers, and diamonds. He stated that Saint Germain had no income or letters of credit but lived in grand style with abundant silver and gold coins that appeared freshly minted.

Madame Pompadour, mistress of Louis XV, testified that Saint Germain gave a lady of the court an "elixir of life" that preserved her energy and beauty for more than 25 years. According to Saint Germain, this "philosopher's stone" contained 777 ingredients. Countess de Genlis and Ninon de l'Enclos both received this youth remedy. One of the most beautiful women in France, the controversial author and courtesan Ninon de l'Enclos was age 80 when her grandson fell in love with her.

Dr. Raymond Bernard's *The Great Secret of Count Saint Germain* reports that the French ambassadress Madame de Gergy saw Saint Germain in 1710 in Venice as Marquis Balletti. At that time he looked 45 years old, and he gave her an elixir that preserved her youth a long time.

Figure 4b. **Ninon de l'Enclos:** "Few people resist age, but I believe I am not yet overcome by it." —Ninon de L'Enclos, in a letter to Saint-Evremond.

About 50 years later Madame de Gergy saw him in Paris and asked if he was the Marquis' son. He replied, "I lived in the previous century and am the Marquis himself." She protested, "You could not be, because you look younger now than you did then. He said with a smile, "Madame, I am very old." When she remarked that he was nearly 100 years old, he replied, "That is not impossible."

The musician Jean-Philippe Rameau also claimed he had met Saint Germain in 1710 at about age 45 under the name Marquis de Montferrat.

Saint Germain always knew, in advance, of every person's arrival, and who sent him. He knew strangers' questions before they were asked. He knew minute details about their lives and associates, even accurately predicting their dates of death. When his presence was needed, he disappeared from one place and reappeared elsewhere.

He had the uncanny ability to write one page with his left hand and another with his right, place the two sheets over each other, shine a light behind them, and the two pages matched exactly, letter for letter, stroke for stroke, as if they were photocopies. He could repeat the entire contents of a newspaper several days later.

Comte de Saint Germain's detailed knowledge of history was baffling to the greatest historians of his time. He predicted the French Revolution to Marie Antoinette, recorded in the book *Souvenirs sur Marie Antoinette* by Comtesse d'Adhemar.

Saint Germain was employed by the French and other European governments as a secret agent and diplomat. He was the guest of Peter III of Russia and the Shah of Persia. Frederick the Great of Germany, Voltaire, Madame de Pompadour, Rousseau, Chatham, and Walpole all knew him and were curious about his origin.

Voltaire bestowed on him the epithet, "a man who knows everything and who never dies." Napoleon was so fascinated with Saint Germain that he formed a special commission to investigate his life, but the collection of memoirs was destroyed in a fire at the Hotel de Ville in Paris in 1871.

Saint Germain was the lord of the Theosophical Illuminists and established a lodge in the Castle of Ermenonville, 30 miles from Paris. He taught the infamous Count Alessandro Cagliostro (1743–1795), founder of the Egyptian Rite of Freemasonry, both alchemy and secret longevity rites. Cagliostro and his wife were initiated into the mysteries of the Illuminists at Saint Germain's castle in Holstein in 1785.

Comte de Saint Germain practiced meditation and was often seen seated in the lotus posture (cross-legged). Sometimes he retired to the Himalayas to a secret retreat. He admitted that he was the servant of a higher power.

At the palace of Prince Carl of Hesse-Cassel in Eckernforde, Germany, Comte de Saint Germain was said to have died February 27, 1784. But his body was seen by no one other than Prince Carl. His body did not lie in state. There was no funeral, no will, no heirs, and no claim to the inheritance. Prince Carl burnt all of Saint Germain's papers for fear of their being misinterpreted. When asked about his death, the prince invariably changed the subject. Many people claimed to meet with Saint Germain or receive letters from him long after his so-called death.

Saint Germain is said to have incarnated as Shakespeare, Francis Bacon, and Christopher Columbus. Some people believe he was Comte de Rochambeau, who served in the Revolutionary War. Saint Germain served as an advisor to the American founding fathers and still serves as America's protector. He was said to be instrumental in the signing of the Declaration of Independence. This is the story as recorded in *Washington and His Generals: Or, Legends of the Revolution* by George Lippard:

Faced with hanging, disemboweling, and quartering for high treason by King George III of England, the courageous founding fathers debated for endless hours throughout the night in the State House at Philadelphia on July 4, 1776, with the lower chamber doors locked and a guard posted. Thomas Jefferson spoke bold words and John Adams poured out his soul. Still the parchment remained unsigned. A pale-faced man, rising in one corner, expressed his terror of "axes, scaffolds and a gibbet."

Suddenly a tall slender man with piercing dark eyes rose, and his words rang through the hall. Here is a brief excerpt from his electrifying speech:

> Gibbets! They may stretch our necks on every scaffold in the land! They may turn every rock into a gibbet, every tree into a gallows, and yet the words written on that parchment can never die!... What! Are there shrinking hearts and weak voices here, when the very dead upon our battlefields arise and call upon us to sign that parchment or be accursed forever?
>
> Sign! If the next moment the gibbet's rope is around your neck. Sign! If the next moment this hall rings with the echo of the falling axe. Sign! By all your hopes in life or death, as husbands, as fathers, as men! Sign your names to that parchment!"[1]

The magic of that speaker's look, the passion in his voice, the prophet-like beckoning of his hand, and the magnetic flame of his eyes soon fired every heart throughout the hall. The delegates rushed forward to sign the document that would change their lives and their country forever.

The signatories then turned to express their gratitude to the un-known speaker. However, he had vanished. How he entered and left the locked, guarded room is unknown.

Signing the Declaration of Independence was a risky, thankless venture. Nearly every one of the signers died bankrupt. The courage it took for these 56 prosperous men to sign away their fortunes and to invite capture and certain death could only be inspired by a master such as Saint Germain.

Saint Germain's violet, purifying flame of transmutation is used by seekers everywhere to lift their consciousness and quicken their bodies, furthering their ascension process. See page 225 for a Violet Flame Invocation.

Dieities of the Classical World

12 Gods of Antiquity

The immortal Olympian deities are said to live on the highest moun-tain of Greece, at the borderline between earth and sky. In their idyllic home, they feast on sumptuous banquets, eat ambrosia, and drink nec-tar, which makes them immortal. Their leader is the all-powerful father of the gods, Zeus.

Figure 4c. **Goddess Athena:** She is the god-dess of wisdom, encouraging law and or-der, and the all-bedewing goddess of mois-ture and agriculture. Her festivals are cel-ebrated during the rainy season. The virgin dawn, she breathed the soul into human beings, and her first duty was to arouse men from slumber. Therefore, the cock and owl, birds of morning and night, are sacred to her. The Medusa head signifies the star-lit night, doomed to die with her arrival as dawn. As earth mother, the snake is sacred to her. She carries an *aegis* (shield) and a golden staff, which symbolize dignity and youth.

Figure 4e (on pages 60 and 61) is an overview of the Olympian deities. The left column of this chart shows both the Greek and Roman names of these deities. They are divided into male and female counterparts. For example, Zeus-Jupiter is associated with his wife, Hera-Juno.

Gaia

The primeval earth mother goddess, mother of the gods, Gaia and her brother Eros were born from Chaos, the great void of emptiness. Gaia then gave birth to the sea, the sky, and the mountains. Gaia married her son Uranus and gave birth to the 12 Titans, six male and six female Elder Gods that were eventually overthrown by the Olympian Gods.

Nourisher and mother of every movable and living being, Gaia also mated with the underworld and bore many demons and more Titans. In ancient Greece, oaths sworn in the name of Gaia are considered the most sacred and binding of all oaths.

Figure 4d. **Gaia:** "Gaia, the beautiful, rose up, Broad blossomed, she that is the steadfast base of all things. And fair Gaia first bore the starry Heaven, equal to herself, to cover her on all sides and to be a home forever for the blessed Gods."—Hesiod. The Greek personification of Mother Earth, Gaia is born of Chaos and Divine Principle. She is the female principle in nature, who bore offspring by her own inherent power. The all-giving and the nourisher-of-all, her emblem is a globe and she is portrayed as the Great Mother, tending the young.

Greek and Roman

TWIN FLAMES	SEX	EPITHETS	SYMBOLS
Zeus Jupiter	Male	King of the Gods, God of the Sky and Thunder, Ruler of Mount Olympus	Thunderbolt, Eagle, Bull, Scepter, Oak Tree
Hera Juno	Female	Queen of the Gods Goddess of Women	Peacock, Cow, Wedding Ring
Athena Minerva	Female	Goddess of Wisdom, Goddess of War, Goddess of Crafts, Savior, Protector, Horse-tamer, Virgin Dawn	Helmet, Spear, Snake, Aegis, Golden Staff, Cock, Owl, Olive Tree, Plow, Loom
Hermes Mercury	Male	Messenger of the Gods, Lord of the Winds, God of Commerce	Gold Staff, Caduceus, Winged Sandals, Winged Hat, Ram, Crane
Poseidon Neptune	Male	God of the Seas	Trident, Horse, Sea Horse, Dolphin, Bull
Demeter Ceres	Female	Goddess of Fertility, Goddess of Agriculture, Goddess of Nature and Seasons	Wheat Seed, Cornucopia
Apollo	Male	The Sun God, God of Light, Eternal Youth, God of Music	Sun, Golden Lyre, Mice, Laurel, Snake, Hyacinth, Tree, Bow, Arrows of Apollo
Artemis Diana	Female	Goddess of Moon, Goddess of the Hunt, Goddess of Maidens	Golden Bow and Arrows, Dogs, Deer, Moon
Aphrodite Venus	Female	Goddess of Love, Goddess of Beauty	Laurel, Ram, Rose, Dove, Swan, Hare, Pomegranate
Ares Mars	Male	God of War	Dog, Wild Boar, Vulture, Wolf, Spear, Shield
Hephaestus Vulcan	Male	God of Fire, Blacksmith to the Gods	Hammer, Pincers, Forge, Anvil, Quail
Hestia Vesta	Female	Goddess of Family Peace and Security, Goddess of Hearth and Home	Sacred Eternal Flame, Fireplace

Figure 4e.

Gods of Olympia

FUNCTIONS
Maintains order, Administers justice, Controls the Gods, Defends Greek cities and dwellings, Father of earth's kings, Origin of heavenly light, Regulates weather.
Sister and wife of Zeus, Patroness of marriage, married life, and motherhood.
Breathes soul into human beings, Arouses humans from slumber. Teaches art of weaving, Created first olive tree, Patroness of crafts, strategic battle, agriculture, victory (Athena Nike), unchanging youthfulness (Pallas Athena).
Runs swifter than the wind, Can become invisible, Patron of writers, orators, philosophers, travelers, commerce, and measures, Invented lyre and fire, Protects herds and flocks.
Calms ocean waves, Summons terrible storms, Causes and prevents earthquakes, Creates mountains, islands, valleys, channels, and horses.
Teaches grain crop cultivation. Patroness of Eleusinian Mysteries—Secret rites where souls of initiates receive redemption and immortality.
Emits solar energy, Overcomes darkness, Founded oracle at Delphi, Physician, Patron of healing, music, prophecy, poetry, archery, truth. Teaches art of prophecy, Shapes Fates or destiny. In his light, all is revealed.
Apollo's twin sister, Patron of pregnant women, Protector of children, nature, rivers, and animals.
Controls humans and gods with erotic powers, female wiles, and deceit, Patroness of desire and fertility.
Spreads war and destruction, frenzy, hatred, and bloodshed.
Husband of Aphrodite, Brother of Hestia, Patron of forges.
Eldest goddess in Olympus, Virgin, Protects eternal sacred fire in hearth of every home and at center of every city. In Delphi, Hestia's common flame of all Greeks burns next to the omphalos, the stone symbolizing the navel of the world.

Lady Liberty

The Roman goddess Libertas (Latin for the word *liberty*) is the embodiment of freedom. The first temple to Libertas was built in 238 BC on Aventine Hill in Rome, and another temple was built about 57 BC on Palantine Hill. This goddess inspired many iconic figures, such as the Statue of Liberty; and coins, such as the United States Peace Dollar, Morgan Dollar, Saint-Gaudens Double Eagle, and Walking Liberty Half Dollar.

Figure 4f. A Vision of Lady Liberty Shining Light upon Manhattan: "Give me your tired, your poor, Your huddled masses yearning to breathe free, The wretched refuse of your teaming shore. Send these, the homeless, tempest-tost to me. I lift my lamp beside the golden door!"—Emma Lazarus. In September, 1990, when I was on Mount Shasta, I saw a vision of Lady Liberty hovering above Manhattan pouring golden light on the city.

Themis

Themis (also Lady Portia and Iustitia) is the goddess of justice and of opportunity. She embodies order, divine law, and justice, and sits beside Zeus as adviser. She creates balance and harmony, and the scales are her symbol. She judges whether the dead go to Tartarus (underworld) or the Elysian Fields (heaven), and is blindfolded to remain impartial. Themis was the first deity of prophecy and oaths, in charge of the Delphic oracle, until she passed it to Apollo. As Portia, she is said to be the twin flame of Saint Germain. She uses the silver violet flame and is a gatekeeper of the mysteries.

Deities of Egypt

In the ancient Western world, Egyptians were more concerned with immortality than any other nation. Their ability to preserve corpses for millennia is legendary. The journey of the soul through the afterlife dominated their religion. The scarab, a beetle that falsely appears to reproduce itself without any visible means, represents resurrection.

The chart in Figure 4g on pages 64 and 65 describes some of the deities of Egypt, along with their names, symbols, and purpose or function.

Native American Divine Beings

White Buffalo Calf Woman

The legend is that about 2,000 years ago, a white buffalo calf descended from a cloud and turned into a beautiful Indian girl, carrying a sacred bundle. She spent four days among the Lakota, teaching the meaning of the sacred bundle, sacred songs, traditional ways, and seven sacred ceremonies.

She instructed the Lakota that, as long as they performed these ceremonies, they would remain guardians of sacred land and would never die. White Buffalo Calf Woman prophesied that the birth of a white buffalo calf would be a sign of her return to purify the world and bring harmony, balance, and spirituality.

Wakan Tanka

In the Sioux tradition, the Wakan Tanka, or "Great Mystery," are a group of sacred entities with mysterious ways. These immortal beings were never born and never die. The Wakan Tanka is also defined as the Great Spirit, the power of the life force and sacredness residing within everything. Before creation, Wakan Tanka existed in a great

Deities of

NAME	EPITHET	DRESS AND SYMBOLS
Osiris	God of the Dead	Mummified man with white cone-like feathered headdress
Isis	She of the Throne	Woman with throne-shaped headress, sun disk and cow horns, wings, Isis Knot: symbol of protection
Horus	The Distant One	Man with head of a hawk, Eye of Horus: all-seeing eye of insight and symbol of protection
Ra	The Sun God	Man with hawk head, Headdress with sun disk
Sekhmet	The Powerful One, Avenger of Wrongs, Lady of Slaughter, Mistress of Dread	Woman with head of lioness
Hathor	Estate of Horus Queen of Heavens	Woman with ears of a cow, Horned headress with sun disk
Thoth	He Who Is Like the Ibis	Man with head of sacred ibis, Baboon
Amun	King of the Gods	Man with ram-head, Ostrich-plumed hat
Anubis	He Upon His Mountain	Man with a jackal head
Atum	The All, Perfection	Man with double crown, Ankh
Nut	Sky Goddess	Woman whose body arches across sky, wearing starry sky
Nun	Waters of Chaos	Man carrying a boat
Hapy	God of Inundation	Man with potbelly, Water plants
Nephthys	Lady of the Mansion	Woman with headdress showing her name in hieroglyphs

Figure 4g.

Ancient Egypt

FUNCTION
God of resurrection, the underworld, afterlife, and fertility, Tests the dead.
Wife of Osirus, mother of Horus, Protective goddess, Goddess of motherhood, Giver of all life, Matron of nature and magic.
Son of Isis and Osiris, God of sky and sun, Protector of the ruler of Egypt, Embodies the Pharaohs.
Most important God, King and father of Gods, God of light, warmth, and growth.
Goddess of war, Protector of the Pharaohs, Leads Pharaohs into battle, destroys enemies with arrows of fire. Divine physician, with doctors and surgeons as her priesthood. Her hot breath is the desert winds.
Protective goddess, Goddess of love, joy, beauty, music, and dance, Mother of Pharaohs, Goddess of Fertility, Helps women in childbirth.
God of writing, knowledge, science, measurement and time, Invented hieroglyphs, God of the moon.
God of creative force, fertility, air, and breath of life.
God of embalming the dead, Protector of the dead.
Creator God, who rose from the waters of chaos and created all the Gods.
Mother of Isis and Osiris, Body creates canopy over the earth.
Associated with chaos at edges of universe, The only thing that pre-exists land on earth.
Brings flood to Nile, Deposits rich silt on banks of Nile, for growing crops.
Protective goddess of the dead.

emptiness called Han (darkness). Feeling lonely, he created companions: rock, earth, sky, and sun. He is worshipped by many different names in Native American tribes.

Quetzalcoatl and Pahana

In legends of the Americas, a fair-skinned, white-bearded god visited their land, bringing culture, art, science, and wisdom. It is believed that this god, Quetzalcoatl ("feather serpent"), will return. Born of virgin birth, Quetzalcoatl is the inventor of books and the calendar, giver of maize, and lord of death and resurrection.

Pahana, the fair-skinned "Lost White Brother" or "Elder Brother" of the Hopi departed for the east when the nation began its migrations during what they call the "Fourth World," our current world cycle. When Pahana returns, the wicked will be destroyed and a new age of peace will begin.

White Eagle

The White Eagle Lodge was founded in 1936 by Grace and Ivan Cooke in England. Grace brought forth messages from White Eagle, a gentle, loving Native American master. He says that the "Christ spirit" of divine love and light in the heart can guide everyone and radiate into the world to bless, heal, and comfort others. White Eagle teaches a gentle way, in harmony with the laws of life.

White Eagle says the ultimate goal of humanity is for the inner light to become so strong and radiant that the cells of the physical body are transmuted into a finer substance that can overcome mortality.

Wiraqocha and Pachamama

The ancient Incans lived in harmony with their surroundings, in communion with nature and the animal world.

Wiraqocha ("vital energy of the sea"), the invisible God, beyond human concepts, is the essence of existence. He represents the universe and is the creator and light-giver to the world. He created humans and ordered their communities to become sacred centers (*Pakarinas*). His physical manifestation and symbol is Inti, the Father Sun.

Pachamama ("mother earth") gives life to human beings. She is mother of all purification, cleansing, and pardon. She bestows the only laws needed by humanity: the law of unconditional love (*munay*), the virtue of service or work (*yankay*) and the value of knowledge (*yachay*).

Other Ascended Masters

Here are just a few more masters you might encounter or call upon as you explore inner space:

- Master Lady Nada, to remove false beliefs and learn unconditional love.
- Great Divine Director, to follow your divine life plan and purpose with divine direction.
- Master Lanto, to materialize objects and desires from cosmic light and substance.
- Zarathustra, to know truth and discern it from untruth.
- Afra, patron of Africa and of the black race.
- Oshun, African goddess of rivers and waters.
- Fortuna and Lakshmi, goddesses of abundance and prosperity.
- Hina, Polynesian and Hawaiian moon goddess.
- Pele, Fiery Hawaiian volcano goddess.
- Amaterasu, Japanese Shinto sun goddess.
- Spider Woman, who creates the web of interconnectivity of all life.
- Aengus, Celtic God who helps soulmates and twin flames meet.
- Lady of the Lake, Celtic goddess, guide to emotion and renewal.
- Lugh, "the shining one," Celtic sun god of harvest.
- King Solomon, embodiment of wisdom, son of King David.
- The Beautiful Many, all the divine and angelic beings that come in the name of God.

Chapter 5

Masters of India

The self-existent Lord pierced the senses to turn outward. Thus
we look to the world outside and see not the Self within us. A
sage withdrew his senses from the world of change and, seeking
immortality, looked within and beheld the deathless self.
—Katha Upanishad, 2.1.1

For 22 years, I studied and served under the guidance of famous
enlightened spiritual master and guru of the Beatles and of Deepak
Chopra—Maharishi Mahesh Yogi. Breathing the holy breath and
drinking the ambrosial atmosphere around such an enlightened being
has transformed my life on every level. Luckily, such blessings have
continued. I have been graced with many meetings with extraordinary
spiritual masters from India. Some of these holy people have lived
well more than 100 years. Some are ascended masters. Some are living legends.

Brahmaveta Shri Devraha Hans Baba

I have been granted several personal meetings with a beautiful
saint named Devraha Hans Baba, a *naga baba* (naked ascetic) who sits
on a high platform, chanting devotional songs to the Gods Radha and
Krishna. These particular songs are in a mysterious language, entirely
untranslatable. In his presence, I entered an ecstatic, altered state of
consciousness, and, amazingly, found myself compelled to dance a joyous dance of divine love.

Hans Baba's guru, Brahmarishi Yogiraj Devraha Baba, was believed to be more than 800 years old when he made his ascension in 1990. This great saint, who required no food and wore no clothing in winter or summer, was said to be the direct disciple of Bhagavan Ramanujacharya of Kanchipuram (1016–1137).

Devraha Baba was one of the most highly revered saints in India. All the presidents, prime ministers, rulers, and politicians sought his counsel. All the Ghandis visited him. King George V met him in 1910. Dr. Rajendra Prasad, India's first president, met Devraha Baba in childhood in the early 1900s, when his father took him to see the saint. Dr. Prasad stated that Devraha Baba was already an elderly man when his father first met him in the 19th century.

Devraha Baba relinquished his body on June 19, 1990. A few months later, his foremost disciple, Hans Baba, the priest in the Radha-Krishna temple in the Vindhyachal ashram of his guru, underwent a metamorphosis. His appearance and behavior changed, and he began to physically resemble his guru. He ascended the platform (*manch*) where his guru had always sat. Apparently, Devraha Baba's soul underwent *parkaya pradesh* (transmigration of the soul) and entered the body of Hans Baba and has since carried on his teaching.

When I saw Hans Baba in August 2001 in Jaipur, I witnessed the following stunning event: A woman from Jaipur stood before the manch, where Hans Baba was meeting visitors. Hans Baba greeted her by name and continued, "I remember meeting you at Kumbh Mela 12 years ago in 1989." The woman answered, "Yes, I met Devraha there." As it turned out, Hans Baba had not attended Kumbh Mela in 1989 and had never visited Jaipur before. It was Devraha Baba who had met the woman.

Many miracle cures and other extraordinary events have occurred in the lives of Hans Baba's devotees. He is like a wish-fulfilling tree who, when asked with a sincere heart and right intention, will grant any boon.

When I told Hans Baba that I would include him in this book, he dictated this message:

"The world cannot be run through anguish, anger, and hatred. Connect with each other and find the right people who can spread love and peace in the world. Connect those people together in a global family. The right people should come forward."

Figures 5a and 5b. **Devraha Hans Baba:** A devotee of Lord Krishna, Hans Baba is one of the most famous saints in India. His guru, Brahmarishi Yogiraj Devraha Baba, was said to be more than 800 years old when he ascended.

Teet Maharaj

When I met Sri Sri 108 Sri His Holiness Swami Prakashanand Ji Maharaj, I examined his passport, which said he was born in 1892. But the late Queen Aishwariya, queen of Nepal, who happened to be visiting him at that time, claimed that he is at least 150 years old, because her grandfather knew him earlier in the 20th century. Teet Maharaj still drives a car. In fact, he drove all the way to Delhi from his ashram in Jageshwar to get a passport and visa for the United States.

At age 4, Teet Maharaj left his parents and traveled to Haridwar, where he became an ascetic. In the Himalayas and Varanasi, he learned Sanskrit, Hindi, and English and studied the ancient scriptures. At age 20, he moved to Gaumukh, the source of the Ganges River.

Figure 5c. **Teet Maharaj:** This photo was taken when his passport said that he was age 108, but his devotees claim that he was at least age 150.

Then he descended to the Himalayan foothills near Nainital, in the Teet Forest. For 30 years he meditated in a cave, where tigers and their cubs guarded the entrance. In 1927 the British government granted him the forest of Teet and the title His Holiness Maharaj of Teet.

Teet Maharaj has traveled the entire length and breadth of India and visited Afghanistan, Sri Lanka, Tibet, Nepal, and Burma. He trekked on foot to every pilgrimage in India and the Himalayas, barefoot, clad only in a loincloth, even at 14,000 feet.

In 1960 he settled near the 4,000-year-old Jageshwar Temple, the only temple in the world where Lord Shiva is worshipped as Maha Mritunjay (the great conquering of death). Teet Maharaj acquired the land next to the temple and created the Mokshdham Ashram.

Ananda Mayi Ma

Figure 5d. **Anandamayi Ma:** With no training or education, "The Bliss-Permeated Mother" was taught by her own inner guru. She never gave formal initiations and refused to be called a guru, as she affirmed, "All paths are my paths," and "I have no particular path."

Nirmala Sundari (1896–1982) was born in what is now Bangladesh. As a child, she frequently experienced God and often went into a state of ecstasy upon hearing devotional chanting. She attended the village school for barely two years.

At age 13 she was married, but remained celibate. She spent her days meditating in God-intoxication. At age 22, rather than seeking a guru, she initiated herself: "As the master (guru) I revealed the mantra. As the disciple (shishya) I accepted it and started to recite it."[1] Her husband sought initiation from her and became her devotee.

Although completely uneducated, she spontaneously chanted Sanskrit hymns. She performed intricate yoga postures and often went without food or drink. In 1926 in Shahbag, she set up a Kali temple. Many people began to be drawn to what they realized was a living embodiment of the divine.

In 1932, she moved to Dehradun with her husband and spent the rest of her life traveling extensively throughout India, founding many ashrams, hospitals, and temples. In 1970, I had the great fortune of meeting Anandamayi Ma, the "joy-permeated mother," and receiving waves of bliss at her ashram in Dehradun, Himalayas, India.

Sri Ramakrishna Paramahansa

Gadadhar Chatterjee (1836–1887) was born in Kamarpukur, in West Bengal, into a poor but pious orthodox Brahmin caste family. He had his first ecstatic mystical experience at age 6. As priest at the Dakshineswar Kali Temple, he longed for the Divine Mother Kali with fervor and passion, until his devotion was finally fulfilled.

Later he became known as Sri Ramakrishna Paramahansa ("always absorbed in meditation"), one of the greatest saints of all time. He was known for accepting and promoting all religious faiths, and his marriage with Sarada Devi is regarded as the ideal spiritual union.

> *Consciously or unconsciously, in whatever way one falls into the trough of nectar, one becomes immortal. Similarly, whosoever utters the name of the Deity voluntarily or involuntarily finds immortality in the end.*
> —Paramahansa Sri Ramakrishna

A *yogini* (female yogi) named Brahmani (Bhairabi) taught Ramakrishna the tantric disciplines. She had learned these secret practices from Mahamuni Babaji (see page 77). In a conference of priests, she proved that Ramakrishna had all the signs of an avatar on his body, and challenged them to accept her opinion.

Ramakrishna often practiced a tantric process called *avishkara*. He entered into "the great mood of perfect serenity" (*Mahabhava Samadhi*), in which he dressed in the clothing of *Bhavatarini*, an aspect of Mother Divine, identified with her, and embodied her completely (see her picture in Figure 5f on page 75).

Figure 5e. Sri **Ramakrishna Paramahansa:** A spiritual master from India, Ramakrishna was believed to be an avatar (an incarnation of God). He practiced *avesha,* a method in which devotees invite a deity to express through their bodies. This process is similar to the Divine Revelation "ecstatic expressions of God."

Ramalinga Swami

Ramalinga Swamigal (1823–1874) was born in Marudur, India. At age 5 he composed beautiful devotional poetry, and at age 12 began teaching in the temple. He was considered an incarnation of divine wisdom. His advanced scriptural knowledge came by grace and meditation, because he had no formal education. He married at age 27, but his wife, Danammal, remained a virgin.

Figure 5f. **Durga, the Divine Mother:** A form of Mother Divine, Durga is a deity of India who rides a tiger or lion. Her *yantra* (symbol) is shown in the circle. She represents *shakti* (the power of God) and is worshipped by Tantrics, who awaken *kundalini shakti,* coiled up like a serpent at the base of the spine. When kundalini shakti rises up the spine and unites with *Shiva* at the crown of the head, then the aspirant attains *yoga*, "union with God."

In 1860 Ramalinga moved to Vadalur and founded a charity house in 1867 to lodge travelers, feed needy elders, and give medical treatment to the poor. Simple, gentle, and loving, his teaching was focused on devotion, kindness, and compassion for all beings.

His collection of poetry, *Thiruvarutpa* ("The Divine Song of Grace"), described his bodily transformation into an immortal body. He wrote that his mortal body transformed into a golden hue, then into a "body of love," and a "body of grace" or "body of light." This new body, imperceptible to the touch, was imperishable and unaffected by the environment. He wrote:

"I prayed for an effulgent body that would endure forever against wind, earth, sky, fire, water, sun, moon, death, disease, weapons of killing, planets, injuries of evil deeds or anything else. He later fulfilled my prayers and I have such a body. Think it not a mean gift. O people, seek refuge in my Father who is the lord of the Beatific splendor that immortalizes even the material body."[2]

Ramalinga's disciples attempted to photograph him, but nothing appeared on the photographic plates except his clothing. Because his body cast no shadow, he always covered his head and entire body with a white cloth. He was slender and of medium height with a long, sharp nose and large, serene eyes emitting divine brilliance. He ate once every two or three days. He easily read other people's minds and performed many miraculous healings.

In Mettukuppam in 1870 he moved into a small hut, now known as "The Sacred Mansion of the Miracle." On January 30, 1874, he told his devotees that he would be leaving to enter into all bodies of God's creation. He told them to padlock his door from the outside and keep the oil lamp in his temple burning forever. He said that if his room were to be opened later, it would be empty.

Later that night his devotees were chanting outside the room. Suddenly they saw a flash of violet light emanating from the Swami's room. When the room was opened, he had disappeared. The police, after searching the area and examining the building, declared the Swami had vanished into thin air.

In July, 1882, Madame Helena Blavatsky (see page 109) stated in her magazine *Theosophist* that Ramalinga Swami was the forerunner of the Theosophical movement.

Nine Naths

In India, there are traditionally nine immortal sages who are un-born and therefore never die. Their consciousness is so advanced that their spiritual stature and the magnitude of their work is unfathomable. These are the Nine Naths, or nine immortal sages.

The primal Nath and direct manifestation of the supreme Godhead is Adi-Nath ("first lord"). Though he is nameless, he is affectionately called Babaji ("father"), or Mahamuni ("great sage") Babaji. Many disputed names are used for the nine Naths in various regions of India. The Nath tradition is also found in the Jain religion.

Figure 5g. Mahamuni Babaji: The immortal saint Babaji, the "Yogi-Christ of India," described in Paramahansa Yogananda's *Autobiography of a Yogi,* is the founder of many great teachings, including Divine Revelation. He is pictured in the Himalayas, where he is believed to reside today. The word *Babaji* is a respectful name for "father," used in India as a title.

Mahamuni Babaji

The ineffable Babaji, the primal Nath, is the collective consciousness and total light of the seven primordial sages born at the beginning of time—the Elohim. In his infinite compassion, Babaji takes human form to evolve, redeem, and liberate humanity, as need arises. He can materialize and dematerialize his deathless light-body, anytime, anywhere, and take any physical form, at will.

In *Autobiography of a Yogi* by Paramahansa Yogananda (1893–1952) several chapters are devoted to Babaji (also Mahavatar Babaji or the Yogi-Christ). He appears as a youth of 25 years or younger, with a strong body, dark lustrous eyes, and long hair, and requires no food.

Babaji is believed to reside in Badrinath, Himalayas, at

10,248 feet, a few miles south of the Tibetan border, on the Alakananda River. He lives in a large cave facing two waterfalls near Badrinath at Gauri Shankar Peeth, an ashram surrounded by sheer rock cliffs with a row of caves at the base. An invisible, mysterious, one-mile perimeter surrounds the area, which averts visitors who lack Babaji's permission. There he dwells with his "sister" (paternal cousin), Mataji "Annai" Nagalakshmi Deviya.

Amman Pranabananda, described by Yogananda as the "saint with two bodies," asked Babaji how old he is. He replied, "It is going on four *kalpa.*" (One kalpa is more than four billion years). Babaji's mission is to assist humans in their desire for God-realization. Usually he does this anonymously. Some of the many manifestations of Mahamuni Babaji, and saints initiated by him, are described in the next section.

Manifestations of Babaji

Matsyendranath (also Mina, Minapa), taught *Hatha Yoga* (union with God through physical culture) to the legendary Goraknath (also Shiva-Goraksha-Babaji and Gorakshanath). Matsyendra learned the discipline of *pranayama* (the science of breath), from Babaji in the Himalayas near Srinagar, Garwal, now Uttarakhand. Goraknath bestowed physical immortality on two men still alive today: Bhartriji and Gopajin.

Bhartriji (also Bhartrihari or Bhartariji), was the emperor of India right before the time of Jesus. At age 300 he wrote *Bhartrihari Shaktam,* a classical scripture of India. His ashram is in Bhartara (named after him), Alwar, Rajasthan, near Sariska Forest Reserve.

Bhartriji meditated for 700 years and lived for centuries without food and water. Seven tombs are in his ashram, because he was buried alive and encased in cement every 108 years for the past 700 years. He dematerializes his body, leaves the tomb, and materializes a new body each time.

Gopajin (also known as Gopichand), Bhartriji's nephew, was an ancient king of Nepal, and is also immortal. Leonard Orr, founder of Rebirthing, met Bhartriji and Gopajin several times.

Kriya Babaji Nagaraj was born in Tamil Nadu in about AD 200. At age 5 he joined some wandering ascetics. He became a scholar and formidable debater, but quickly realized he was no closer to God-realization. At age 11 Nagaraj traveled on foot from Varanasi to the southernmost tip of Sri Lanka, and became a disciple of Siddha Boganath (see page 83). Nagaraj sat under a banyan tree for six months and began to incarnate the eternal youth Lord Muruga (son of Lord Shiva).

At Boganath's request, Nagaraj trekked back to Courtrallam, Tamil Nadu, where he prayed continually for Siddha Agastya to initiate him. He subsisted on donated scraps of food for 48 days. Weak and emaciated, he was near collapse when the sage finally emerged from the forest, embraced and fed him, and taught him *Vasi Yogam*, a *pranayama* technique (breathing exercise).

Agastya sent Nagaraj to Badrinath, to "become the greatest *siddha* [perfected being] that the world has ever known." Nagaraj made the grueling, treacherous journey to the Himalayas. After 18 months of rigorous discipline, he entered *soruba samadhi* (immortality), and his body ceased to age.

Lord Adi Shankara (509 BC–477 BC), founder of monism and *Vedanta* (*Advaita* or non-dualism) was initiated into Raja Yoga (royal yoga) by Babaji in Varanasi and practiced this discipline in Kedarnath, Himalayas. The "mystic of the soul," he taught that individual and universal souls *(Atman* and *Brahman)* are fundamentally identical. He revived Hinduism in India and founded the *Swami* order with its four *maths* (monasteries) and four *Shankaracharyas* (enlightened teachers) in four corners of India.

Figure 5h. **Lord Shankara:** A child saint, Adi Shankaracharya was destined to live only 16 years, but he was given a 16-year life extension by the immortal Veda Vyasa (see page 81), in order to continue his commentaries on the *Brahma Sutras*.

Kabir (born circa AD 1398), weaver, saint, and poet, was initiated into Raja Yoga by Babaji at Varanasi. He sought to bring harmony between Hindus and Muslims, and preached monism and the avoidance of idol worship. His corpse awoke after death and gave his quarreling Muslim and Hindu disciples instructions about his last rites. Then he vanished from under the shroud. Nothing was left but flowers, half of which were buried by Muslim rites and half cremated by Hindu rites.

Hairakhan Baba lived from the early 1800s until 1922 near Hairakhan village, Nainital district, Uttar Pradesh, on the Gautama Ganga River at the foot of Mount Kailasa, Himalayas, near the Nepal border. In 1922 he died while crossing the Kali River to Nepal. He reappeared from 1924 until 1958 in Dhanyon Village near Almora in Uttar Pradesh.

He reappeared in Hairakhan in 1970 as a youth by manifesting a body from the ethers in a cave near his old ashram. There he sat for 45 days in motionless meditation, not eating, drinking, or sleeping. People from all around the world visited him.

In 1972 he proved to Indian courts that he was the same Hairakhan Baba, more than 100 years old (although he looked 20), and therefore the legal owner of his property. He taught Mansa Yoga (dissolving the mind) to his devotees. Many people who stayed with him in Hairakhan claim he is Mahamuni Babaji himself. He left his body again on February 14, 1984. Leonard Orr and Sondra Ray were his most famous devotees.

Nim Karoli Baba, saint of the 20th century who taught Mantra Yoga (use of sacred sounds), was initiated by Mahamuni Babaji into the Rama Mantra. He was the guru of Ram Dass (Richard Alpert). When I visited his camp at the Kumbh Mela (see page 188) and his ashram near Jageshwar, I experienced the palpable energy of his immortal being.

Ann and Peter Meyer of San Diego, California, founders of Teaching of the Inner Christ and Teaching of Intuitional Metaphysics (parent organizations of Divine Revelation), were initiated by Babaji, who often appeared to Ann in physical form and to Peter in spiritual form. They write in their book, *Being a Christ*:

"On October 19, 1962, the Master Babaji, manifesting a physical body, visited Ann Meyer and awakened her to a new teaching. Babaji had been teaching and guiding Peter Meyer from deep within himself for many years. In December of 1963, Peter and Ann were married and had begun to give courses, passing on the new teaching which Babaji had and was imparting to them, both through many physical visits and also inwardly through their minds."

Veda Vyasa

It is said that Krishna Dwaipayana has lived for thousands of years and is still alive today. As Veda Vyasa ("splitter of the *Vedas"*), he divided the Vedas into four sections. Because average people could not understand the Vedas, he composed 18 Puranas (the great epic storybooks), which include the *Mahabharata*, the story of the great war between the Kauravas and the Pandavas, with its profound scripture *Bhagavad Gita*, and the *Srimad Bhagavata Mahapurana*, the story of Lord Krishna.

These Puranas are tales of sages and kings, which teach Vedic wisdom to the masses. The scribe for the *Mahabharata* was Lord Ganesh, the elephant God, who agreed

Figure 5i. **Veda Vyasa:** The immortal sage Vyasa made Vedic wisdom accessible to the masses by writing epic tales of kings, sages, and immortal beings. © Copyright 2009 B.G. Sharma; published by Mandala Publishing. All rights reserved. Used with permission. *www.mandala.org*

to the task only if Vyasa dictated it all in one sitting. At one point, Ganesh broke off his tusk to use as a pen when his quill broke. The scribe for the *Srimad Bhagavatam* was Vyasa's son, Shukadeva, also said to be immortal.

Markandeya

Lord Shiva blessed a childless, pious couple with a son, but prophesied that the child would not live past age 16. The youngster traveled to Varanasi, where Lord Shiva instructed him to proceed to Tirukkadavur, Tamil Nadu, and worship him at the shrine.

While in Tirukkadavur, Markandeya turned 16 years old, and Yama, Lord of Death, came to claim him. But Markandeya embraced the Shiva Linga (egg-shaped symbol of Lord Shiva). The enraged Yama threw his noose around both Markandeya and the Linga and tried to pull them together. Lord Shiva emerged from the Linga and destroyed Yama instantly. Shiva promised Markandeya that he would be immortal and ever remain 16.

The Markandeya Mantra, known as Maha Mrityunjaya Mantra (literally, "The great conquering of death"), is a prayer to overcome death. Here is the mantra: *aum trayambakam yajaamahe, sugandhim pushtivardhanam; urvarukamiva bandhanaan, mrityormukshiye maamrtat.* The translation is as follows:

We worship Lord Shiva, the three-eyed one (the sun, moon, and fire), who is fragrant and who nourishes all beings. As the ripened cucumber is liberated from its bondage to the vine, may he liberate me from death, for immortality.

Learn how to pronounce this mantra correctly by using the book and CD, *Mantra—Power of Sound*. It is available at *www.divinerevelation.org*.

Immortal Siddhas of Tamil Nadu

In Tamil Nadu, India, there are 18 legendary siddha alchemists. Here are stories about some of the most renowned.

Siddha Thirumoola

Rishi Sundaranatha was worshiping at Tiruvavaduturai temple in Tamil Nadu. As he left the temple, he encountered herds of cows, crying at the death of their cowherd Moola. Sundaranatha became so empathetic that he left his body in a hollow log and entered Moola's body, restoring him to life. The cows rejoiced. The next day he searched for his body, but it was gone. Sundaranatha then served in Moola's body and became known as Thirumoola (*thiru* means "holy").

Thirumoola settled near Chidambaram—the temple of Nataraj (the dancing Lord Shiva). He meditated near a banyan tree for 3,000 years. At the end of each year he came out of silence long enough to speak one verse of four lines, imparting his teaching for the year. Nine books comprising 3,000 verses were recorded under the name

Mantra Malai (garland of mantras). Today this book is known as *Thirumandiram*.

Thirumoola stated in verse 80, "I lived in this body for numberless crores of years [one crore equals 10 million]. I lived in a world where there is neither day nor night."[3]

Thirumoola is known as the greatest mystic of Tamil Nadu and the supreme preceptor and originator of the esoteric school of siddhas.

Siddha Agastya

One of the *rishis* ("seers") who cognized the Vedas, Agastya ("mountain-thrower") was less than 5 feet tall, but none could match him in strength. A great fighter, hunter, and archer, he killed many demons and protected the region from enemies. Agastya is known for drinking the waters of the ocean to enable the gods to kill their enemies, who were hiding under the sea.

Agastya founded the first Tamil Academy. His treatise on Tamil grammar contains 12,000 aphorisms. He wrote works in science, medicine, philosophy, yoga, education, history, religion, mysticism, exorcism, alchemy, pharmacy, and magic. He is as renowned a physician in India as Hippocrates is in the West. Agastya was the royal chaplain of the divine line of Pandiyan rulers. After leaving that court, he became an ascetic and has since lived in anonymity.

The demon Ilvala hated Brahmins, because they refused to fulfill his demands. He often took vengeance by transforming his brother Vatapi into a goat and then serving the goat to Brahmins to eat. When Ilvala called Vatapi back to life, the Brahmins' stomachs ripped open as Vatapi emerged, laughing. However, when the goat was served to Agastya, the only risk to Agastya was a burp, because he had digested the goat.

Today Agastya is said to reside near Coutrallam waterfalls in the Pothigai mountains of southern Tamil Nadu. This is where Babaji Nagaraj was initiated by him.

Siddha Boganath

Boganath (also Boga) was born in Varanasi. At Palani Malai mountain in southwestern Tamil Nadu, near Kumaraswamy temple, he attained the immortal state of *soruba samadhi* through the grace of Lord Muruga, the eternal youth (son of Lord Shiva).

At age 315, Boganath left for China. It is said his journey was made via aircraft. He demonstrated to the Chinese details of its construction and later built a ship with a steam engine. In China he was instructed by the saint Kalangi Nath into the *siddha* sciences ("supernormal powers") and *kaya-kalpa* ("rejuvenation") herbal formulas.

He entered the body of a deceased Chinese man, regenerated him, and prolonged his life through kaya-kalpa herbs. He became known as Wei Poyang, famous Taoist alchemist of the Eastern Han dynasty, who wrote an ancient treatise on immortality.

As an alchemist, Boganath used 4,448 rare herbs to create a master medicine that cures all diseases. He formed this medicine into a substance harder than granite and molded the idol of Muruga for the Palaniandavar temple in northern Chennai, India. Its composition is still a mystery today. When the idol is washed, a medicinal substance is extracted from it.

In Assam near Mt. Kailasa, Boganath composed *Boga Saptha Kandam*, with 700,000 verses. Upon returning to Tamil Nadu, he introduced Chinese salts, chemistry, and porcelain. Later he established a Yantra shrine in Sri Lanka at Katirgama, where Babaji Nagaraj met him about AD 211.

Four Saivite Saints

Four immortal saints were among the 63 Nayanars (also Nayanmars), devotional Shaivite (devotees of Lord Shiva) poets of Tamil Nadu, India. It is believed that these four saints left the physical plane by vanishing into thin air. None of them left his body behind or was buried or cremated.

Thirugnana Sambandha or Campanta (7th century AD), a child saint, vanished at age 16 into a divine light, which appeared at his marriage ceremony. He sang his first poem at age 3 and sang a total of 10,000 poems. He wrote the first three volumes of *Tirumurai*, the canon of the Tamil Shaivite school.

Appa (7th century AD), who composed 4,900 hymns of 10 verses each, merged with the form of the Absolute Lord at Pugalur.

Sundaramurti or Cuntara (8th century AD), who prophesied the names of all 63 future Nayanars, merged with Lord Shiva at Mount

Kailasa, or, in another version, was taken to heaven on a white elephant. He wrote the seventh volume of the *Tirumurai*.

Manickavasaga or Manakanychara (8th century AD) merged with the idol of Nataraja, the form of Lord Shiva as a cosmic dancer, in the Chidambaram temple.

Sadguru Dattatreya

The celestial sage Narada knew it was God's will to descend onto earth as a *sadguru* (great teacher). The saint Atri was so powerful that the gods were concerned he might usurp their thrones. His wife Anasuya was pure of heart, loving and devoted. They lived a celibate, meditative life in the Himalayas. Narada decided that no woman was equal to Anasuya and chose her as the mother of the coming *sadguru*, So the goddesses Saraswati, Lakshmi, and Durga sent their husbands, Brahma, Vishnu, and Shiva, to Atri's hermitage.

While Atri was meditating by a holy river, the three Gods arrived, disguised as three old begging priests. The priests told Anasuya they could not accept food from a woman with her clothes on! She recognized these priests as the three Gods, and sprinkled holy water with magical healing properties onto them. They were reduced to little babies crying "OM, OM, OM."

When the sage Atri returned, Anasuya told him the story, and he was grateful that for this extraordinary visitation. But the goddesses were dismayed about their husbands being turned into babies. They requested Anasuya to restore them. She sprinkled the same miracle water on the babies, and the three Gods reappeared full-grown.

The Gods granted any wish to Atri and Anasuya. The couple asked them to appear as a *sadguru* to bless humanity forever. The three Gods joined together into a child and gave *datta* (adopted child) to Atri, exclaiming, "I have given Myself as a son to you." Datta-Atri (adopted son of Atri) or Dattatreya became the son's name.

Dattatreya teaches that God is the guru and the guru is God. He is the Guru of gurus and he lives forever as an *avadhuta* (beyond all disciplines and formalities). He embodies the highest teaching of non-attachment, not only from desires and karma but also from fanaticism. He teaches that God is the great self within everyone and everything.

Lord Dattatreya is now an immortal sage, said to reside on Girnar mountain in Gujarat, India. Seekers of many religions live in caves and the forest on that mountain. Above the timberline are temples to

Dattatreya and a sacred spot where his feet are imprinted. Every year seekers from all over India march around the mountain on a five-day pilgrimage.

Chapter 6

Incarnations of God

O Bharata, whenever there is decline of righteousness, and an exaltation of unrighteousness, then I Myself come forth in body.
—Lord Krishna

Avatar is a Sanskrit word that literally means "descent." It is a divine incarnation—God appearing in an embodied state. A full avatar is God in physical form, which appears whenever the earth needs divine intervention. Lord Krishna states in the *Bhagavad Gita*:

"For the protection of the virtuous, for the destruction of evil-doers, and for firmly establishing *Dharma* [righteousness and virtue], I am born from age to age. Arjuna, My birth and activities are divine. He who knows this in reality does not take birth again on leaving his body but comes to Me."[1]

There is only one God, known by many names, and it causes the creation, preservation, and destruction of the universe. It takes on the personas of the Hindu trinity: Lord Brahma (creator), Lord Vishnu (preserver), and Shiva (destroyer). This one consciousness incarnates into physical form at crucial junctures in human evolution.

Lord Brahma creates the universe and Lord Vishnu preserves it. Then, at the end of one day in the life of Lord Brahma, Lord Shiva swallows up the universe. At that point, dissolution (*pralaya*) occurs. The physical and subtle worlds are absorbed into the causal world, symbolized by one vast primordial ocean, while Brahma sleeps. At the start of each new era, Brahma wakes up, and the universe manifests

Figure 6a. **Dasavataram:** Ten incarnations of Lord Vishnu are mentioned in *Garuda Purana* 8:10–11. © Copyright 2009 B.G. Sharma; published by Mandala Publishing. All rights reserved. Used with permission. *www.mandala.org*

again, with the cycle repeating infinitely. To learn about the deep esoteric meaning of the creation and dissolution of the universe, read my book *Exploring Chakras* (New Page Books, 2003).

Matsya (The Fish)

Nighttime approached at the end of Lord Brahma's day, and dissolution was about to begin. As Lord Brahma was falling asleep, the demon Hayagriva seized the Vedas and drowned them in the primordial ocean. In order for Brahma to re-create the universe, he needed these precious instruction books. Lord Vishnu took the form of the fish Matsya, who dove into the waters and restored the sacred texts to Lord Brahma.

Matsya revealed to King Satyavrata (later named Manu Vaivasvata— father of all humans) that the earth was about to be inundated by a flood. He instructed the king to collect all varieties of plant, seed, animal, and the seven sages (*rishis*) that cognized the Vedas, so life could begin anew after the flood.

As the rains poured and the ocean rose to swallow the earth, Matsya arrived with a boat, which Satyavrata and all the creatures boarded. Matsya then towed the boat, sailing the primordial waters during the entire dissolution, throughout the night of Brahma. Finally they landed on a high mountain peak.

To learn more about the days and nights of Lord Brahma, read *Exploring Chakras.*

Kurma (The Tortoise)

Near the beginning of creation, the demons and the gods were churning the primordial milk ocean in order to recover the nectar of immortality for the purpose of restoring strength to the gods. As the churning progressed, Mount Mandara, used as a churning rod, began to sink into the soft ocean bed.

Lord Vishnu took the form of a tortoise avatar, Kurma, and dove to the bottom of the ocean, where his back was used as a pivot for Mount Mandara so the churning could continue. (See page 188 for the entire story.)

Varaha (The Boar)

A demon named Hiryanyaksha was intoxicated with power. He abducted the Earth and hid it at the bottom of the primordial ocean, where it was submerged during the entire dissolution. Lord Vishnu appeared as the boar avatar Varaha, who dove to the bottom of the sea and lifted up the submerged Earth with his tusks.

As Varaha rose from the ocean, ready to offer the earth to Lord Brahma, Hiryanyaksha ordered him to put it back. When Varaha did not comply, a brutal battle ensued for a thousand years. Finally the boar avatar Varaha killed the demon. Varaha then lifted the Earth out of the primordial ocean and prepared it to support life by shaping the mountains and continents. Thus the Earth was restored and life could begin again.

Narasimha (The Half Man, Half Lion)

After the boar Varaha slaughtered Hiryanyaksha, his brother Hiranyakshipu became furious. He plotted revenge on Lord Vishnu. Hiranyakshipu practiced years of severe austerity, whereby he convinced Lord Brahma to grant him a blessing that he could never be killed by any human or animal, during daytime or nighttime, indoors or outdoors, on the ground or in the sky. He could not be killed by any weapon or natural calamity. Thus Hiranyakshipu's immortality seemed guaranteed.

Lord Vishnu took the form of the avatar Narasimha (neither human nor animal), who outwitted the demon by killing him at twilight (neither day nor night) on the threshold of a courtyard (neither indoors nor outdoors). Narasimha placed the demon on his thighs (neither ground nor sky). Using his sharp nails (with no weapon), he disemboweled and killed the demon.

Vamana (The Dwarf)

King Bali or Mahabali was filled with pride and ambition. He conquered the Earth, the underworld, and then ousted the king of gods, Indra, from his celestial throne and declared himself ruler. In order to restore order, Lord Vishnu incarnated as a priest, the dwarf Vamana.

King Bali invited all the priests of his kingdom to a great religious ritual and gave them generous gifts. When Vamana's turn came, Bali promised him whatever land he wanted. Vamana humbly asked Bali for three strides of land. The king laughed and told Vamana to measure whatever land he could cover in three strides. But the dwarf grew to mammoth proportions. He crossed the sky and heaven in his first stride, and traversed the Earth and the netherworld in his second.

Vamana then asked Bali to give him space to measure his third stride. The humbled King realized his folly and offered the deity his own head to set his foot on. This symbolized his surrender to the Lord. As a result, Mahabali attained immortality.

Parashurama (Axe-Wielding Rama)

Through devotion to Lord Shiva, Parashurama acquired great skill in warfare. When his father was beheaded by greedy warriors, Parasurama avenged his father's death by killing their entire clan, and thereby conquered the entire earth. Then Parashurama demanded that the corrupt Haihaya-Kshatriya kings submit to his imperial position. They refused. As a result, Parashurama exterminated the Haihaya-Kshatriya kings and warriors 21 times, thus fulfilling a vow to his mother, who had beat her chest 21 times over the loss of her husband.

Later, remorseful about his wanton killings, Parashurama offered penance. The sea god Varuna responded, and promised him land equal to the distance he could throw his axe. Thus the state of Kerala, India, was born.

Lord Rama (Ramachandra, King of Ayodhya)

Lord Vishnu became a full avatar as Lord Rama along with his partial manifestations as his brothers Bharata, Laksmana, and Satrughna. Rama's father sent him into exile in the forest, accompanied by his spouse Sita and younger brother Laksmana.

There the 10-headed monster Ravana appeared as a beautiful golden deer to lure Sita away from Rama. The demon kidnapped Sita and carried her to Sri Lanka, where she was imprisoned in the demon's garden. Rama, with the help of Laksmana and his devotee Hanuman, the monkey-god, flew to Sri Lanka and fought a battle that ended Ravana's life. The history of Lord Rama is recorded in the Indian epic story *Ramayana*.

Lord Krishna (The Black)

In order to relieve the oppression of the Earth, overrun by armies of kings who were incarnations of demons, Lord Vishnu incarnated partially as Sri Balarama with fair complexion, and his younger brother Sri Krishna, with black complexion. The exploits of Lord Krishna are written in the epic *Srimad Bhagavatam.*

Even as a baby and in childhood, Krishna resurrected many people from the dead and killed several demons. At age 7, he held Mount

Govardhana above the land as an umbrella for seven days while torrential rains poured down.

When the entire world was at war between the Pandavas and their stepbrothers, the Kauravas, Krishna was charioteer for Arjuna, leader of the Pandavas, and Krishna gave his army to the Kauravas. Many demons were killed on the battlefield, all of which attained the Lord's divine abode. Lord Krishna was said to leave the Earth on February 16, 3102 BC.

Figure 6b. Lord Krishna: "Though unborn and immortal, the Imperishable Self, and also the Lord of all beings, I manifest Myself through My own Yogamaya [divine potency]." —*Bhagavad Gita* 4:6. The word *Krishna* means "black," representing the impersonal God, formless and attributeless, beyond all phenomena. He stands in the golden egg of creation, *hiranya garba*. His flute plays the sacred sound of OM, the vibration at the basis of the universe. He is a cowherd. The cow represents the senses, which must be mastered to attain enlightenment. His dalliances with the *gopis* (milkmaids) represent the *lila* (play) of the Vedas, subtle sound vibrations that are the building blocks of creation.

Lord Buddha (The Enlightened)

Lord Vishnu incarnated as Lord Buddha in 563 BC. He was born Siddhartha Gautama, Prince of Patliputra. His horoscope foretold that he would witness four signs and, as a result, renounce the world. Worried about losing an heir to his throne, the king arranged Siddhartha's marriage at age 16. He kept the boy in a sheltered environment with every luxury available.

At age 29 Siddhartha took four journeys in which he saw four sights: an old man, a sick man, a dying man, and an ascetic. Shocked at humanity's suffering, he resolved to locate its root, seek its escape, and alleviate suffering from all living beings. On the day his son was born, Siddhartha renounced his throne and became a wandering monk.

Under a guru's instruction, he practiced severe austerities, but after six years, he collapsed in frustration and realized the futility of asceticism. After regaining his strength, Siddhartha vowed to sit under a fig tree and not move until he achieved God-realization. After attaining his supreme goal, he remained in *nirvana* (transcendental awareness) for 49 days.

For 45 years he wandered throughout India, teaching *Dhamma* (universal doctrine) to those of all castes. At age 80, Buddha was inadvertently served poisonous mushrooms by a blacksmith. He became ill and gave final instructions to his closest disciple, Ananta, and to Maitreya, whom he prophesied would become the next Buddha thousands of years hence. Then he lay on his right side and entered the final Nirvana.

Kalki (The Eternal)

The present world age, Kali Yuga, is said to be the time of deepest human ignorance, with righteousness at its nadir. The avatar Kalki is predicted to appear at the end of this age, when moral excellence has decayed, the rule of law has disappeared, and the human mind is in total darkness. In the village of Shambal, India, Lord Vishnu will incarnate as Kalki, into the family of the Brahmin Vishuyasha.

With a huge army of Brahmin warriors, riding a white steed named Devaduta, he will travel throughout the world, punishing all evildoers, reestablishing righteousness, leading the universe into dissolution, and heralding the Golden Age in the next cycle of time. The Kalki avatar is predicted to be the last incarnation in this age.

Chapter 7

Buddhist and Taoist Masters

*A spiritualized man [shen jen]...who does not eat the five
grains, but inhales air and drinks dew, he can mount the clouds
and drive flying dragons; He can save men from disease and
assure a plentiful harvest; he is immune to flood and fire.*
—Chuang Tzu

The Eight Immortals

The ancient Taoist tradition in China reveres eight immortal sages. Their images are found in homes, grottos, temples, and Chinese restaurants. The Tiger Balm Garden in Hong Kong exhibits their sculptures and scenes of their legends.

Eight trigrams are the basis of the *I Ching*, an ancient book of divination. Each of the trigrams is associated with one of the immortals. Taoists invoke the eight immortals, eight trigrams, and eight directions in a powerful form of magic that controls spirit forces and fights evil—the *Pa-chen T'u*: Battle Chart of the Eight Trigrams.

The Eight Immortals attained immortality through ancient Taoist practices. The most famous, Lu Tung Pin, born AD 798, is associated with medicine, healing, and the elixir of immortality. His large sword captures and tames evil spirits. His bushy flywhisk symbolizes his power to fly at will. He is the patron saint of barbers and the sick.

Born into a family of high-ranking government officials, Lu Tung Pin was expected to become powerful, wealthy, and famous. But his interest was in spiritual life. One day he stopped at an inn where the sage Han Chung Li invited him to drink warm wine.

95

The wine put Lu Tung Pin to sleep. He dreamt that he held the highest post in the emperor's court, and served in fame and fortune for 50 years. But when he offended the new emperor, he was exiled and disgraced as an enemy of the state. Every member of his family was executed. Alone, weeping bitterly, he awoke. After this dream, Lu Tung Pin followed Han Chung Li into the Ho Ling mountains to learn the secrets of immortal life.

When a disease seems incurable, people visit shrines or grottoes of Lu Tung Pin, where they receive a prescription or a charm, and drink the healing spring water.

The other seven of Eight Immortals are the following:

Ti Kuai Li is a healer and exorcist and is the champion of the downtrodden. His symbol is an iron crutch. He gained immortality by taking a pill from Lao Tzu. He is unpredictable and takes the form of a beggar.

Chang Kuo Lau rides backwards on a donkey and carries a bamboo musical instrument. He is the bringer of offspring, especially male. A renowned musician, he was born at the end of the 7th century.

Ts'ao Kuo Chiu carries a pair of castanets or an imperial tablet of recommendation. Born in the 10th century, he was a member of the imperial court, the son of Ts'ao Pin of the Sung dynasty. He is a reformed murderer and is patron saint of the theatrical profession.

Han Hsiang Tzu is depicted with a jade flute and is the patron of musicians. He is a poet and lover of solitude and beauty.

Han Chung Li was a military man in imperial service during the Han dynasty. He is an alchemist who invented the pill of immortality. He carries a feathery fan, which controls the seas, or the peach of immortality.

Lan Ts'ai Ho represents the lunatic and is seen holding a basket of flowers. He is the patron saint of florists.

Ho Hsien Ku, a female, was granted immortality by the other seven immortals, who were disguised as beggars, when she welcomed and fed them in a house where she was severely mistreated as a servant. She carries a lotus flower, symbolizing openness and wisdom.

TI KUAI LI
1. South

HAN HSIANG TZU
2. Southeast

HO HSIEN KU
5. Southwest

HAN CHUNG LI
3. East

LU TUNG PIN
6. West

TS'AO KUO CHIU
4. Northeast

LAN TS'AI HO
7. Northwest

CHANG KUO LAU
8. North

CH'IEN
TUI
SUN
LI
K'AN
CHEN
KEN
K'UN

Figure 7a. **The Eight Immortals:** Eight sages, recognized as immortal, are worshipped in China. In the center is the *Tai Ji Tu*, "the diagram of the supreme ultimate," representing the union of pairs of opposite principles, yin (female/earth) and yang (male/heaven)—duality merging into wholeness. Yin is represented by the black half of the circle and yang by the white half. Within each half is a dot of color of the other half, representing that each force contains its opposite. These two forces are opposite, yet originate from each other and flow into each other, interacting perpetually in a cycle. Around this symbol are eight trigrams, representing eight directions. The immortal saints are shown next to the trigrams associated with them.

The Dhyani Buddhas

The Five Dhyani ("meditation") Buddhas, or Great Buddhas of Wisdom, are primordial Buddhas, the central deities of Mahayana Buddhism. Each represents a different aspect of enlightened consciousness to aid in spiritual transformation. They are represented in Buddhist art in mandalas and thangkas. Each Buddha overcomes a specific evil with a particular good, and each has a complete system of symbolism.

The chart on the next page summarizes qualities of the Dhyani Buddhas.

The 84 Mahasiddhas

Traditionally, 84 great *siddhas* from India founded the Buddhist tantric lineages of Tibet. The word *siddhi* means "perfection," or "spiritual power," and siddhas are those who have realized perfect spiritual awakening. Nearly all of them lived for many centuries and then left the Earth by ascending bodily into heaven. These remarkable beings attained enlightenment, supernormal powers, and immortality by disregarding convention and penetrating to the core of reality. They show us the way to the spontaneous, free state of mystical attainment. Here are just a handful of the most renowned:

- Luipa (late 8th century): "The Fish-Gut Eater."
- Saraha (late 8th century): "The Great Brahmin."
- Ghantapa (9th century): "Bearer of the Bell," who rose into heaven, and, with his young consort, became the deities Padmasambhava and Vajravarahi, joined in union (see Figure 7c on page 100).
- Dombipa or Dombi Heruka (10th century): "The Tiger Rider."
- Tilopa (989–1069): "The Great Renunciate."
- Naropa (1016–1100): "The Dauntless Disciple."

The Five Dhyani Buddhas

Buddha	Vairocana	Akshobhya	Amitabha	Ratnasambhva	Amoghasiddhi
Epithet	Buddha Supreme and Eternal, The Radiant One	Immovable or Unshakable Buddha	Buddha of Infinite Light	Source of Precious Things or Jewel-Born One	Almighty Conquerer or Lord of Karma
Family	Buddha	Vajra	Padma	Ratna	Karma
Wisdom	All-Accommodating	Mirror-Like	Discriminating Awareness	Equanimity and Equality	All-Accomplishing
Evil	Ignorance	Hatred and Anger	Desire	Greed and Pride	Envy
Skandha, Aggregate	Form	Consciousness	Perception	Sensation	Mental Formation
Action	Turning Wheel of Dharma (teaching)	Protecting, Destroying	Magnetizing, Subjugating	Enriching, Increasing	Pacifying
Symbol	Wheel	Scepter, Vajra	Lotus	Jewel	Double Vajras
Element	Space	Air, Wind	Fire	Earth	Water
Color	White	Blue	Red	Gold, Yellow	Green
Season		Winter	Spring	Autumn	Summer
Direction	Center	East	West	South	North
Mudra, Gesture	Dharmachakra (Wheel-turning Gesture)	Bhumisparsa Mudra (Gesture of Touching the Earth)	Dhyana mudra (Gesture of Meditation)	Varada Mudra (Gesture of Giving)	Abhaya Mudra (Gesture of Fearlessness)
Consort	White Tara	Locana	Pandara	Mamaki	Green Tara
Vehicle:	Lion	Elephant	Peacock	Horse	Garuda
Dhyani Bodhisattva, Spiritual Son	Samantabhadra	Vajrapani	Avalokiteshvara	Ratnapani	Vishvapani
Pure Land, Sect	Central Pure Land Akanistha Ghanavyuha	Eastern Pure Land Abhirati	Western Pure Land Sukhavati	Southern Pure Land Shrimat	Northern Pure Land Prakuta
Mantra, Syllable	Om	Hum	Hrih	Trah	Ah

Figure 7b.

Figure 7c. **Yab-Yum:** A Buddhist *Mahasiddha* (great perfected saint) named Padmasambhava (the Lotus-born) is shown in *Yab-Yum* (father-and-mother) position with his mystic consort, Vajravarahi. The Yab-Yum position is also called the Great Pose, *Mahamudra*, the closest embrace between man and woman. The male and female are inseparable; one cannot exist without the other. Together they symbolize the highest spiritual unity of contrasts, the resolution of duality into divine wholeness. Another symbol representing this concept is the Confucian *Yin-Yang* symbol.

Kuan Yin

Kuan Yin ("one who hears the cries of the world") is the most popular religious figure in China. She embodies the female form of the *bodhisattva* ("enlightened being") Avalokitesvara, known as Padmapani, born from a tear shed by Lord Buddha at the sight of humanity's suffering. The goddess of mercy and compassion, she helps people escape impossible or awkward situations. She is often portrayed rescuing the Jade Emperor from his predicaments.

Kuan Yin rejected marriage and joined the nunnery of the White Bird in Lungshu Hsien, against the will of her father, Miao Chuang Wang, ruler of a northern Chinese kingdom about 696 BC. Infuriated, he ordered her execution, but the sword chosen to carry it out shattered into a thousand pieces. Then he ordered her suffocation. Her soul descended into hell and transformed it into paradise. She was carried on a lotus flower to the island of P'ootoo, near Nimpo, where she healed the diseased and saved mariners from shipwreck for nine years.

In order to raise money to build a bridge at Ch'uan Zhou near Lo-Yang, Kuan Yin posed as a beautiful woman. She stood on a boat and vowed to marry any man who could throw coins onto her body from the riverbank. The coins always landed in the boat or in the river, and were later recovered by children diving into the water.

Figure 7d. **Kuan Yin:** "In the lands of the universe there is no place where She does not manifest Herself.... Compassion wondrous as a great cloud, pouring spiritual rain like nectar, quenching the flames of distress!" —The Lotus Sutra.

Wei T'o, a straw shoe vendor, outwitted Kuan Yin by smashing a coin into powdery fragments with a rock, and hurling the powder at her. Wei T'o and the boat's helmsman built the bridge. After the opening ceremonies, Kuan Yin asked Wei T'o to take her hand. They rose off the ground and flew to Pu T'o Shan, Kuan Yin's home. She asked Wei T'o to sit opposite her and promised they would face each other eternally, because he had won her heart.

In temples throughout China, statues of Kuan Yin and Wei T'o face each other and are worshipped as a symbol of undying love. Thus, the Chinese say that couples are "face-to-face husband and wife."

Figure 7e. Lao Tzu: "The Tao that can be told is not the eternal Tao. The name that can be named is not the eternal name. The nameless is the beginning of heaven and earth." —Tao Te Ching, 1

Lao Tzu

Lao Tzu (604 BC–531 BC?), founder of the Tao-chia school of Taoism, kept his identity secret in order to test his students. His name means "old master." The *Tao Te Ching*, the foundation of Taoist philosophy, is attributed to him. Its message is to live a simple life of moderation and peacefulness, in tune with natural law.

Lao Tzu is said to live on the magical, fertile mountain Hua Shan, also called the Western Mountain or Flower Mountain. Near its summit is the temple of Lao Tzu. In front of the temple is the great furnace where Lao Tzu created his pill of immortality. Pilgrims visit this mountain in hopes of meeting Lao Tzu or gaining his blessing. Mushrooms growing on this sacred mountain are believed to grant immortality.

Li Ching Yuen

A legendary Chinese herbalist, Li Ching Yuen was born in 1677, in the mountains of southwest China. Later he moved to Szechuan province. At age 11, he met three traveling herbalists and joined them to learn the art of medicinal herbs. They journeyed in high mountains, through many countries, where they encountered lions, tigers, and poisonous snakes.

When Li was collecting herbs, he met an herbalist who walked very quickly. Li wanted to know how he could move so fast. The herbalist told him that he ate one-third ounce of Gou Qi Zi (goji berries or wolfberry fruit) daily. Li took his advice. He married 14 times, and lived to see 180 descendants covering 11 generations.

In 1749, at age 71, Li joined the Chinese army as a teacher of martial arts and tactical advisor. At age 130, while traveling in the K'ung-T'ung mountains, he met a 500-year-old Taoist. Li asked him the secret of longevity, and the Taoist taught him an exercise called Ba-Kua (eight trigrams) exercise, similar to Tai Chi Chuan.

Li Ching Yuen sold medicinal herbs and taught many disciples in the Oh-Mei mountains of Szechuan province. Those disciples lived more than 100 years. The oldest men of the district could recall stories about Li Ching Yuen from their grandfathers. Even at age 248, Master Li had good eyesight and a quick stride.

In 1927, General Yang Shen described Master Li in his report, "A Factual Account of the 250-Year-Old Good-Luck Man": "He can walk very quickly in the mountains, even though he's almost 250 years old. He is seven feet tall. His complexion is ruddy, but he is completely bald. His fingernails are very long. In one meal he eats three bowls of rice, chicken, and another kind of meat."

The New York Times reported his death on May 6, 1933, as *"The Amazing 250-Year-Old Man."*[1] Professor Wu

Figure 7f. **Master Li Ching-Yuen:** This photograph of Master Li was taken in 1927 at the residence of General Yang Shen.

Chung-Chien, dean of the department of Education in Minkuo University, found records showing that Li was born in 1677 and that the Imperial Chinese Government congratulated him on his 150th and 200th birthdays. At the time of his death, he looked to be a man of 50.

Master Li's secret: "One should have a quiet heart, sit calmly like a tortoise, walk sprightly like a pigeon, and sleep soundly like a dog." He attributed his longevity to peace of mind and said everyone could live at least a century by attaining inward calm.

Silent Master of Tengboche

Figure 7g. Rinpoche Lopsang Thundun: When Sean David Morton arrived at the Tengboche monastery, Rinpoche gave him a box containing a brush, mirror, some beads, and other trinkets. He told Sean that the monastery had been keeping it for him. When Sean refused the gift repeatedly, finally Rinpoche punched Sean in the third eye with his knuckle, which awakened Sean's memory of his past life in the monastery. Photo courtesy of Sean David Morton, *www.seandavidmorton.com.*

In 1986, in Dharamsala, India, my friend Sean David Morton was directed personally by the Dalai Lama to study at the Buddhist monastery in Tengboche, Nepal. So Sean made the grueling two-week trek to 12,687 feet, on the border of China, at the foot of the mountain Ama Dablam, near Mount Everest. Rinpoche Lopsang Thundun, head of the monastery, accepted Sean as a novitiate, because he recognized that, in a past life, Sean had been a young monk there.

One morning before sunrise, an unusual little man from the mountains barged into the monastery, as if he owned the place. He rambled on, making chirpy sounds, yammering like a monkey, waking up everyone, bellowing, "Hello I'm here! Hello everybody!"

That day the monastery took a vacation. There were no exercises, chanting, or prayers. It was a feast day. The monks ate, played games, and, for the entire day, listened to this man talk. He spoke part Nepalese, part Tibetan, and part Chinese, with a weird dialect. Sean did not understand a word. He kept asking the English-speaking monks to translate, but they just patted him on the head and laughed.

All day long, the man sang songs, told stories, and acted things out—as if a drive-in movie had showed up at the monastery. From what the monks translated to Sean, the man related his adventures in underground caves, his travels to other worlds, and all he learned in meditation.

Legend says that there are two great subcontinents: Agartha Major underneath the Himalayas in Tibet, and Agartha Minor below the Gobi Desert in China. These continents are supposedly inhabited by two races, associated with extraterrestrials: (1) "Royal Serpents" (*Nagas Hirachi*), or serpent-men; tall, thin bipeds with tails and large eyes, which evolved from surviving dinosaurs that were driven underground after an ancient meteor collision, and (2) "Sons of the Original Son," blond-haired, light-blue-skinned giants, between 9 and 16 feet tall, which are remnants of the primal, original humans.

So the mystery man rambled on all day and well into the night. Finally everyone went to sleep. The next morning, Sean was making breakfast. The man came into the central kitchen, the Great Hall. Sean greeted him, but the man said nothing. Instead, he pointed to things he wanted. Sean served him tea. When the other monks arrived, they were reverential toward him, but he did not answer. The monks gave him food, supplies, and blankets. Then everyone gathered and sat for a very long time, with hands folded, as the man walked up into the mountains and disappeared.

Sean inquired about the man, but received no response. Finally, after Sean pestered Rinpoche sufficiently, he conceded: "He has been coming here every year since I was age 5 or 6, when I came to the monastery." Sean realized that Rinpoche was in his 60s, but the man looked younger than that. So he asked, "How old do you think he is?" Rinpoche replied, "He says he's 450, but he doesn't look a day over 300." Sean thought it was a joke.

But Rinpoche continued, "He looks exactly the same as when I first met him as a young boy, and he hasn't aged a day. He says he's 450 years old, and I have no reason to disbelieve him. He said that he probably stopped counting around then, so he's probably older than that."

Sean asked, "Have you any proof?" Rinpoche replied, "The only proof I have is that I knew him. The people in my village knew him. My family knew him. My father's father knew him, and he seems to have a connection with my family."

Sean then asked, "Why does he come?" Rinpoche answered, "He comes to the monastery because he takes a vow of silence in the mountains. He gets to speak one day out of the year, and that was his day." Rinpoche then explained why the monastery took a vacation that day: "It is more valuable to be in the presence of one of those men than any prayers or any work we can do."

Figure 7h. **Monastery at Tengboche.** Photo courtesy of Cheryl Goodwin, *www.good2gophotgraphy.com.*

Bo Min Gaung

The Kung Fu teacher of my friend Andrew Blagg advised him to seek out the legendary *weikzas* (wizard monks) of Burma, whose lineage predates Buddhism by thousands of years. Under mysterious, uncanny circumstances, Andrew met and studied with an amazing weikza named Abun Wanta, whose body houses the soul of another legendary weikza, Bo Min Gaung.

Bo Min Gaung had lived in northern Burma, at Mount Popa. He was renowned for his spiritual power, strength, and supernormal abilities, and is famed for leading a nonviolent resistance against the Japanese during World War II. He harbored thousands of people against persecution. Three times the Japanese publicly tried to be-

Figure 7i. **Bo Min Gaung:** A famous weikza of the 20th century who is worshipped in Burma.

head him, and each time hundreds of witnesses saw the Samurai sword blade break over his neck. The third time the Japanese gave up and said, "Okay, this is a man of power."

In the early 20th century, Abun Wanta meditated in a cave for 10 years, then came out of his cave and worked as a civil engineer in the 1920s, repairing Shwedagon Pagoda. He returned to the cave in the late 1920s and emerged again in 1951, the very day that Bo Min Gaung passed from his body. At that moment, Bo Min Gaung's spirit passed into Abun Wanta, who has since then carried on Bo Min Gaung's teachings.

All the weikzas Andrew met in Burma had three things in common: Firstly, they were all vital for their ages, which was well beyond 100 years. Secondly, they had incredible strength. And finally, they were all tremendously funny.

Figure 7j. **Abun and Andrew:** Abun Wanta, well more than 100 years old, is the embodiment of legendary weikza Bo Min Gaung, and was Andrew's mentor in his previous life.

Chapter 8

Madame Blavatsky's Teachers

*For Earth is only the footstool of man in
his ascension to higher regions.*
—Helena Petrovna Blavatsky

Madame Helena Petrovna Blavatsky, founder of the Theosophical Society and author of *The Secret Doctrine*, was born in 1831 in southern Russia. As a child she was thrown from a horse, when a tall, mysterious man from India miraculously appeared and saved her life by reining in the horse and lifting her head, so her skull would not hit the ground.

She moved to London in 1851 and once again met this same man, Master Morya Khan, whom she had seen in dreams since childhood. He told her that he had come to London to meet her personally. He was in Hyde Park, accompanying the Premier of Nepal to the first great International Exhibition. Seventeen years later, in 1868, Morya sent her a message while she was in Florence, instructing her to meet him in Constantinople and travel with him to Tibet.

Master Morya, known as El Morya, lived about 150 miles southwest of Lhasa, near Tashilhunpo Monastery, seat of the Panchen Lama, spiritual leader of Tibet. Morya's house was in a narrow, steep ravine with a stream, flanked by high mountains covered with pines. It was near the town of Shigatse, on the River Nyang, about four miles above its confluence with the Tsang-po (Brahmaputra) river. Blavatsky stayed with Morya's friend Koot Hoomi (also known as Kuthumi or K.M.), on the other side of the ravine. She studied with her teachers Morya and Kuthumi from 1868 until the end of 1870.

Kuthumi

Figure 8a. **Master Koot Hoomi:** Painted by Hermann Schmiechen in 1884 in London.

Master Kuthumi Lal Singh is a Sikh, from Nepal, of Kashmiri and Rajput extraction. He lived in India as Sirdar Thakar Singh Sadhanwali. Ever youthful, his complexion is light, and he wears no turban. He has long brown hair with red and gold strands. His beard is parted in the middle and fanned out in Rajput style. His nose is chiseled, and his eyes are large, liquid blue, and full of joy and love.

It is said that Kuthumi's previous incarnations included Thutmose III, Pythagoras (582–507 BC), Saint Francis of Assisi (AD 1182–1226), and Shah Jahan (AD 1592–1666). Kuthumi took a university degree in Europe in the mid-1700s. That made his age more than 100 when Blavatsky met him. A scholar in English, French, and German, he studied at the University of Leipzig during the 1870s.

He plays celestial music on an unusual organ, which sends healing to those in transition, and inspires architects, poets, and scientists.

Master Morya

Master Morya, from Nepal, was a Buddhist, belonging to the Shivabhavika sect. A Rajput king by birth, Morya has a commanding, overwhelming presence. Of dark complexion, he has a black beard divided into two parts, in Rajput style, long, flowing black hair in a turban, and dark, piercing, powerful eyes. His height is 6 feet 6 inches. He speaks in short, terse sentences. Morya was a few hundred years old when Madame Blavatsky first saw him in childhood, and his appearance never changed.

Master Morya lived as Ranbir Singh, a member of Kashmir's royal family. It is said his other embodiments included the Hebrew patriarch Abraham, Akbar the Great (1542–1605), Thomas Becket (1118–1170), and Thomas More (1478–1535).

Along with Master Kuthumi and Saint Germain, Morya founded the Theosophical Society. He ascended in 1898 and continues his great work for humanity. He says that it is impossible to make progress on the spiritual path without a sense of humor.

Figure 8b. **Master Morya:** "Each man of us has gone this ceaseless round and will repeat it for ever and ever." —El Morya

Djwal Khool

At his home, Kuthumi received various young Tibetan *chelas* (pupils) from the Lamasery. One of them was Djwal Khool (or Khul), age 15, known formerly as Gai Ben-Jamin. He is said to have a Tibetan face with high cheek bones, and be somewhat rugged in appearance.

Known as "The Tibetan," he is called the "Messenger of the Masters." He dictated much of H.P. Blavatsky's *The Secret Doctrine*, plus volumes through Alice A. Bailey. Morya, Djwal Khul, and

Kuthumi are believed to be the three Magis or Wise Men who followed the Star of Bethlehem to Jesus. Djwal Khool now works with healers, medical researchers, and philanthropic organizations associated with healing.

Hilarion

In 1860 Madame Blavatsky first encountered Master Illarion (Hilarion Smerdis), the "Greek Brother," in Armenia. She met him again in Greece in 1871. According to Mr. Leadbeater (Blavatsky's student, who wrote about the masters), he appears as an Arab: young, handsome, with a slightly hooked nose, a low, broad forehead, dark skin, dark eyes, and a black beard. He wears white robes and a turban.

Leadbeater says that Hilarion lives with the Druze sect, the mystics of Mount Lebanon, an Islamic monotheistic order, incorporating Gnostic, neo-Platonic, and other philosophies. Colonel Olcott, one of the founders of the Theosophical Society, refers to Hilarion as a "representative of the Neo-Platonic Alexandrian school."

Some believe that his previous lives included the Apostle Paul of Tarsus, the Assyrian Neo-Platonic philosopher Iamblichus Chalcidensis (circa AD 245–325), Smerdis the Magian of Cyprus (AD 6th century), and Archbishop Hilarion Cigalen of Cyprus (born 1660). Some people also believe he was Saint Hilarion (AD 291–371).

Hilarion is the guardian of ancient Egyptian mysteries, including medicinal remedies. He is recognized as a proponent of the Orpheus tradition, and he introduced the science of divination into Cyprus in 2000 BC. He is a master of devotees, with intense purity and a fiery devotion that overcomes all obstacles.

Serapis Bey

Serapis was the Greek god of Alexandria and chief deity of Ptolemaic Egypt. Ptolemy I, the first Greek monarch of Egypt (305–283 BC), was told in a dream to obtain a statue of Serapis from Sinope, on the Black Sea, and to promote the cult of Serapis to unite his Greek and Egyptian subjects. Serapis is the Egyptian god of ascension and the bridge between heaven and earth.

In 1871 Blavatsky went to the pyramids and, in Luxor, met the Coptic Master Serapis Bey and his brother Tuitit Bey. Serapis is described by C.W. Leadbeater as tall and fair in complexion, with a distinguished, ascetic appearance. He is Greek by birth although his work is done in Egypt.

One evening Blavatsky was traveling with Serapis in the desert and camped for the night under a tent. After their evening meal she joked about wanting a café au lait. The master rose and went to a camel, drew a liquid out of a water skin, and brought it to her. It was the steaming hot beverage she had asked for! As she drank it, the liquid turned back into water.

Master P., The Venetian

Hilarion visited Egypt and worked with Serapis, as well as Master P., the Venetian. While Madame Blavatsky was in Egypt, she met Master P. Described as the most handsome of the members of the Brotherhood by Mr. Leadbeater, he is about 6 feet 5 inches, with a flowing beard, golden hair, and blue eyes. Although he was born in Venice, his appearance is Germanic.

His previous incarnations included "Minister of Culture" in the government of Atlantis, an architect of the Egyptian pyramids, and an Incan mural painter. Many people believe he was Paolo Veronese (1528–1588), a Venetian Italian Renaissance painter.

Lord Maitreya

Madame Blavatsky stated that Maitreya ("loving kindness") is the secret name of the Kalki avatar and fifth Buddha, who comes at the culmination of this world cycle (see page 93). This new messiah, or next advent of Lord Maitreya, will be a great spiritual teacher, bringing a new religion that would unify all religions.

According to traditional Buddhism, Maitreya will appear when the teachings of the current Buddha are completely forgotten. The event will allow the unveiling of true dharma to the people, ending humanity's current age of ignorance, and birthing a new world. It is said that Gautama Buddha visited Maitreya in his celestial abode and commissioned him to come to Earth as his successor 5,000 years after Buddha's death (see Figure 8c on page 115).

The Mahachohan

Morya and Kuthumi referred to the Mahachohan ("great master") as their guru. He was the Chief of the Archive Registers of the Dalai Lama and the Panchen Lama. Kuthumi called him his "Great Master." Madame Blavatsky called him the "Chohan Rimpoche" or the "Chohan Lama Rimpoche."

Mr. Leadbeater describes him as having the personality of a statesman or military man in an Indian body, tall and thin, wearing Indian robes and a white turban. He has a strong, square chin and sharp profile. His eyes are deep and penetrating. His clean-shaven face is stern, and he speaks abruptly.

One of his former incarnations is thought to include Homer, the Greek poet (circa 8th century BC). He is said to represent the Holy Spirit, and is chief master of the Great White Lodge.

The Four Mind-Born Sons of Brahma

Madame Blavatsky wrote about a master who, she believed, came from the planet Venus: Sanatkumara. He is referred to as lord of the world, spiritual king of the world, and director of the evolution of the planet. Madame Blavatsky said he appears as a dignified, handsome youth with omniscient majesty. He is said to reside with Lord Buddha and Lord Maitreya in Shambhala, legendary celestial city above the Gobi desert. These three masters form the Triumvirate of Shambhala.

According to ancient scriptures of India, Lord Brahma, the creator, practiced austerity for the purpose of creating various worlds. As a result of his penance, he had four "mind-born" sons—born as ideas in his mind, without human birth. They appeared at the beginning of creation, 5 years old, blazing with spiritual energy. Their names were Sanaka (ancient), Sananda (joyous), Sanatana (eternal), and Sanatkumara (eternally young).

Sanatkumara is often worshipped in the Hindu religion as the eternal youth Lord Muruga, otherwise known as Kumaraswamy, Skanda, or Kartikeya, one of Lord Shiva's sons. He is believed to be the Buddha of this present age, and brings eternal youth.

Figure 8c. **Triumvirate of Shambhala.** Tibetan Buddhists believe Shambhala is a mystical kingdom guarding sacred, secret spiritual teachings, a heaven of the gods, hidden by mists deep within the Himalayas, encircled by a ring of snowy mountains, and shaped like an eight-petaled lotus. Only accomplished yogis can locate and enter it with the supernormal powers of flying. Lord Gautama, the past Buddha, is on the left, depicted in his teaching posture. Lord Sanatkumara, Buddha of the present, is in the center. Lord Maitreya, the future Buddha, is on the right.

Figure 8d. **Sanatkumara:** In the present *kalpa* (an age that lasts more than four billion years), Sanatkumara and his three brothers expounded the truth, which was lost during the dissolution at the end of the preceding age.

Figure 8e. **Sananda:** *"OM Bhoor Bhuvah Svah, Tat savitur varenyam. Bhargo devasya dheemahi diyo yonah prachodeyaat."* I meditate on the spiritual effulgence of that adorable light, the ultimate reality, source of the universe, which is worthy of praise. Unveil to me the face of the true spiritual sun, the supreme Self, which appears through a disc of golden light. May that divine being bless me, purifying and illuminating my intellect, that I may realize the ultimate truth." —The *Gayatri* Mantra, Rig-Veda, III.62.10

Sananda is the universal, cosmic Christ. He embodies the universe. All the stars, galaxies, and solar systems are contained within his being. He brings universal light, love, wisdom, power, and healing.

The Seven Rays

In the third volume of the *Secret Doctrine*, Blavatsky described "Seven Primeval Rays" as a group of celestial beings. She stated that this symbolism was "adopted later on by the Christian Religion as the 'Seven Angels of the Presence.'" These seven rays, which, according to Theosophy, convey divine qualities, are the seven types of light-substance that compose the universe.

Alice A. Bailey (1880–1949), whose books are based on Theosophy, believed the Seven Primeval Rays originate within the "Solar Logos"— the consciousness of the Sun—and are then transmitted through Sanatkumara, the Buddha of this age (see Figure 8g on page 118).

Madame Blavatsky's Contribution

Madame Blavatsky did more to popularize ascended master teachings than any other writer. At the same time, much controversy abounds around her. Some of her claims have been investigated and exposed as false. However, she inspired many generations and made a great contribution toward bringing the ancient teachings of India to the West, as no other person before her.

Blavatsky's teachers were immortalized in the writings of various members of the Theosophical Society. Because of the

Figure 8f. Blavatsky and Her Teachers: This photo is believed to be a group portrait of Blavatsky in the foreground, with masters Kuthumi, Morya, and Saint Germain, from left to right, in the background. Whether there is any truth to this is anyone's guess.

The Seven Rays
According to Alice A. Bailey

NO.	RAY	COLOR	ASCENDED MASTER	ASCENSION RETREAT	PLANET RULER	CHAKRA	JEWEL
1	Will - Power	Blue	Morya	Darjeeling, India	Pluto/Vulcan	Vishuddha (5) Throat	Diamond
2	Love - Wisdom	Indigo	Kuthumi	Shigatse, Tibet	Sun/Jupiter	Sahasrara (7) Crown	Sapphire
3	Active Intelligence	Green	Venetian	Chateau de Liberté, France	Earth/Saturn	Anahata (4) Heart	Emerald
4	Harmony thru Conflict	Yellow	Serapis	Luxor, Egypt	Moon/Mercury	Muladhara (1) Base	Jasper
5	Concrete Science	Orange	Hilarion	Island of Crete, Greece	Venus	Ajna (6) Brow	Topaz
6	Love - Devotion	Red	Master Jesus	Mount Lebanon, Lebanon	Mars/Neptune	Manipura (3) Solar Plexus	Ruby
7	Ceremonial Order	Violet	Saint Germain	Transylvania, Romania	Uranus	Swadisthana (2) Sacral	Amethyst

Figure 8g. The Seven Rays: Alice A. Bailey, Theosophical author of the early 20th century, wrote about the esoteric meaning of the seven rays in her books.

fame surrounding these masters, many mediums have claimed to "channel" them during the past century. A few of the many ascended master societies include the following:

- The Theosophical Society, founded in New York City in 1875 by Helena Blavatsky, Henry Steel Olcott, and William Quan Judge. *www.theosophical.org.*

- The Agni Yoga Society, originated in 1920 by Nicholas Roerich and his wife Helena, who published messages from Master Morya. *www.agniyoga.org.*

- The Lucis Trust, established by Alice A. Bailey and Foster Bailey in 1922. Alice Bailey published messages from the Tibetan teacher Djwhal Khul in 24 books. *www.lucistrust.org.*

- The "I AM" Religious Activity, created in 1934 by Guy W. Ballard and his wife Edna Ballard. They received 3,834 dictations from many ascended masters and published the monthly periodical, *The Voice of The "I AM,"* and *The Saint Germain Series* books. *www.saintgermainfoundation.org.*

- White Eagle Lodge, established by Grace and Ivan Cooke in 1936 to spread the teachings of a Native American ascended being. *www.whiteeaglelodge.org.*

- The Bridge to Freedom, started by Geraldine Innocente in 1951. In 6,000 pages of dictation, she received messages from the masters and published under a pseudonym, Thomas Printz.

- The Summit Lighthouse, founded by Mark Lyle Prophet in 1958. After he died, Elizabeth Clare Prophet continued his work and founded the Church Universal and Triumphant in 1975. She also founded the Royal Teton Ranch and wrote many books. *www.tsl.org.*

- Ascended Master Teaching Foundation, created by Annette and Werner Schroeder in 1980 to propagate the dictations received by Geraldine Innocente. *www.ascendedmaster.org.*

- The Temple of the Presence, established in 1995 by Monroe and Carolyn Shearer, in Tucson, Arizona. *www.templeofthepresence.org.*

- Ascension Research Center, an Internet resource for ascended master teachings. *www.ascension-research.org.*

AUTHOR'S NOTE: I am not endorsing any of these organizations. I am simply providing information so you can come to your own conclusions. Messages from divine beings might be inspiring and enlightening, but they are only as clear and accurate as their messengers. Wisdom and discernment are required when approaching them. You can learn how to distinguish true divine message from other messages by studying my books *Divine Revelation* and *How to Hear the Voice of God*.

Part III

Mystical Encounters

Chapter 9

Ascended Masters Among Us

*Immortality is the great world of light that
lies behind all human destinies.*
—Henry W. Longfellow

In this section of the book, you will meet some rare, extraordinary
people who are walking the path of ascension, or who have had direct
experiences and physical encounters with the ascended beings and divine masters.

Only a handful of individuals are attempting to make the leap of
faith to walk beyond death and realize physical immortality. I have
had the opportunity to meet a few of these precious beings. Now we
will explore some of their experiences.

Joanna Cherry

My first mentor in the ascension field is a beautiful being of light:
Dr. Joanna Cherry, founder of Ascension Mastery International, an organization that promotes teachings of ascension and distributes beautiful artwork of the ascended masters. I consider Joanna one of the
foremost authorities on ascension. Here is how Joanna describes her
first ascension experience:

> In 1983, after visiting Mount Shasta and reading about the as-
> cended masters in *Unveiled Mysteries* by Guy Ballard under the pen-
> name Godfre Ray King, I returned home to San Francisco, on fire. I
> began to share the possibility of ascension for humanity. I began to

meditate, nearly every day, to experience ascension, with the help of my two closest inner friends: Saint Germain and Babaji, the Yogi Christ, the immortal master of the Himalayas.

I had in mind a most definite picture of how my ascension would look: My body would become invisible and turn into light. I would float off to an ascended master retreat, where there would be a party. "Welcome!" and "Congratulations!" the masters would say. After the party I would float back home and be an ascended master on earth.

I had some fears to overcome: I feared death; I feared being non-physical (which equaled death in my mind); I feared flying through the air. So I worked to heal these fears.

For a year or more, I could point to no progress in my ascension meditation. I had received one clear guidance only, which was to open all my chakras. Finally, I began to see light in my third eye, and it was growing brighter.

One day I had this thought: "I think I can ascend today. I think I've worked through my fears enough—let's give it a try." So I opened my chakras, and welcomed the light. My third eye grew increasingly brighter, began to blaze, and suddenly I felt afraid. "I could be annihilated by this light!" Very forcefully, I said "No!"

The light immediately receded.

I felt a sense of great disappointment, which was not my own. I saw Saint Germain (I did not even know he could feel disappointed), who said, "You were so close! If you had just gone a little farther, you would have experienced an ascension." But I had frightened myself with the thought of annihilation.

For a few months, I did not call in the light. But I was learning something vital to the ascension process. I kept asking, "How do you ascend? Exactly what do you do?" The answer was surprisingly simple. You declare it. You say, "I am ascending now. I am quickening. I am lighter and lighter. I am the light of my own God-being," and other statements of truth.

When I began to say these statements, I felt an immediate shift— a rush of speed—an upliftment. These words became an essential part of my meditation. I later learned to add a spinning energy, which makes the words even more powerful.

After a few months, I felt the energy build and had the thought again: "I think I can ascend today." So I sat down as before, opened my chakras, called in the light, and spoke the words. Again the light grew in brightness until it was a great blazing sun in my forehead. Once again I began to feel afraid.

I was just on the verge of saying "No!" when—and I cannot tell you how this happened—my breath imploded, and I surrendered. The light washed over me, through me, and I became light. It was me, and I was it, and there was nothing to fear. Here I was, still present, still being. And I was in pure bliss.

A great grin appeared before me in my inner eye. It was Saint Germain. Never in all my work on ascension had he smiled so at me. "Congratulations!" he said. "This was your first ascension experience."

"But how could that be?" I cried. "I'm not floating off to the retreat, and I can still feel the things around me." He laughed. "You are ascending in your own way, step by step," he explained. "Not only is this best for you, but you have come to be a teacher of ascension. You want to create techniques that help others ascend."

My expectation of ascension was so rigid that I had trouble believing my master friend. I was in confusion when Babaji appeared. He said sternly, "Do not underestimate this experience. You have had your first ascension experience today." I realized something really significant had happened, though it did not fit my anticipated picture.

I began to teach this meditation in my ascension workshops. I have realized, from the feedback I received, that it is a practice of great power. Many people now use it as an ascension tool. When you are ready to leave the earth plane, you can use it to ascend. Your body will come with you or remain on earth, according to your readiness.

You will learn this powerful ascension meditation in Chapter 18 on page 219 of this book.

Annalee Skarin

Annalee Kohlhepp was born on July 7, 1899, in American Falls, Idaho, the ninth child of Frederick John Kohlhepp and Mary Ella Hickman. Unwanted and unloved, Analee suffered a painful upbringing. In fact, her mother had worn a girdle so her pregnancy would be hidden. Her father, a Jewish convert to Mormonism, died when Annalee was 19.

Annalee's first marriage to William Gorman ended in annulment. Their son died at the age of nine months. After her marriage ended, she served in a Church of Latter Day Saints mission in California where she met Reason Skarin, whom she married 21 years later.

After her mission, Annalee wed Hugo Avarell in 1922 and bore a stillborn son and two daughters, Linda Moat and Hope A. Hilton. That unhappy marriage ended in 1943. When her daughters were teenagers, Annalee left for Buffalo, New York, and married her true love, Reason Skarin, who had waited for her and kept her photo on his mantelpiece.

Annalee was dedicated to the LDS Church and served in many capacities for decades. She was spiritual, mystical, devoted, and possessed a keen sense of humor. After she wrote the magnificent book *Ye Are Gods*, her son-in-law wrote a cutting exposé of the book and submitted it to Mark E. Petersen, an LDS Church elder. Annalee's daughter Hope, who believed her mother was paranoid schizophrenic, fully supported her husband's actions.

The Mormon Council of Twelve declared Annalee to be anti-Christ, because, as Apostle Mark E. Peterson of the council reported, her teachings nullified the Atonement of Jesus Christ in her claim that "there shall be no more death, that death is unnecessary and that we ourselves can overcome and avoid death." The Council, consisting primarily of men who had not read Annalee's book, excommunicated her from the church.

In a letter dated June 7, 1951, Annalee wrote to a friend: "All I am trying to do is to teach mankind that it is possible for every child of God to be so in tune with Him and His Holy Spirit that they can be directed in all that they do, in all that they say, and that their lives can become a melody of living glory as they learn to abide completely and fully in His Holy Spirit. It is such a breathtaking glory every moment of every day that it is almost unspeakable in its power."[1]

Annalee's heart was broken, because she was entirely devoted to the church and had served in every way—teaching, heading organizations, and filling missions. She had given a tenth, and sometimes half, of her income to the church.

At age 52, Annalee found herself living in the home of a friend in Salt Lake City. On the morning of June 16, 1952, Annalee hinted to her friend, "Mrs. B.," that the previous night she had received a revelation that the angels might be coming for her soon. She left instructions with Mrs. B. for her books and personal belongings to be sent to her daughter.

That evening Mrs. B. noticed a bright light flash from under Annalee's bedroom door but did not disturb Annalee, thinking she was studying. Late that night, at 1:10 a.m., Mrs. B. suddenly awoke and felt impelled to rush to Mrs. Skarin's room. Annalee was gone!

Figure 9a. **Annalee Skarin:** Photo courtesy of Ascension Mastery International.

All her clothing was still there and her dentures were lying on the bedside table. A strong yet delicate scent filled the house, and Mrs. B. thought this fragrance had awakened her.

The same day, June 17, at about 10:30 p.m., Mrs. B. was sitting in her living room with her grown son and two daughters. Annalee Skarin suddenly entered the house wearing a plain blue dress. Her legs were covered with dust and her hair was disheveled.

Annalee asked them, "So you believe I have translated?" Mrs. B. and her family members replied, "Yes." Annalee then praised them for their faith and asked God to bless them. Suddenly, before their eyes, Mrs. Skarin transformed into a shining being in a white garment, with her hair in golden light. Annalee smiled with shining white teeth, even though her dentures still lay on her bedside table. Mrs.

Skarin continued to utter blessings and prayer, as she slowly disappeared from sight.

Annalee did not return. Her husband Reason, a New York policeman, disappeared six months later. The FBI investigated both cases, but they had to drop them for lack of evidence. Anthony Brooke personally interviewed several people in Salt Lake City, including Mrs. Skarin's lawyer, officials from the Mormon church, and Mrs. B. herself. Brooke published his findings in *Fate Magazine.*

Only the first of Annalee's books, *Ye Are Gods*, was written before her ascension. She continued to write seven other books until 1972. Her books have been a powerful catalyst in the ascension movement.

Bonnie Johnson

In 1994, Joanna Cherry interviewed Bonnie Johnson and her friend Billie Stearns, who had studied with Annalee Skarin for three years, starting in the summer of 1966. Annalee and Reason Skarin were using the names John and Nan Mathews, as "the Mormon Church was trying to track them down." The study group met weekly with up to 50 people in attendance.

Bonnie narrated her first ascension experience, which led her to Annalee:

> It was back in '53. The twins were 3 years [old] and my little boy just 4 months. One day we had a big earthquake, and I took out the Bible and began to read. I said, "Lord, how is it your coming will be?" Then I quit reading and began to contemplate. All at once I was lifted off the divan, and my clothes fell off like veils to the floor. The most [beauteous] white robe was put on me, whiter than any snow I ever saw, and stars sparkled all over this garment, just like real stars. My face shone like light, and the knowledge was so great.
>
> I looked up and saw Jesus, and I became filled with him. It was such a thrill, but I said, 'But I can't go, I've got these little children.' Then I found myself back on the divan. I was lifted in love for seven days. Angels would come and pat me on the head. It was ecstatic. It was a whole year before I said anything to anybody, because I knew they wouldn't believe me.

One day Bonnie and Billie went to visit Annalee in her trailer, but she was nowhere to be found. They waited an hour. Then, as Bonnie describes:

> It wasn't too long after that, I heard a great big boom coming through the atoms of her trailer. I went around to the side, and Annalee opened the curtains [of the glass door], and there she was, standing in the air about [8 to 9 inches off the floor]. She was putting on a sweater, and she turned her head and nodded. Two hands appeared over her shoulders—there weren't any feet—and helped her with her sweater. When she got it on, she nodded again and the hands disappeared.

On another occasion, Bonnie and Billie and their husbands were returning home from a bowling tournament in Chico. They were driving along Highway 99, talking about Annalee. Suddenly, Annalee and Reason's car appeared ahead of them, but as they followed the car off the Cypress Street exit onto the city streets, Annalee's car disappeared.

Bonnie described one of her recent experiences to Joanna:

> The other day I was in the mall, close to Sears. I was blessing everybody, and all at once I saw golden stairs, and I could see...right through them to the top. Oh, they were beautiful! I went running up there. Down below they were shooting pictures of Santa Claus, and I thought "Well, I wonder if anybody saw me go up here?"
>
> By looking down and wondering about what happened there, [I was let] down on the floor again, but on this side, not where I'd been. I thought, "My land, why didn't I go on and get my mind where I was going?!"

Bonnie then shook her head in regret. Annalee had told Bonnie that she is headed for translation in "not too long a time."

Libby Maxey

Libby Maxey, who attended one of my Ascended Master retreats in Mount Shasta, authored the book *I Am Liberty: One Mind's Journey through Ascension*, where she describes many of her amazing ascension experiences. Libby was kind enough to share some for this book:

Light of God's Love

[Once], in September 1995, I was coming out of a meditation. Upon opening my eyes, I perceived a great white-gold light both with my physical eyes and my spiritual vision. I looked deeply at the light, my consciousness drawn irresistibly toward it. Bands of energy, waves and bands of pulsating, undulating, spiraling light beamed from a central light core of immensity beyond description.

Each pulsation of energy was brought about by a tone—a deep, all-encompassing sound—a thought from the mind of God. Each thought contained universes and worlds, eons and forevers, completed. Each tone was a song of new creation. God gazed upon the entirety of her creation, and divine love flowed in a cascade of light, igniting all the other thoughts as they cavorted and pulsated, responding in kind to this grandest vibration.

This tone of love moved out further, birthing new colors in the waves of light, new resonance in the undulations, heading directly to the minds and hearts of God's beloveds of earth, circling the planet in spiraling tendrils of God's own love thought.

I saw the limitless light, the very light that is God—light so completely engrossing, such a totality of experience. At its most transfixing, the light was an intensity of violet, a shimmering fire that burned all around and through me, yet it was just before me, about a foot from my third-eye chakra, where it burned most brilliantly. The light was also like a diamond, a jewel of transparency and translucency at the same time, but without edges of any kind.

I could feel the energy vibrating everything in me, and all around me. The light had depth and breadth, vibration, sensation, sound, voices, laughter, and song—the perfection of harmony. The light had fragrance, like wondrous newness, reborn continually—like flowers and sunshine, like frankincense, like God. The light is indeed all in all. The light of God lingered, wave after wave of bliss crashing over me.

Every organ of sensation in my body was supercharged with presence, power, and glory. I could see, hear, feel, smell, taste, and *know* that God *is*. I saw the light of my own resurrection. I stood and declared: "I AM the resurrection and the light."

Seamless Garment of Light

[During another group meditation], Melchizedek [appeared] before us. We were suddenly standing, tall in our physical bodies and in our bodies of light. The fantastic light of Melchizedek's being filled the room, our consciousness, everything, yet this time his appearance was different [than we had experienced on previous occasions]. Though far beyond our kindergarten spirituality, he was our peer. "I have something for you," he conveyed to me, and at the same instant, he casually yet purposefully tossed something over me. I saw and felt a substantial sort of light falling around me with a softly rustling whoosh.

The light covered my body entirely, all the way to the floor. Still standing, I was breathing very deeply, tremendously exhilarated, feeling this wonderful, substantial, gorgeously color-filled fabric of light envelop my body like a robe. I opened my eyes and the light garment remained. My hands, lifted in praise, moved to touch the fabric covering my arms. I twirled around, feeling the light garment move with my body, the folds wrapping around my legs and falling straight again. I knew it was a seamless garment.

Melchizedek's thoughts entered my consciousness, his great pleasure with my readiness, his joyful merriment billowing around me like the garment. I could feel his tender gaze upon me, yet it was not just me he gazed upon, but me enveloped in this special, wonderful light. Then I knew—this is the coat of many colors, the woven cloak of souls, the very same garment of light I once saw Christ Sananda wear, and know he wears forever.

Chapter 10

Miraculous Visitations

And there appeared an angel unto him
from heaven, strengthening him.
—Luke 22:43

An ascended master, deity, divine being, angel, or aspect of your higher self might sometimes appear in physical form. Such incidents are usually considered miracles, because they are outside our "normal" realm of perception. But they may be more common than you think. The next two chapters describe many such meetings. This chapter is about some of the more famous visitations. The following chapter is about visitations ordinary people have reported.

Ascended masters often leave two proofs of the incident: The first is that they are an ascended being rather than just an ordinary human, and the second is that they visit in a material body rather than an ethereal or astral body (a ghost).

Jesus fulfilled both these criteria when he visited his disciples after his ascension. The fact that he appeared after death was proof that he was more than human. By eating food, and by asking one of his disciples to touch his wounds, he proved that he appeared in physical form rather than as an apparition. In all my visitation experiences with ascended masters, they ate food with me to prove they had manifested a corporeal body.

Visitations From Babaji

Lahiri Mahasaya's Visitations

In 1861 Mahamuni Babaji first appeared to Lahiri Mahasaya (1828–1895), Paramahansa Yogananda's *paramguru* (guru of his guru). Lahiri, age 33, was working as an engineer in the government and was transferred to Ranikhet in the Almora district, Himalayas, at the foot of the Nanda Devi mountain, at 25,661 feet.

He was walking up Dunagiri (Drongiri) Hill and suddenly encountered a beautiful, youthful ascetic in a cave on the Gogash River. This ascetic, the great Babaji, had suggested to the mind of Lahiri's employer to transfer him to this secluded Himalayan outpost. Babaji had been saving Lahiri's cave, blanket, bowl, and brass cup, which Lahiri had used in his previous lives as Babaji's disciple.

That night Babaji materialized a magnificent, golden, jewel-encrusted palace and initiated Lahiri into Kriya Yoga (tranquility of mind through stillness of breath). Lahiri stayed with Babaji 10 days and then was instructed to take the teachings of Kriya Yoga to the masses of humanity. Upon returning to the office, Lahiri was transferred from Ranikhet and informed by his employer that he had been sent there in error.

After returning home to Moradabad, Lahiri told his friends about his experience. These skeptical businessmen dismissed the entire vision as a hallucination. Lahiri recklessly claimed, in defense, that he could ask Babaji to appear in his house. Immediately he regretted his promise, but he realized he would have to follow it through.

He asked his skeptical friends to leave the room and began to pray for Babaji to appear. Soon Babaji materialized, but, displeased by his disciple's injudicious claims, he stated, "Truth is for earnest seekers, not for those of idle curiosity." However, Babaji agreed to stay so Lahiri would not be humiliated by his friends. When the only entrance to the room was opened, his friends were stunned to find a young stranger, glowing with a brilliant aura, sitting next to Lahiri on the floor.

Babaji shared a bowl of *halva* (pudding) with these seven men and then invited them to prove he was real by touching him. He blessed them, and, to their amazement, he vanished with a brilliant flash of light that faded into countless tiny sparks.

Babaji subsequently appeared to Lahiri Mahasaya many times to assist in his teaching of Kriya Yoga. And Babaji personally knocked on Yogananda's door as he was about to travel to the West to spread Kriya Yoga to America. In *Autobiography of a Yogi* by Paramahansa Yogananda are many stories of visitations by Babaji.

After Lahiri Mahasaya's death and cremation, Lahiri appeared to three of his disciples in different cities, saying that he resurrected his body from the disintegrated atoms of his cremated body into a remodeled, youthful, radiant form. In every case, he asked the disciple to examine his body and touch its flesh.

Figure 10a. **Lahiri Mahasaya:** Those who have met Babaji in the flesh say that his appearance greatly resembles Lahiri Mahasaya.

Satyeswarananda's Visitations

Swami Satyeswarananda Giri received several inner revelations, which he had compiled into a book.

In a hut near the Vaisnabi Mata Temple in Dunagiri Hill, Himalayas, on October 18, 1974, Mahamuni Babaji appeared in the middle of the night as a tall, muscular man with long hair and a beard. Babaji informed Satyeswarananda that the revelations had been sent by him, and he would have to take the messages "far away." Babaji embraced him and lifted him to a higher state of consciousness. Then he said, "I am with you," and he disappeared into bright light. Satyeswarananda was very moved by this encounter, because he had been following Lahiri Mahasaya's teachings of Kriya Yoga for 24 years.

Satyeswarananda left for Europe soon afterward, where he taught Kriya Yoga for one year. Upon the Swami's return to Dunagiri hill,

Mahamuni Babaji appeared and lived in a cave adjacent to the Swami's hut. Babaji stayed there secretly from August to November in continuous meditation and silence. He required no food but occasionally accepted rice pudding or halva out of kindness. Babaji returned each year and stayed during the same period.

One season Satyeswarananda took a remarkable pilgrimage to Badrinath, a sacred shrine high in the Himalayas, with Babaji. At that time he met Mataji (Babaji's sister) as well as other amazing yogis, including some who appeared out of nowhere. The Swami discovered that Mahamuni Babaji and other members of their party were invisible to those they met on the road.

After their sojourn to Badrinath, Babaji flew, with Satyeswarananda locked in his arms, back to his hut 300 miles away. Satyeswarananda quickly arrived in his hut by this method, called *atibahik* (clairportation). Often Babaji appeared to the Swami as a bright star that traveled towards him and then materialized into a physical body.

Yogiraj Gurunath Siddhanath's Visitation

In 1967, Yogiraj was on a quest to meet Shiva-Goraksha-Babaji, whom he calls the "visible and invisible savior of humanity." He traveled to the sacred city Badrinath, Himalayas, on foot and by hitchhiking. The cave called Jilmilee Gufa was located at the foot of the Neelakanteswar ("Blue-Throated Shiva") Mountain. As Yogiraj ascended the trail in silence, he felt he was entering a heavenly sphere. When he reached the top, he viewed the entire snow-capped Himalayan range from the lower mountains near the cave.

Exhausted, he lay down to watch the setting sun pass behind the clouds. Suddenly a light appeared. He thought the sun had returned. A voice said, "Indeed, if you think it is the sun, it is." A shimmering, otherworldly light filled the whole area. Yogiraj turned onto his stomach, joined both hands in *pranams* (prayer position) and prostrated on the ground.

He asked the nameless Great Presence, "Who are you?" The answer came: "Whoever thou thinkest me to be, that I am for thee. I AM That I AM." Yogiraj then said, "Shiva-Goraksha-Babaji." The voice of the Great Presence rang out, "Tathastu, Tathastu, Tathastu!" That Sanskrit word means, "So be it" or "It shall be so."

Yogiraj described, "He was non-being, egoless, the formless, eternal unborn Self who had no identity, not as any human understanding is concerned."

Yogiraj then experienced a cold/warm current running from the top of his head to his toes, as though he were being revamped and cleansed. He gradually expanded into boundless awareness. Soon the trees, birds, clouds, sky, planets, stars, galaxies, and sun's rays were him and breathing his breath and prana—a vast unity within diversity. Babaji's message was not in words, but in shafts of light, which embodied blessings and wisdom transmitted into the superconscious no-mind of Yogiraj.

Yogiraj described Babaji's appearance: "His hair touched his heels and was ablaze with a radiant fire. His countenance had a heavenly luster and his body appeared wet as though he had a bath in the Alakhananda river, and yet was dry."

Yogiraj felt the oneness of all creation in him and the deathless fragrance of Babaji's body. As the soul of Yogiraj returned after the experience of both his form and formless Self, he felt, "Oh Lord! This universe, a bubble in my consciousness, a nothing in Thy Nothingness! Only the Lord God may comprehend Thee, oh Lord, thou about whom naught may be said!"

Guy Ballard's Meetings With Saint Germain

In August, September, and October of 1930, Guy W. Ballard (1878–1939), whose penname was Godfre Ray King, received extraordinary visitations from the ascended master Saint Germain on Mount Shasta, California. He recorded these in *Unveiled Mysteries* (1934). A few months later, Saint Germain visited him in the Wyoming Rockies and Teton National Park. He reported these in *The Magic Presence* (1935).

Mr. and Mrs. Ballard had been searching 30 years for the truth of life. Their answer came with the visitations of Saint Germain. Guy returned to Chicago and founded the "I AM" Religious Activity, Saint Germain Press, and Saint Germain Foundation in 1932. Saint Germain continued to teach Guy the law of life, the "Mighty I AM Presence," and the use of the creative words "I AM"—God in action.

A series of discourses from the ascended masters appeared to Guy in words of "living light." These discourses were compiled into the *Saint Germain Series*. Guy received the dictations in public, and thousands of people attended. By 1938, three million people followed their teachings. I have met several elderly people who witnessed these dictations firsthand. They described the exalted feeling in the room, charged with electric divine energy. The Ballards founded a second center in Los Angeles, and many reading rooms, study groups, and schools. After Guy's death, his wife Edna continued to receive the dictations, under the name Lotus Ray King.

Guy's first visitation occurred one morning on a hike up Mount Shasta from the town of McCloud, California, where he was stationed on government business. He started at daybreak. By noon he had climbed high up the mountain. As he bent over a mountain stream to get water with his cup, suddenly an electric current passed through his body from head to foot.

A young hiker stood directly behind him. Upon second glance, Guy realized this was no ordinary person. The stranger asked Guy to give him his cup and he would fill it with a more refreshing drink than water. His cup was immediately filled with a creamy liquid. Guy was astonished at the revivifying effect of the liquid. The stranger stated that the liquid came from universal supply, which is life itself.

The man went on to explain the law of precipitation, in which anything can be instantaneously materialized through commanding in love. He materialized a gold disc in the palm of Guy's hand. Then he explained that God's intention is only to give good to his children, and we must accept God as the source, owner, giver, and doer of all the good we have ever received. He said that everyone is a perfect temple of God.

After instructing Guy on the laws of life, Saint Germain showed his true form, a magnificent saintly figure in a white, jewel-bedecked robe. Guy immediately recognized him, because he had seen him in his inner vision many times.

After more teachings, Saint Germain took Guy on a journey in his subtle body while his physical body rested on the mountainside. Saint Germain put his arm around Guy and they lifted high off the ground and traveled through space to the south of France. There Saint Germain showed him one of Guy's past lives. They traveled on to Egypt, while Saint Germain described another of Guy's embodiments.

After much instruction about universal truths, Guy found himself back on the hillside, with the sun setting in the distance. He was concerned that he would not make it back to his hotel until midnight. Saint Germain told Guy to put his arm around his shoulder and close his eyes. Guy felt himself lifted off the ground, and then suddenly felt his feet touch the floor. He found himself in the lodge at the foot of the mountain in McCloud. Then Saint Germain disappeared.

For the next few days, Guy recorded his experiences in writing. One day, upon waking, he found a metallic gold card lying on his bedside table. Written in violet script, a note instructed him to be at their meeting place on the mountain at 7 a.m.

The next morning he hiked for 10 miles to the spot. As he climbed, his feet became increasingly lighter. He sat to rest, when suddenly a panther appeared. Guy panicked at first, but then realized this animal was part of God's life. With this thought, all fear left, and he was at peace.

Saint Germain then appeared. He congratulated Guy on overcoming fear, and stretched out his hand, offering four cakes. Guy was immediately rejuvenated by them and felt a tingling sensation throughout his body. Saint Germain then sat next to him and began his instruction. Guy was taken on many journeys and saw past lives from ancient times, long before recorded history.

Guy met Saint Germain several times that year. He was shown numerous secret retreats and buried civilizations through personal physical visitations. Believed to be a reincarnation of George Washington (there is an astonishing physical resemblance), Guy Ballard granted to the world a great treasure of wisdom in his writings.

O mighty God in me! I face thy eternal sunrise and receive its mighty radiance and activity, visibly manifest in my experience.
—Guy Ballard

George Washington's Visitation

An extraordinary vision received by George Washington was reported in the *National Review*. Anthony Sherman, age 99, described it to Wesley Bradshaw in Independence Hall, on July 4, 1859. A first-hand witness, Sherman claimed to be the only person alive who knew of the incident.

Sherman recounted that Washington resolved to spend the winter of 1777, the darkest period of the Revolution, at Valley Forge. One day, Washington related that a beautiful female appeared in his private office, even though he had given strict orders not to be disturbed. Though he asked several times why she was there, she did not respond.

Then a voice said, "Son of the Republic, look and learn," and the woman extended her arm toward the east. Out of a mist, Washington saw all the nations of the world. A dark, shadowy, angel-like being floated over the ocean between Europe and America, and a dark cloud enveloped America. Flashes of lightning gleamed through the cloud, and smothered groans and cries came from the American people. The cloud withdrew into the ocean, and cities sprang up all the way from the Atlantic to the Pacific.

Then an ill-omened specter from Africa approached America, and flitted slowly over every city. The inhabitants went to battle. A bright angel placed the American flag between the divided nation, and said, "Remember ye are brethren." The inhabitants then made peace and united around the National Standard.

Then, from Europe, Asia, and Africa, thick black clouds joined together. A dark red light gleamed, and hordes of armed men marched into America by land and sea. These vast armies devastated the country, burning the cities.

A light of a thousand suns then shone down from above, and broke the dark cloud into fragments. An angel bearing the national flag and a sword descended from heaven, along with legions of radiant spirits. The Americans, who were nearly overcome, immediately took courage again and renewed the battle. The dark cloud rolled back, leaving America victorious.

Once more the cities sprang up, and the bright angel cried loudly: "While the stars remain, and the heavens send down dew upon the earth, so long shall the Union last."

The mysterious female visitor then said, "Three great perils will come upon the Republic. The most fearful is the third." Washington felt that he had seen a vision of the birth, progress, and destiny of the United States of America."[1]

Visitations From Madame Blavatsky's Teachers

H.P. Blavatsky received countless ascended master visitations. Although she rarely talked or wrote about visitations from the masters, *Blavatsky and her Teachers* by Jean Overton Fuller describes a few of them.

Master Morya and Master Kuthumi

Madame Blavatsky stayed in a ravine in Tibet, studying with her gurus Morya and Kuthumi, from 1868 to 1870. During that period, her relatives were anxious about her whereabouts. Her aunt received a letter at home, hand-delivered, from an Indian man who disappeared in front of her eyes as soon as he had given it to her. The letter, stating Helena was safe and in good hands, was unsigned but in the same handwriting as the letters in the British museum signed K.H. or Koot Hoomi.

One day Madame Blavatsky told Colonel Olcott (one of the founders of the Theosophical Society) that Master Morya wished him to do some business for Morya in another town. The colonel was concerned because he knew he would lose $500 per month if he left New York. Nevertheless he went, even with his financial obligations. Upon his return, he asked his bank for a statement. He saw two mysterious bank deposits, each for $500, and thought there must be an error. He was told that both deposits had been paid over the counter in cash by an unusually tall gentleman with brown skin, long, black, flowing hair, and piercing eyes. This mysterious man had asked the teller to help him fill out the deposit slip because he could not read English.

In 1878 Colonel Olcott was reading a book in his bedroom in his New York apartment when he suddenly caught the glimmer of a white flash out of the corner of his eye. A very tall Indian man, about 6 feet, 7 inches tall, was towering over him in white garments and an amber turban. He appeared without entering through any door. His black hair hung to his shoulders. His beard was parted on the chin with the ends twisted up and hung over the ears, Rajput style. He had piercing, benign eyes.

The spiritual presence of the man was so overwhelming that the colonel fell to his knees in awe. The man placed his hand on the colonel's head. He stayed for about half an hour, explaining the colonel's mission and his relationship with Madame Blavatsky. Just before he left, the man unwound his turban and left it on the table as proof that he had come in physical form and not as a hallucination. Then he vanished into thin air. This was Colonel Olcott's first visitation by Master Morya.

Leadbeater's Visitations

Mr. C.W. Leadbeater first encountered Djwal Kul in 1884 in Cairo on his way to India with Madame Blavatsky. The master appeared in Madame Blavatsky's hotel room, without the use of a door or by making any entrance, while Leadbeater was seated on the floor, cutting out newspaper articles. He was so startled that he jumped to his feet. Madame Blavatsky scolded him that he would not go far in occult work if he was startled by a small trifle such as that.

Mr. Leadbeater first met Master Morya passing through a room on his way to meet Madame Blavatsky in her bedroom. He also reported seeing Kuthumi on the roof of the Theosophical Society Headquarters. Djwal Kul appeared to him several times on that same roof, both of them materializing out of nowhere. Mr. Leadbeater claimed that he received many visitations from the masters throughout a period of 40 years.

Madame Blavatsky, C.W. Leadbeater, Dr. Annie Besant, and other members of the Theosophical society had numerous visitations from Saint Germain. It was said that Madame Blavatsky spent the good part of 1885 in Wurzburg, Germany, with Saint Germain. Mr. Leadbeater reported that he encountered Saint Germain walking down the Corso in Rome, dressed as any other Italian gentleman.

You might enjoy reading of 62 more visitations of Blavatsky's teachers at *www.blavatskyarchives.com/mastersencounterswith.htm*.

Marian Visitations

Volumes have been written about visitations from Mother Mary, the mother of Jesus. Let us mention just a few of them here.

Lourdes

Saint Bernadette Soubirous (1844–1879) was the visionary at Lourdes, France. From February 11 to July 16, 1858, when Bernadette was 14 years old, she reported that "a small young lady" in white, standing in a niche in a rock, appeared to her 18 times. The lady held a rosary of pearls and wore a white veil, blue girdle, and golden roses on her feet.

During the ninth visitation, the lady told Bernadette to drink from the spring flowing under the rock, and eat the plants growing there. But there was no spring. Bernadette assumed the spring was underground, so she clawed at the ground unsuccessfully. However, in just a few days, a freely flowing spring appeared, which proved to have healing properties. On the 16th visitation, the lady identified herself as "The Immaculate Conception." Since that time, the Lourdes Medical Bureau has verified 67 local cures as inexplicable.

Fatima

On May 13, 1917, three children—Lucia de Jesus, age 10, and her cousins Francisco and Jacinta Marto, ages 9 and 7—were tending their flock in Cova da Iria, parish of Fatima, town of Vila Nova de Ourém, Portugal. At midday, they saw a brilliant light. Assuming it was lightning, they started back home. As they walked down the slope, another flash occurred, and they saw, atop an evergreen tree, "a Lady dressed all in white, more brilliant than the sun, shedding a light that was clearer and more intense than that of a crystal goblet filled with crystalline water and sruck by the rays of the most brilliant sun" (as described by Lucia). The Lady was holding a white rosary.

The Lady invited them to return to the Cova da Iria for five consecutive months. On the 13th of June, July, September, and October, the Lady appeared and spoke to them again. On the 19th of August, the visitation took place at Valinhos, because on the 13th the children were not in their home area.

On October 13, with about 70,000 people present, the Lady said she was the "Lady of the Rosary." She asked for a chapel to be built there in her honor. After the apparition, all present witnessed the miracle promised to the three children: The sun, resembling a silver disc, could be gazed at without difficulty. Whirling as a wheel of fire, it appeared to nearly fall upon the Earth.

Since 1917, pilgrims have flocked to the Cova da Iria from all parts of the world. Pope Pius XII noted that the message of Fatima is one of the greatest interventions of God through Mary in world history since the death of the Apostles.

Our Lady of Guadalupe

In 1531 at Tepeyac, a hill northwest of Mexico City, a Lady from heaven appeared to a humble Native American, Juan Diego, born in Cuautitlan. She identified herself as the ever-virgin Holy Mary, Mother of the True God for whom we live, of the Creator of all things, Lord of heaven and the earth. She requested that a church be built on the site.

When the local Bishop hesitated, and requested a sign, Mother Mary sent Juan Diego, in mid-December, to gather a bunch of impossibly out-of-season roses for the Bishop on a hilltop where no flowers could ever grow, due to crags, thistles, thorns, nopales, and mesquites. As Juan approached the top of the hill, he found himself among a great variety of exquisite, fresh, fragrant Castilla roses, which he immediately cut.

After Juan Diego gave the roses to Mary, she used the actual physical hands of her ascended body to place and arrange the roses in Juan Diego's tilma (cloak). At the same time, her image was miraculously imprinted on his tilma.

This rough-quality maguey cactus cloth, which should have deteriorated in 20 years, shows no sign of decay 475 years later. The image has undergone intense scientific testing. The conclusion is that the image is not painted by human hands, and the pigments are not of this world. It is also said that on the cloth, the Lady's eyes reflect what was in front of her in 1531.

An incredible list of miracles, cures, and interventions are attributed to Our Lady of Guadalupe. Ten million people per year visit her Basilica—the most popular Marian shrine in the world, and the most visited Catholic church in the world outside the Vatican.

Chapter 11

Meetings With the Masters

Be not forgetful to entertain strangers; for thereby
some have entertained angels unawares.
—Hebrews 13:2

When ascended masters wish to bless you, they may visit you in physical form. These beings often appear out of nowhere when you least expect it, and they disappear again. You may have already had an extraordinary visitation that seemed quite ordinary at the time.

Perhaps while you were taking a walk, someone approached and spoke loving, comforting words of profound truth that touched your heart. Perhaps you were in trouble or danger, and someone came to your assistance. These ascended beings appear as average human beings—anyone you might encounter on the street, even a homeless person. They may materialize in any form whatsoever, even an animal.

When you receive a visitation, you accept and trust it without question as perfectly natural. You find yourself inviting a total stranger to walk with you or assist you. Ascended beings often make contact by touching you or gazing into your eyes. They involve you in conversation that seems mundane at the time but that, upon reflection, has deep spiritual significance. Rarely will such beings make their identity known until they are gone.

Ascended beings may come to teach you, guide you onto a new path, provide inspiration, feed spiritual power, make spiritual contact, deepen communication with them, or give love, protection, encouragement, or proof of their existence. After such a visitation, your consciousness is lifted, or you may take a new life direction.

Dr. Joanna Cherry says, "You may have had a visitation without realizing it. You can ask about it later in meditation. It is not necessary to receive visitations to receive all the teaching we need, because we each learn in our own way. But if you do not think you have received one and would like to, just ask for one."

The rest of this chapter details stories of visitations from divine beings, angels, and ascended masters to ordinary people, just like you and me.

Maitreya

Curt de Groat, New York, New York

In the early 1980s I was sitting in a car in New York City, saving a parking space for a friend, when I decided to spend this time praying for the world. I remembered thinking, "I don't know if my prayers will do any good. But I'll pray anyway."

The next day I was waiting for my boss to open the store where I worked, a used clothing store on the lower east side of Manhattan. I decided, while I was waiting, to pray for each person who passed by. I visualized each person surrounded in golden light. It was a beautiful day, and I enjoyed seeing each passerby filled with light.

All of a sudden I saw, out of the corner of my eye, a man who looked like a homeless vagrant. I knew the panhandler was going to ask me for a handout, so I decided to avert my gaze. But the man came right up to me and looked straight in my eyes, saying, "What you're doing with your mind is good for the world." I immediately went into a space of golden light, and when I turned to look for the man, he had disappeared.

A Man Who Wasn't There

Craig Sim Webb, Quebec, Canada; Speaker, Trainer, Author[1]

One summer night, I was walking towards the subway. A car approached, with dogs barking out the window. The barking reminded me of a quote about "listening to the barking dogs of the unconscious"; that is, subtle experiences that try to catch our attention with an important message.

The driver stopped and asked directions, and I gladly helped him. I continued to the subway, contemplating a principle symbolically exemplified by the car and barking dogs, about how it is wise to help people when they ask for it, along the lines of why Jesus said, "Ask and ye shall receive, knock and it shall be opened."

As I descended the subway stairs, I was lost in my thoughts when I saw an old gentleman slowly hobbling down the steps with a cane. Without thinking twice, I asked him if he needed help. He did not look at me, but he said something very odd: "As I was walking down the stair, I met a man who wasn't there."

He had a British accent, which is quite unusual in Montreal. I was confused by his response, yet out of good will, I repeated my offer to assist him. He shook his head and said, "It might be a little convoluted, but hopefully you get the point." Well, I did not get it, but I wished him well and continued down another couple of flights.

Then it stuck me that perhaps the old gentleman was trying to help me learn the precise lesson I was contemplating as I entered the subway, since I twice offered him help when he had not asked for it. I immediately ran back up two long flights of stairs to speak to him again. At the speed he was hobbling down the steps, there was no way he could have either passed me or even turned back and left the subway. But in the 20 or 30 seconds it took to sprint back to where he should have been, amazingly, there was nobody there. His peculiar statement suddenly seemed to make sense.

The Gold Lady

Rima Granados, Atlanta, Georgia

My daughter Grace was born with Tetralogy of Fallot, a disease with four heart defectss, including a hole between the two lower chambers of the heart. This caused oxygen-starved blood to pump through her system, which made her skin appear blue. Still, she would laugh and babble, often when no one was near her. She would smile and stare and wave to a fixed point in the room long before she could speak. At 6 months, with many resulting complications, her heart was repaired. Even covered in tubes and wires, she continued to smile.

Eighteen months later, healthy and happy, Grace and I were playing "plane" on the carpet. She would lie facing the ceiling on my bent knees and pretend to fly. At one point, she smiled and waved at a point on the ceiling. I asked, "What are you waving at?" She giggled and looked at me as if I had three heads, "To the Gold Lady, Mama. She said she has to go help other kids now, so she went away."

Babaji's Blessing
P.J. Worley, Woodside, California

I was reading one of my favorite books, probably the first metaphysical book I ever read: Yogananda's *Autobiography of a Yogi*. I have read it about seven times. That is how I first met Babaji—in that book.

I was rereading the chapter in which Lahiri Mahasaya bi-located: During a meeting with his disciples, he told Ram Gopal to go to one of the bathing areas on the Ganges River. As Ram Gopal waited by the river, a huge stone slab lifted and hovered, suspended in the air, while Babaji's sister Mataji levitated out of an underground cave. Then Lahiri Mahasaya arrived, hovering over the Ganges and appearing in a ball of light. Afterward, Babaji appeared like a whirlpool of light from the cosmos.

Babaji began telling his sister that he had decided to shed his form and leave the planet. They discussed it, and she asked him not to. He asked, "What is the difference if I wear a visible or invisible wave on the ocean of my Spirit?" Then she said, "Since it doesn't make any difference, and I am asking you to stay, then will you stay?" So he committed to remain in an immortal body on this planet forever.

The impact of that commitment really made a tremendous impression on my entire being. I just started sobbing. I must have sobbed for 10 minutes or longer, because I felt it was such a gift of love to the planet. It made a huge impact on me.

When Ram Gopal returned later that night, he found that Lahiri Mahasaya had not left his dais the entire evening. He had been giving a discourse on how a realized saint can appear in several places at once.

Later in the book, on page 348, Lahiri Mahasaya is quoted: "Whenever one utters with reverence the name of Babaji, that devotee attracts an instant spiritual blessing." I felt moved to call upon Babaji, so I did. I then received one of my most magnificent spiritual experiences. My body began to rise up off the chair, and I levitated. It was an experience of indescribable bliss and joy and happiness.

I wanted to open my eyes because I wanted to look down and see everything. But my eyes were shut. I could not open them. They were sealed shut. They just would not open. I got so excited that I insisted that they be opened. I wanted to see. The minute I got them open, that ended the experience.

Lighten Up
Rev. Rian Leichter, Woodside, California

Babaji visited me one time while I was driving. As I drove down the expressway in my car, someone or something suddenly whizzed by me on a purple motor scooter, similar to a Vespa. The creature was dressed totally in purple. He had a purple hat and purple glasses, like Elton John. As he drove by, he looked into my eyes and gave me a big smile. At the time, I thought this encounter was really strange. Later, in our group meditation, I asked whether it was Babaji, because I had a suspicion that it was. I was right.

At that time I was going through a divorce and a difficult period in my life. I was feeling very serious, upset, and weighed down by the divorce and by my financial situation. Babaji's visitation was a reminder to lighten up and to not be so serious. The message was to be free, enjoy life, and not be so overwhelmed. Soon after that, I began using positive affirmations, and my life took an entirely different, positive direction.

"It's a Beautiful Day, Isn't It?"
Marissa Bracke, Ossian, Indiana[2]

I was a freshman at college, living away from home for the first time, desperately homesick for my parents and brothers, and the safety of all I knew. I was depressed, finding it hard to even get up and go to class. I just ached so deeply inside, missing my home and my comfort zone.

One morning, as I walked from my dorm to class, the university trash disposal truck pulled up alongside a neighboring dorm. Nothing unusual there; it was their weekly pick-up day. Two guys were always on the truck—I saw them every week as I walked to class. But that day I saw neither of them. Instead, there was this new fellow.

He had an extra pip in his step and was whistling—in the rain, on a chilly morning, while picking up trash. Whistling. Because he was a different guy than those I usually saw, and because his incredibly happy demeanor so starkly contrasted with the day and his tasks, I paused and took notice of him for a few seconds before continuing on my way.

After I took a few steps, his whistling stopped, and I heard him say, "It's a beautiful day, isn't it?" I turned around, and he was looking right at me. He waved. Then repeated his sentence, "It's a beautiful day, isn't it?"

I looked around at the grey sky, the pouring rain, students hustling to class under umbrellas and raincoats, and feeling this knot of depression in my chest. I shrugged at him and mumbled, "I guess so."

He laughed, this full, deep laugh. He shook his head, and the rain was dripping off of his hair. He looked at me again, winked, and said, "Oh it is. It's a beautiful day. Just let it in." Then he went back to the truck, and I turned to keep walking.

I could not believe how much lighter and more okay I felt. The knot of depression was loosening, and I felt...just really okay, as if I had just gotten a hug from a loved one.

I turned to wave to him, to say thank you. But when I turned back, he was not there! The two fellows who usually worked on that truck were there, but he was not. I turned back on my way and walked to class.

Every week that semester I made sure to get out to the sidewalk in time to see the truck pull up to the neighboring dorm, hoping to catch this new fellow again so I could thank him and let him know how hugely his greeting had affected me—and how I was doing great in school, joining groups, making friends, feeling really happy—and that somehow his greeting had been the turning point.

But I never saw him again.

I later told my mom and dad this story. Mom said, "He was an angel." I agreed, "I think so too. I'm just glad I was on this angel's trash truck route that day!"

Gift of a Mother Mary Medallion
Maryam Balbed, Silver Spring, Maryland

I delivered newspapers when I was 12. On Sunday mornings, delivery was 4 to 5 a.m. One Sunday when the papers seemed particularly heavy and it seemed especially dark out, I had an interesting encounter.

I delivered to a building where only seniors lived. Many of the residents often seemed crabby, and they gave me a hard time when I came around to collect payment every month.

That morning, when I entered the building lobby, a really nice elderly lady started talking to me. I immediately thought it was odd, because no one in that building had ever spoken a kind word to me before. The lady said something about how good it was to see a kid working so hard, and that I should be careful, because it was so dark out when I delivered on Sunday mornings. The lady then handed me something. I looked down for just a second to see what she put in my hand. It was a small Mary medallion, like Catholics wear. Then I looked up to thank the lady. She was gone.

To this day I still have the Mary medallion. I did not understand the significance of it at the time, but my name Maryam is the Muslim name for the mother of Jesus (my father is Muslim)—so I was named after her. And I have always felt a strong affinity for Mary. [See page 206 for more information about the Miraculous Medal.]

Mr. Jupiter
Colin Maxwell, Louisville, Kentucky

In the summer of 1977, I scraped together some money to buy a four-story building to house a meditation center in Louisville, Kentucky. The center was located in a rundown section of the downtown inner city. Even from the first evening of the center's operation, my colleagues and I were plagued by disturbances, vandalism, and theft.

One evening I was in the kitchen near the back door when I heard loud music, revving engines, and squealing tires. I raced out into the twilight, hoping to identify the culprits, but I found nothing there. The noise sounded as if it were coming from the back porch. I had 50 yards of unobstructed view and felt certain I should have seen something as I ran toward the parking lot. I was scared and angry, with my heart pumping and legs trembling. I thought, "Where are these crazy people out to harass us?" It was getting dark so I walked back to the house.

As I started up the porch steps, I heard a deep voice say, "Yo, yo, hey now, wait up! I gots to talk with ya." I turned around and saw what I thought must be the biggest black man south of the Ohio River strolling up the flagstone path like Master Po, trimmed out at 6 feet 10 inches and 375 pounds.

A huge, friendly, toothy grin broke out on the man's face as he extended his hand out to me and said, "I'm Mister Jupiter, and I live jus' down the way there. I was hopin' to meet with ya 'fore too long. Y'all is with them meditation folk, ain't ya? I knows and I sees y'all comin' in for meetin's and such, and I jus' wanted to tell ya I'm real happy ya'll is here in this neighborhood. I think y'all is doin' a real good thing here. Helpin' those whose is seekin' to find their way and all. Now ya know, the folk livin' 'round here, they's all good people and they's has love in them too, so don't ya worry none no mo'. They all give a listen when I talk, and I'll be spreadin' the good word about ya. Things'll be okay from now on."

All the while he spoke, Mr. Jupiter pumped my hand up and down. This handshake embodied immenseness, magnanimity, wisdom, acceptance, and unconditional, mutual positive regard. I felt inspired, enwisdomed, assured, and very lucky while in Mr. Jupiter's presence—like a favored child being praised by a strong, loving father.

After Mr. Jupiter spoke, he smiled. I noticed an exquisitely cut gem-quality amethyst hanging from a thick gold chain around his neck. It sparkled, picking up reflections from the streetlights. He wore a yellow jumpsuit and a yellow baseball cap. On his cap was a logo that said "Victory All-Stars."

Then Mr. Jupiter said, "Well, I gots to go now. Hope to see ya 'round." I felt really happy and did not know what to say. Mr. Jupiter smiled again and turned away. I turned and started up the stairs. At that moment, I thought to ask Mr. Jupiter where he lived. But when I turned around, he was nowhere to be seen.

From that evening until I finally left the building two years later, there was no more theft, vandalism, or disturbances. No one ever saw Mr. Jupiter again.

Two Days Before 9/11

Laurie Nadel, PhD, Journalist, New York City, New York

I was filing a story about a surfing contest to my editor at the *New York Times* Long Island Section around midnight on Sunday, September, 9, 2001. I turned off my computer and went to my bedroom where my daughter was asleep with her cat.

Suddenly an angel appeared in front of me. She said, "Whatever happens, I want you to know that I will keep you and your daughter safe." She stretched her right wing over my daughter and the cat.

I thought I was hallucinating and my voice barely squeaked, "You're in my imagination, right? I am making you up?"

"No, I am real." She smiled. My room was flooded with shimmering gold light for a second or two.

Then she was gone.

Temple of Garuda

Sean David Morton, Hermosa Beach, California[3]

In 1985, on my way to India, I visited friends in England, where we used some stones with mystical properties and a planchette to try to contact angelic entities. I asked a youthful, naïve question: "Where would I find God in India?" The prophecy I received was, "That which you seek, you will find in the Temple of Garuda. It will be in the last place that you look, and a blind man will teach you."

At the library we discovered that Garuda is a half-man, half-eagle god that Lord Vishnu rides on. There were only two temples in India dedicated to Garuda—nowhere near where I was traveling.

So off I went to India, to the Kumbh Mela in Haridwar. I lived in Dharamsala, in the Dalai Lama's complex, and worked in the orphanage. The Dalai Lama instructed me to go to Nepal, where I was accepted into the Tengboche monastery and lived there for eight months under the guidance of Rinpoche Lopsang Thundun. All the while, I wondered whether the prophecy would be fulfilled.

Finally, in early December 1986, I left Nepal, and, at the airport in Delhi, I boarded a Pan-American flight for home. I was left thinking, "So much for that prophecy. After all the meditation I did, the experiences I had, the pilgrimages and shrines I visited, there was no Garuda temple and no blind man. And I did not find God."

I was lost in this thought as the plane taxied onto the runway. All of a sudden, one of the engines dropped from the plane and caught fire. It was the last Pan-Am plane that week, and the plane had to be replaced. So we returned to Delhi. Meanwhile, I wandered around the city, still hoping for a blind man somewhere.

After four days, Pan-Am replaced the plane. But there was another delay. We waited in the Delhi airport for eight hours. I sat by the window, watching airplanes taxi back and forth. Across the field, a plane approached—Garuda Airlines, decorated with an eagle-headed, winged man. But I did not even notice it. By that time, I had completely dismissed the prophesy as utter nonsense.

An annoying woman with two babies screaming their heads off sat right next to me. One of them threw up. She jumped up, grabbed the babies, and left, leaving her chair open. I turned, and a man was sitting there. I never saw him come, and did not see him go.

The man had large coke-bottle lens glasses, as in a Jerry Lewis movie. He was dressed in a royal blue suit, white shirt, and red striped tie, exactly like Clark Kent in Superman comics. I thought, "Does this guy work for the *Daily Planet* or something?"

He greeted me, then took a big handkerchief out of his pocket and flourished it above his head. He started cleaning his coke-bottle glasses and said, "Oh my goodness gracious me, you know I am completely blind without my glasses."

Garuda planes going to and fro, blind men sitting next to me— the universe was hitting me on the head, but I was totally clueless. I was the blind one.

The man put on his glasses and said, "You are a very interesting young man, so what are you doing in India?" I sighed and said, "I don't know whether you want to hear this story. It would take a long time, after all I've been through." He replied, "Apparently we have some time before our plane. Please, I love long stories, tell me." I said, "You would only laugh, because I don't think you would believe it." His voice grew low and deep, and he said, "Oh I would believe a great many things."

I said, "Well, I came to India seeking God." He said, in a low voice, suddenly losing his Indian accent, "And is it God you are finding?" I answered, "To tell you the truth, after all I have been through—No. I have had a lot of experience. I have learned many things. But I haven't had what you consider that feeling, that essence, of who and what the creator and the creation is."

We talked about my experiences. He reached into his pocket, handed me a card, and said he was a doctor from Bombay. I have no recollection of what was on that card. Then he said, "Come with me." He stood up and started to walk away. I noticed it would be a long time before the plane came, so I followed him.

An entire wing of the airport was taped off, under construction. As if he owned the place, the doctor parted the curtain of clear plastic tarp and walked into the construction area, all the way to the end of a long hallway. He picked up a chair and sat across from me. Then he guided me into the meditation that I teach people today.

The doctor led me through an open space, a beautiful perfect beach, a waterfall, walking down a path, seeing a beautiful glowing white temple in the distance, walking up seven steps to the porch, and meeting a great spiritual master, which, during this first experience, was Rinpoche Lopsang Thundun.

The golden door opened and I entered a fabulous temple with a black curtain at the other end. I sat in front of the curtain. The doctor asked me to focus on the curtain and tell him what I saw. The curtain became alive. It was all the things I fear—all my doubts, anger, hatred, contentions. I clapped my hands, put my hands on my forehead, ran my thumbs down the center of my body, opened up my chest, and opened the curtain. When the curtain opened, the doctor said, "Behind the curtain is God."

I was gone. I traveled at thousands of times the speed of light, to the center of the universe, and had a Godhead experience. I was at the stationary Isle of Paradise, on Havana, at the center of all time, all space, all super-universes, filled with whatever that power was. My body started shaking, almost convulsing, from this power, force, and energy moving through me.

This essence, which I realized was this path of bliss, was at the center of, not only all religions, but of the human heart, all time and space, the hologram, and the holographic existence that we are.

Finally, the meditation ended itself. The curtain closed by itself. After walking out of that temple and seeing my master there at the front porch, Rinpoche asked, "Do you understand now?" I replied, "Yes, now I get it!"

I opened my eyes. I was stunned to see this entire deserted part of the terminal filled with hundreds of Hindus. They had torn through the tarped-off section and were now sitting cross-legged in meditation before me, with their hands up in the air, doing this snakelike motion with their heads, bathing in the glow of waves of ecstatic energy coming off me. I was completely freaked out.

Dressed in army khaki pants, with my hiking boots, trench coat, and bag, I stumbled through these people. They lay on their faces, touching my feet and grabbing my legs—not because of who I was, but because of the energy.

So, after weaving through these people, I made my way back to the terminal. In a complete daze, I searched the entire airport for the doctor from Bombay. You would think a man dressed as Superman with bottle glasses would be easy to spot. But he was gone.

The flight left about half an hour later. The doctor from Bombay was not on the flight. He had completely disappeared. I never saw him again. And it was probably better that way.

Almost all students who have taken Divine Revelation classes, when asked to describe their experiences of visitations from the ascended masters, have revealed that at some time they had such mysterious encounters. Have you experienced this phenomenon in your life? If so, send me an e-mail at divinerev@aol.com, and tell me your story.

Part IV

Building Your Light Body

Chapter 12

What Does It Mean to Ascend?

This body Sri Ma always advises: become an explorer of eternity, not a drifter to mortality.
—Sri Anandamayi Ma

In this section of the book, we will explore the possibility of attaining ascension in this very lifetime. To understand ascension more deeply, let us get a better understanding of what is the supreme reality, what is permanent and impermanent, what choices you can make in the course of your evolution, and how you choose your process of life and death. Just as in every other experience in your life, ascension is a choice.

What Is Real?

There are two aspects of life: the unmanifest absolute and the manifest relative creation. Our universe is made of duality, or pairs of opposites: light/dark, male/female, yin/yang, up/down, right/wrong, happiness/sadness. In order for a manifest universe to exist, duality is a prerequisite.

However, beyond these pairs of opposites, there is oneness or wholeness, which is the ultimate reality. Some people call it God. Others call it the absolute, infinite, transcendent, the gap, the void, being, awareness, consciousness, the unified field, Brahman, Tao, Yi, nirvana, *satori,* or *satchitananda*. This absolute oneness is permanent, immortal, nameless, formless, beginningless, endless, unborn, undying, eternal, and imperishable.

159

The absolute reality is one. It has no opposite. In the ancient Upanishads it is described as "Only that which is, was in the beginning, one only, without a second."[1] In the Bible is said, "Hear, O Israel: the Lord our God, the Lord is One."[2]

Among all the creatures in various spheres, humans have a unique ability. They can experience this absolute oneness, and they can merge with this oneness. The experience of oneness is the only reality. There is no permanence and therefore no ultimate reality in the impermanent relative creation.

Anything with a name and form is therefore dual and is not that oneness, although it may embody that oneness—as much as anything in relative creation can. Until an enlightened or ascended being merges fully with the absolute and thereby completely relinquishes its individuality, it still operates in *leshavidya*—the faint remains of duality that maintains individuality in an enlightened soul.

Therefore, anything that can speak to you and give you a message, such as divine beings or ascended masters, still lives in the relative world. In contrast, the absolute non-dual reality is silent and does not speak.

Choosing Your Pathway

Your soul has lived for millions of years in myriad forms. You have incarnated as minerals, plants, animals, and possibly other creatures. Finally you became a human and have already lived as a human for thousands of lifetimes.

When you began to incarnate as a human, you were granted a precious gift by the creator. It is called "freedom of choice." You are the director and sole determiner of your life. Therefore, you can make limitless decisions about life and death in the course of your evolutionary process. These choices affect whether your life is ordinary or extraordinary, whether your lifespan is short or long, and whether you live a mortal or immortal life. Surprisingly, you have the power to choose perpetual life.

Here are seven different examples of possible life-and-death options you might select. You may choose any one of these paths to follow.

Choice 1: The Slow Road of Evolution

You have already lived countless lifetimes as minerals, plants, animals, and humans, and you could choose to live many more, climbing the slow ladder of spiritual evolution. If you continue to walk this prolonged, snail's pace path of evolution, and if you do nothing to change it, you will maintain the same evolutionary process that nearly all living things undergo.

When you walk this slow road of evolution, you are born, you live, and you die. At the time of death, you move into a great light (a heavenly realm) until the time comes to take birth again. Your soul then chooses a particular womb and you are reborn into a family most suited to your spiritual development.

You continue to incarnate into a series of human bodies, until you are finally ready to take higher birth in the celestial realm as an angel. Once you graduate to angelhood, you continue to move up the celestial ladder, eventually becoming a deity or another divine being. There you end your course of evolution. You never attain liberation (*moksha*), and you never become fully self-realized in supreme consciousness.

Choice 2: Becoming an Earthbound Spirit

You may be lost, confused, stubborn, or ignorant at the time of death, and therefore incapable of entering God's light. You may instead dwell in the astral plane (an illusory, gray level of existence) as a ghostly, earthbound, discarnate spirit, lost and alone, until you somehow find your way to the light and then wait for human rebirth.

You might live in the astral world for a long time before finding the light, perhaps hundreds, even thousands of years. There are 15 reasons why a soul would not enter the divine light after death. Please refer to page 87 in my book *How to Hear the Voice of God* to learn those reasons.

Choice 3: Possessing a Human Body

If you are a lost soul or earthbound spirit and are overly attached to the earth plane, or addicted to pleasures of the flesh, then you might want desperately to continue in human form in order to perpetuate your addiction. However, because you cannot revive your dead body, you may try to attach yourself to the body of a living human.

An individual in a weakened condition (such as a drug or alcohol abuser or sickly person) might be susceptible to such astral possession or oppression. By attaching yourself to such a powerless, depleted individual, you would share his or her body and continue to live as a kind of astral freeloader. You might live in that deplorable state as an energy vampire for a long time, seeking various living humans to hook into. If this condition seems familiar to you, please read my book *Exploring Auras* to learn how to heal energy vampirism.

Choice 4: Becoming a "Walk-In"

You may decide that you do not want to undergo the lengthy process of rebirth, childhood, youth, teenage years, and so forth. Therefore you might make a contractual agreement with a human who is on the verge of death or who just died. Just as that person's soul departs from the body (often during an accident or "near-death" experience), with permission from that soul, you might enter his or her body and take it over. Meanwhile, the person's soul leaves the body and moves into the divine heavenly light. In the West this is called a "walk-in." In India it is called *parkaya pradesh* or "transmigration of souls."

Choice 5: Achieving Spiritual Enlightenment

You may attain spiritual enlightenment or liberation during your human embodiment. In this higher state of consciousness you realize your true nature and unite your awareness with supreme Spirit. You no longer have "seeds of *karma*" (human attachments, known in Sanskrit as *samskaras)* binding you to the earth plane, so you can choose to never take human birth again.

In this case, if you decide to "drop the body" (leave the body behind) at the time of death, then your soul can make one of two choices:

1. Merge with absolute *Brahman*, the supreme Godhead, an undifferentiated state of consciousness, and thereby forgo your individuality altogether, or you may

2. Live in a celestial world or *loka* (realm) with the personal God or deity of your choice and maintain your individuality.

Choice 6: Attaining Ascension While Alive

After attaining enlightenment while in human embodiment, you may de-densify your body and transform it into finer material—a light body. This is called "ascension," "translation," or "physical immortality." Your immortal body is not subject to illness, aging, or death. Through this ascension process, you escape bodily death altogether, and you leave no physical body behind to die or decay.

As an ascended master, because you have kept your subtle body and therefore not fully merged with the absolute, you maintain your individuality through *leshavidya*.

Choice 7: Attaining Ascension Near or After Death

Once you have attained enlightenment and are near death or have died, you may resurrect the body at will and create an ascended body of light. This is how Jesus and the Dzogchen practitioners attained their ascension. (See page 195 of this book.)

Mechanics of Ascension

Quantum physics has proven that matter is mostly empty space. The solidity of particles that constitute the universe is an illusion, concocted by the electromagnetic force that binds atoms together. Atomic particles are composed of waves of energy called quanta—from 10,000,000 to 100,000 times smaller than the smallest atom.

Theoretical physics, with superstring, brane, and M-theories, now postulates that the material world consists of the solidified vibrations of various frequencies. The elementary particles observed in particle accelerators are nothing more than excitation modes of elementary strings—vibrating waves of energy.

Your physical body, like all matter, is nearly empty. Between the subatomic particles of your body is space. The area occupied by your body has virtually no substance whatsoever. It consists of congealed energy made of rays of living light.

It was observed in a large cyclotron at Brookhaven Institute in Upton, New York, that if subatomic particles travel near the speed of light, they do not collide, but instead pass through each other. The higher the speed of particles, the more dematerialized they become, and the more they spread out over time and space, without any specific location or time.

By the same principle, you could conceivably raise the vibrational frequency of the matter composing your physical body into a higher octave of energy. It could theoretically be converted into pure energy, a "light body." Such a body already exists as part of your subtle body—your etheric soul self body, your immortal soul. (Read my book *Exploring Auras* to learn more about your subtle bodies.)

Lifting the vibrations of the physical body to the octave of the soul body is called "quickening." The vibrational frequency of your physical body speeds up until it makes a quantum leap into coherent light waves. Thus a flash of light appeared upon the ascension of Jesus, Ramalinga Swami, Annalee Skarin, and other ascended masters. This is similar to the quantum leap, known as the Meissner Effect, that ordinary light takes when it becomes coherent laser light.

Quickening reverses the slowing-down, cooling-down process by which light congeals into matter to create the physical universe (according to the "big bang" theory). This is related to Einstein's equation $E=MC^2$. As mass speeds up, greater energy is created. By reversing the slowing-down process of aging, it is possible to start "youthing" instead.

> *For as the Father raiseth up the dead, and quickeneth*
> *them; even so the Son quickeneth whom he will.*
> —John 5:21

When you ascend, your body's frequencies speed up so much that you step into a lighter dimension, a higher-frequency realm than the material world. You can vanish into thin air and reappear to anyone, anywhere, instantly. You can move without restrictions of time or space, casting no shadow and making no footprint.

Figure 12a. **Susan's Etheric Soul Self:** My etheric soul self represents the true nature of my being, my true physical form and true heart's desires. My perfect idealized form, the etheric soul-self body, represents who I really am, symmetrical, youthful, and beautiful. The physical body should ideally have the same form as the immortal soul body. However, we distort the form of our physical bodies with error-beliefs, including limitation, illness, aging, and death.

*The wind bloweth where it listeth, and thou hearest the
sound thereof, but canst not tell whence it cometh, and
whither it goeth: so is every one that is born of the Spirit.*
—John 3:8

After attaining ascension and full mastery over death, you can return to a physical body by a process called *vyutthana* in Sanskrit. You can resurrect your body and reappear to others, as Jesus did. Or you can manifest any other physical form, at will.

*There are also celestial bodies, and bodies terrestrial: but the
glory of the celestial is one, and the glory of the terrestrial
is another.... So also is the resurrection of the dead. It is
sown in corruption; it is raised in incorruption.... It is
sown a natural body; it is raised a spiritual body. There
is a natural body, and there is a spiritual body.*
—I Corinthians 15:40,42,44

Beyond Death

Everyone is eternal, and no one ever dies. Your soul lasts forever. But ascension is something different. It is eternal life *with* your body—not apart from it. Your body was not created for death. It was meant for eternal life. You have the inherent, God-given power over death. Death does not have to be your pathway. You can enjoy eternal, imperishable glory in the light of God almighty.

Ernest Holmes, founder of the Church of Religious Science, said in *The Science of Mind*:

There is every reason to suppose that we have a body within a body to infinity.... The "resurrection body"...is already within and we may be certain that it will be a fit instrument for the future unfoldment of the soul...the future body will resemble this one, except that it will be free from disease, old age, or whatever hinders a more complete flow of the Spirit.... We have a spiritual body now, and need not die to receive one...we are not going to attain immortality...WE NOW ARE IMMORTAL! Our contention is not that dead men live again, but that a living man never dies."[3]

You are promised eternal life, though you may not believe it. An everlasting kingdom is offered, yet perhaps you reject it. You might seek for immortality, yet maybe you lack faith that it exists. The prophet Isaiah wrote: "I will ransom them from the power of the grave; I will redeem them from death: O death, I will be thy plagues; O grave, I will be thy destruction."[4] And "He will swallow up death in victory; and the Lord God will wipe away tears from off all faces."[5]

Few believe in immortality, because few are aware that such a state exists and that any ordinary person has attained it. Because it is so rare, it is assumed to be impossible. We are so accustomed to watching people grow old, get sick, and die, that it seems inconceivable to imagine youthing instead of aging, or living forever instead of dying.

Enter ye in at the strait gate: for wide is the gate, and broad is the way, that leadeth to destruction, and many there be which go in thereat: Because strait is the gate, and narrow is the way, which leadeth unto life, and few there be that find it.
—Matthew 7:13–14

Your Power to Ascend

We take false comfort in the belief that only glorious beings such as Jesus, Babaji, and Saint Germain can ascend—not us. We enjoy the assumption that their special powers could never be possessed by ordinary humans. That is because it is just too terrifying to imagine that we possess such power ourselves. That responsibility is overwhelming, and way beyond our comfort zone.

To arouse your inner power and take your place as a son or daughter of the living God might be a lot to swallow right now. But eventually you will ascend, whether it takes a lifetime, a hundred lifetimes, or an eon. Finally you will return home. Few pass through the straight and narrow gate that leads to eternal life, but it is *not* impossible to enter. For it is said that even fools shall not err therein: "And an highway shall be there, and a way, and it shall be called The way of holiness; the unclean shall not pass over it; but it shall be for those: the wayfaring men [who are traveling the straight and narrow path of purifying their hearts], though fools, shall not err therein."[6]

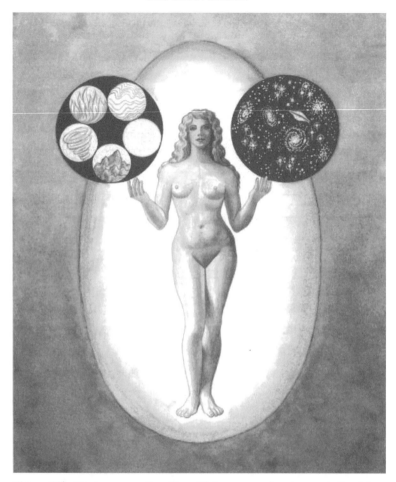

Figure 12b. **Mastery over Creation:** This woman has immortalized her body and enlightened her mind. She juggles the five material elements in one hand and the universe in the other. Therefore she has attained mastery over all of creation. She stands in the golden egg of creation, (*hiranya garba* in Sanskrit) which represents the seed of the universe.

Ascension means freedom. You can live anywhere and materialize anything. You can continue to serve on the earth plane or another plane. You can travel anywhere at the speed of thought and materialize your desires instantaneously.

Are you ready to live as an immortal being? After all, your higher self is as spiritual now as it will ever be, and you are as immortal today as you will ever be. Your soul lives eternally. It is possible to become an ascended master right now.

In my ascension workshops, students have quickened the vibrations of their physical bodies and united with their light bodies during our meditations. This experience is intense bliss, with waves of energy, vibrancy, and joy rushing through the body, in the rapture of ecstatic union. Tingling and electricity is often accompanied by a vision of brilliant inner light. You can practice such a meditation on page 219 of this book.

As the Earth clears negative beliefs that have plagued humanity for eons, the concept of physical immortality will grow. Divine light is growing daily, and the Earth is becoming a sphere of light. Many are waking to their heart's desires and true identity. You can manifest your divine purpose, which may include becoming an ascended master, the highest aspiration a human can attain.

I shall not die, but live, and declare the works of the Lord.
—Psalm 118:17

*In the way of righteousness is life; and in the
pathway thereof there is no death.*
—Proverbs 12:28

*The law of the wise is a fountain of life, to
depart from the snares of death.*
—Proverbs 13:14

Whosoever believeth in him should not perish, but have eternal life.
—John 3:15

*This is Brahman, the Supreme, the Great. Hidden in all
things, body by body, the One embracer of the universe—
By knowing him as Lord, men become immortal.*
—Svetasvatara Upanishad 3:7

Being one with Nature, he is in accord with Tao.
Being in accord with Tao, he is everlasting.
—Lau Tsu, Tao Te Ching

Why Die?

Contrary to popular belief, it is not necessary to die in order to attain eternal life. You can live forever and never die. Death is not real. Yet the belief in death has perpetuated the so-called reality of death generation after generation. The belief in death is the most deeply ingrained of all human beliefs.

The last enemy that shall be destroyed is death.
—I Corinthians 15:26

Death is so far-reaching and gripping that nearly everyone knows it is inescapable. But a few rare individuals have realized it is no more inescapable than bad luck from walking under a ladder—it is simply superstition. Ideally, without the mental programming of death in your subconscious computer, you could live forever.

Annalee Skarin stated in *Beyond Mortal Boundaries*: "Death is the dreary, back door entrance into the other world. It is the servant's entrance. But there is a great front door of glory for those who OVERCOME."[7]

The concept of death stems from a mistaken way of thinking. It is the fantasy that "you" are solely the body. Your erroneous identification with material life programs your subconscious computer for death. What is made of the elements of nature must eventually, according to the first law of thermodynamics (entropy), return to the elements of nature, "dust to dust."

But you are not this earthly housing. You are a divine Spirit that built this physical body from thought vibrations—seeds of desire congealed into physical form. You created this material illusion to achieve your *prarabdha karma,* the set of beliefs used to fulfill your life plan. (Read more about this in my book *Exploring Meditation.*)

Your physical body is just one of many bodies you inhabit. You have many identities on different levels of consciousness, and each identity forms a subtle body. On various levels of awareness, you have separate identities and distinct subtle bodies. Figure 12c shows some aspects of your higher self.

Figure 12c. Aspects of Your Higher Self.

This picture shows a woman standing on Earth. Aspects of her higher self surround her. Floating just above her head is her immortal, etheric soul-self. Two figures above that represent her male and female Christ selves. The figures above that are her male and female "I AM" selves, holding a scroll with the Hebrew letters YOD HE VAV HE, meaning "I AM THAT I AM." Above that, the two aspects of her God self are shown with crowns. The female figure just below the dove is the feminine aspect of God, the Holy Spirit. The stars and galaxies represent the cosmic self. The golden sun symbolizes the impersonal supreme Godhead, "God I AM," shining its radiance everywhere.

You can see this picture (and other pictures in this book), and order prints in full color, at *www.ascendedmasterpainting.com*. The Divine Revelation Guided Meditation CD, available at *www.divinerevelation. org*, brings you, step-by-step, through all the layers of the higher self pictured in this illustration.

Identifying Who You Really Are

Your physical body is manufactured from subconscious beliefs about yourself. Therefore, by identifying yourself as your immortal body of light rather than as your physical body, you could live forever. By transforming your physical shell into its true, ever-youthful embodiment of the immortal soul body, you would not age.

Your ego-identification has created bondage to your body with its beliefs in suffering, old age, and death. You may see yourself as this small, pathetic physical frame in the mirror. But that is not your true nature. You are not this tiny, insignificant bag of bones, blood, flesh, and phlegm. You are the immutable Spirit, without birth or death. You are created in the likeness and image of the almighty, imperishable, everlasting God.

You are immortal right now!

Chapter 13

Conquering Death

The wages of sin is death; but the gift of God is eternal life.
—Romans 6:23

Although nearly everyone believes that it is impossible to overcome death, we are promised eternal life repeatedly in the Bible and other ancient scriptures. We read the words, yet we do not believe them. Perhaps we believe they are applicable to ancient times, but not today. Here we will begin to understand that ancient wisdom is not just for legendary iconic figures of the past. It still lives today and is practical for everyone.

The Bible contains secret information about how to attain immortality, if we just learn how to read between the lines.

Returning to Eden

The concepts of "judgment," "sin," and "death" are clearly depicted in a story from the book of Genesis. Adam, the first man, lived in the Garden of Eden, the garden of immortal life. God told him he could eat the fruit of every tree in the garden except one—the tree of "knowledge of good and evil." God warned that if Adam were to eat from that tree, he would "surely die."

God created Eve, the first woman, out of Adam's rib, and they "were both naked" and "were not ashamed." Eve was tempted by a serpent to eat the fruit of the forbidden tree. The serpent told her she would not die. So she ate the fruit and shared it with Adam. Then their "eyes were opened, and they knew that they were naked." They made garments out of fig leaves. Of course, God caught them in the act.

This story is not a history lesson. It is an allegory about the human condition right here, right now, every day. The meaning of this parable is as follows:

The birthright of Adam and Eve (humanity) is to live eternal life in paradise—a state of oneness with God, without shame, guilt, or other negative beliefs, habits, and conditions. This is eternal life, without "sin" (false beliefs). Adam and Eve represent two aspects of consciousness: the male, *Purusha*, or *Shiva* aspect, and the female, *Prakriti,* or *Shakti* aspect. This is called *yin* and *yang* in Confucianism.

Figure 13a. **Ardhanarishvara:** The two aspects of God, the male *Shiva* and female *Shakti*, are depicted as a hydrogenous being. Ardhanarishvara represents the eternal union of male and female aspects of creation, duality melded into wholeness with opposites coexisting in perfect equilibrium. Night and day are represented in the background, echoing the idea of duality. Many names in different cultures represent these two elements of God, such as the Elohim, twin flames, yin/yang, Adam/Eve, Parusha/Prakriti, Hashem/Shekhinah, or Yab/Yum.

When Eve is created out of Adam, duality is born from oneness. Still they live in paradise, because yin and yang are in balance, harmony, and equilibrium. Adam and Eve live in innocence and contentment, without guile, greed, or need. They know who they really are—immortal divine beings, one with God, at peace with themselves, and harmonious with nature.

Then a serpent tempts Eve to eat the fruit of the tree of condemning judgment. This serpent represents *avidya* (ignorance), the ego, and false identification with limitation. Disobeying God and eating the fruit opens Adam's and Eve's eyes to shame and destroys their innocence. This is called the "fall of man" or "fall from grace."

The belief in "good and evil" is born. This belief is erroneous, a delusion of false identification with duality—*pragya aparadh* in Sanskrit, "the mistake of the intellect." They no longer see the truth. Instead they mistake themselves as limited, isolated, and separate from God.

When the apple is eaten, the ego is born. Isolation from God is born. Thus, suffering is born. Shame is born. The façade is born. Adam and Eve search for fig leaves to cover their inadequacies. By eating from this tree, they will "surely die." The false identification with ego is the "sin" of dual thinking, which separates humans from their true nature of immortal, pristine purity. Thus death is born.

God drives Adam and Eve out of Eden, which is paradise and immortal life. God expels them lest they also "eat of the tree of life and live forever" in their state of "sin" (ignorance). Cherubim and a flaming sword are placed at the gate so they cannot sneak back into the garden. Immortal life is thus closed to anyone who eats of the tree of good and evil—those who falsely identify with ego and thereby judge themselves and others.

Only by remaining in the state of eternal paradise (oneness with God) are you granted the privilege of immortality. The gate to the garden is the "psychic barrier" or "façade barrier"—the false belief in separation from God, which separates your mind from Spirit. By experiencing oneness with God, you are admitted back into the garden, and eternal life is yours.

To Him that overcometh will I give to eat of the tree of life, which is in the midst of the paradise of God.
—Revelation 2:7

"Sin" is a mistaken belief that isolates you from your true nature. It is the mind, separated from God, living in dual thinking, such as "good and bad," "right and wrong," and "reward and punishment." "Sin" means identifying yourself with the dualistic ego rather than the true immortal oneness of divinity.

> *For when ye were the servants of sin [living in ignorance of your true nature], ye were free from righteousness [not following your true purpose]. What fruit had ye then in those things whereof ye are now ashamed? For the end of those things is death. But now being made free from sin [free from ignorance], and become servants to God [experiencing oneness with Spirit], your fruits are holy, and the end thereof is life everlasting. For the wages of sin is death: but the gift of God is eternal life.*
> —Romans 6:20–23

Your "sin" is rejecting and disobeying your true, higher nature, and instead embracing the duality of ego, which is ignorance and illusion. The wages (result) of that mistaken belief is death, because you are identified with your mortal body and your limited mind, rather than with Spirit—your true, immortal higher self. By returning to innocence and living in harmony and oneness with God, you accept the truth that you are already eternal life.

> *Having realized the soundless, unmanifest, formless, imperishable, and tasteless, odorless, eternal Self, that which is without beginning or ending, beyond the Great, and unchanging—one is freed from the jaws of death.*
> —Katha Upanishad 1.3.15

Overcoming the Karmic Law

> *For the law of the Spirit of life in Christ Jesus hath made me free from the law of sin and death [the law of karma].... And if Christ be in you, the body is dead because of sin; but the Spirit is life because of righteousness. But if the Spirit*

of him that raised up Jesus from the dead dwell in you,
he that raised up Christ from the dead shall also quicken
your mortal bodies by his Spirit that dwelleth in you.
—Romans 8:2,10–11

What is the "law of sin and death"? It is the law of karma. *Karma* is a Sanskrit word meaning "action." Through the law of karma, humans manufacture mental laws that lead to so-called sin and so-called death.

Many people believe that the law of karma means the following: If you "sin," you are paid back with "punishments." Yet, who is committing the so-called sin, and who is punishing the so-called sinner? No one but yourself.

In every moment, through every thought, word, and deed, you engage in karma (action). Every action has an effect, not only upon yourself, but also the entire universe. Your actions do not stop with the boundary of your skin. They affect everyone. Every positive or negative thought, word, or deed contributes to either positive or negative vibrations in the universe. Every action has consequences for everyone and everything.

Your subconscious mind is the repository of every piece of karma you create. Throughout your life, a memory bank filled with every experience gets stored in your subconscious mind. Those memories establish habit patterns. You habitually act in certain ways, because you were taught to act that way by parents, role models, and society.

Your patterns create a "mental law"—a set of rules you have accepted through time. Your mental law may consist of many statutes, such as, "I am always prosperous," or "I am not very popular," or "I am beautiful," or "I am fat." Your mental law could not exist without the karmic law, which states that every thought, word, and deed has consequences.

You are responsible for creating every action, and your mental law, or set of mental beliefs, manifests every one of your experiences. These might be so-called rewards for your so-called good deeds, or so-called punishments for your so-called sins. Both rewards and punishments are solely your creations, magnetized by your own set of beliefs.

Living in Eden means dwelling in a paradisiacal state of awareness, free from the law of karma. In that state, duality does not exist.

Your mind is at peace, content, and one with God. No matter what happens, still you experience internal serenity. However, when your mind falls from this state of grace, then you are subject the law of karma. Dualistic thinking is born. You are ousted from the Garden.

> *There is One Path, the annihilation of the*
> *false ego in the real, which raises the mortal to*
> *immortality, in which resides all perfection.*
> —Hazrat Inayat Khan

You are either living in wholeness, free from the law of karma, or you are embroiled in the "tree of good and evil," which is dual thinking—the fall from grace. Then, rather than wholeness, your mind sees only contrasts.

Dual thinking means you judge everyone and everything. You start to form strong opinions. You put boxes around people and place them into categories. You compare yourself with others and perceive them as more successful than you. You become jealous of what they have. You think life owes you more. You resent your position and feel cheated. You place blame and want vengeance. You feel frustrated from not getting what you want. You become obsessed with things you cannot get.

This is the path of internal conflict, your own personal hell. Here you are subject to the chains of your personal mental law, born of the law of karma.

In contrast, there is a "law of grace" that can overcome this hell. The law of grace says, "With God, all things are possible."[1] This law is the key to your return to Eden. It is your way to climb out of the depths of hell and return home to oneness. It is your entrance to the mansion of eternal life, in the glory of the holy presence of divinity.

In short, hell is duality, and heaven is unity. Hell is born of the law of karma, and heaven is born of the law of grace. Through grace you can reach the heavenly shore of paradise. The mistaken way of thinking called "condemning judgment" has enslaved humanity for millennia, but the wondrous gift of the "law of grace" can unlock the secret of eternal life.

For sin shall not have dominion over you: for ye are
not under law [law of karma], but under grace.
—Romans 6:14

As the blazing fire turns fuel to ashes, O Arjuna, so does
the fire of wisdom turn all actions (karma) into ashes.
—Bhagavad Gita 4:37

Divine Love Is the Way

Religious scriptures of all cultures say that surrendering to God
and putting your faith solely in God is the pathway to life eternal.
By spiritualizing your life and transforming your physical body into
Spirit, immortality is attained. When Spirit fully overtakes you, then
you have built a body of divine light.

The path is to transform every aspect of your life—mind, body,
emotions, and consciousness—into pure Spirit. It is your birthright
to live in the light of God. This can be accomplished by inviting God
into your life, right here, right now, and in each moment.

For he that soweth to his flesh shall of the flesh reap corruption; but
he that soweth to the Spirit shall of the Spirit reap life everlasting.
—Galatians 6:8

Being born again, not of corruptible seed, but of incorruptible,
by the word [essence or Spirit] of God, which liveth and abideth
for ever. For all flesh is as grass, and all the glory of man as
the flower of grass. The grass withereth, and the flower thereof
falleth away: But the word of the Lord endureth for ever.
—I Peter 1:23–25

How can you be "born again" of incorruptible seed? How can you
transform your body, which is "born of the flesh," into Spirit, which is
"born of the Spirit"? It is by loving God with all your heart and humbly surrendering to God. It is by doing your best to follow the will of
God.

As Moses said to his people Israel (*Israel* means "shining ones of light"): "Hear, O Israel: The Lord our God, the Lord is One. And thou shalt love the Lord thy God with all thy heart, and with all thy soul, and with all thy might."[2]

This law, the most sacred in Judaism, is regarded with such sanctity for good reason. It is the most fundamental law upon which all other laws are built. Jesus declared it to be the greatest commandment. By practicing this, you automatically fulfill the second great commandment: "Thou shalt love thy neighbor as thyself."[3]

By mastering the greatest commandment, you master life, for divine love is the primary, essential form of love. Love is the magnet that binds you to divinity and glorifies life. Ecstatic union with your divine lover brings immortality. This oneness, the fulfillment of *yoga* (union with God), is the essence of eternal life.

The immeasurable love of a devotee for God is the glue that solidifies a bond without boundaries, seams, or cracks. By unifying your individual soul with universal Spirit, you realize God-consciousness. In that state there is no lack—only the fullness of divine union. On that level of love, death has no place—only the abundance of joy. An overflowing cup has no space for emptiness.

The sun shall be no more thy light by day; neither for brightness shall the moon give light unto thee: but the Lord shall be unto thee an everlasting light, and thy God thy glory. Thy sun shall no more go down; neither shall thy moon withdraw itself: for the Lord shall be thine everlasting light, and the days of thy mourning shall be ended.
—Isaiah 60:19–20

Holy communion—union with the secret place of the most high God—is the "fountain of living waters," the eternal fountain of youth. That innermost dwelling place within the sacred chamber of your heart is your doorway to immortal life. Walk through that door and approach the throne of almighty God. Surrender yourself before the indwelling presence and realize that you are the Christ ("the anointed").

If you love God with all your heart, soul, and might, then you live in the fullness of love. That means accepting the very essence of divine love and transforming your being into a love-being. You train every cell of your body to overflow with the juice of love and radiate the fullness of love.

A lawyer asked Jesus how to inherit eternal life. Jesus asked the lawyer what is written in the law. The lawyer answered by stating the two greatest commandments: loving God with all thy heart and loving thy neighbor as thyself. Jesus answered him, "Thou hast answered right: this do, and thou shalt live."[4]

By radiating love continually from every pore of your body, your cells of flesh are transformed into cells of pure Spirit. Your cells clothe themselves in the raiment of divine light, erasing all marks of illness and death. Nothing can rend a garment woven in immutable fabric. Your mortal frame is transformed into luminous, effulgent blazing light, deathless and imperishable. Your inheritance of eternal life is bestowed.

> *But lay up for yourselves treasures in heaven, where neither moth nor rust doth corrupt, and where thieves do not break through nor steal: For where your treasure is, there will your heart be also. The light of the body is the eye: if therefore thine eye be single [one with God], thy whole body shall be full of light.*
> —Matthew 6:20–22

> *And they that be wise shall shine as the brightness of the firmament; and they that turn many to righteousness as the stars for ever and ever.*
> —Daniel 12:3

"Born of the Spirit"

As yogis and siddhas have demonstrated, spiritualizing the body is key to immortal life and to the reversal of aging. Every atom of the body glows with brilliance of eternal splendor. The gross physical frame of blood, muscle, and phlegm transmutes into its fundamental precursor—rays of living light. This full translation of flesh into Spirit is what Hindus refer to as "twice-born" and what Jesus called "born again" and "born of the Spirit": "Except a man be born of water and of the Spirit, he cannot enter into the kingdom of God. That which is born of the flesh is flesh; and that which is born of the Spirit is spirit. Marvel not that I said unto thee, Ye must be born again. The wind bloweth where it listeth, and thou hearest the sound thereof, but canst not tell whence it cometh, and whither it goeth: so is every one who is born of the Spirit."[5]

The ideal God-seed is your immortal light-body—your true form, in which God intends you to dwell. It is your perfect divine body, as God sees you. To be "born again" is to outpicture this perfect ideal image conceived by God. You are created in that perfect image and likeness. Your soul is as God sees itself—perfect and whole. Being "born of the Spirit" means allowing Spirit to express through you in the ideal way of perfection that God conceives for you.

> *I will pour out my spirit upon all flesh; and your sons*
> *and your daughters shall prophesy, your old men shall*
> *dream dreams, your young men shall see visions.*
> —Joel 2:28

You deserve to live immortal life in the bliss of eternal divine union. God is imperishable life. Your soul is incorruptible and immortal, without beginning or end, indestructible. Death has no power over you when you fully realize your higher self, your truth of being.

> *He who has realized the eternal Truth does not see death, nor*
> *illness, nor pain. He sees everything as the Self, and obtains all.*
> —Chandogya Upanishad 7.23, 7.27

> *So when this corruptible shall have put on incorruption,*
> *and this mortal shall have put on immortality, then shall*
> *be brought to pass the saying that is written, Death is*
> *swallowed up in victory. O death, where is thy sting?*
> *O grave, where is thy victory? The sting of death is sin;*
> *and the strength of sin is the law [the law of karma].*
> —I Corinthians 15:54–56

Chapter 14

Elixir of Immortality

Flow Soma, in a most sweet and exhilarating stream, effused for Indra to drink. The all-beholding destroyer of Rakshasas has stepped upon his gold-smitten birthplace, united with the wooden cask. Be the lavish giver of wealth, most bounteous, the destroyer of enemies; bestow on us the riches of the affluent.
—Rig Veda: 9.1.1.1–3

Legends of the fountain or pool of immortal life have been passed down throughout human history. Bathing in the ambrosial waters washes away mental impurities and brings new life and eternal youth. The Greek philosopher Herodotus writes of a fountain that generated extraordinary longevity in Ethiopia. The *Alexander Romance* describes the mythical exploits of Alexander the Great crossing the Land of Darkness, along with his servant, to find the immortal spring.

Muslim mystics speak of a fountain of ambrosia and tank of paradise. Spiritual masters of India seek the pool of nectar and the lake of honor. Water of life or living waters of everlasting life are also mentioned in the Bible: "But whosoever drinketh of the water that I shall give him shall never thirst; but the water that I shall give him shall be in him a well of water springing up into everlasting life."[1]

Nectar of the Gods

The ambrosial elixir of life, or Philosopher's Stone, is a potion that, when ingested, is believed to grant eternal life. The word *ambrosia* derives from the Greek root *ambrotos*: *a-* (not) and *mbrotos* (mortal).

183

Amrita is a similar word in Sanskrit, meaning "without death." The term *nectar* comes from the Latin *nek-* (death) and *-tar* (overcoming). The word *elixir* derives from the Arabic *al-iksir* (miracle substance).

In myths of Enoch, Thoth, Hermes Trismegistus, and Al-Khidr (The Green Man), the immortal white drops, liquid gold, or dancing water is drunk. In Homer's poems, nectar is the drink of the gods and ambrosia is their food. *Amrita* is the Sanskrit equivalent, which is consumed by the gods of India.

According to Robert de Borón's tale of the 12th century, when Joseph of Arimathea was imprisoned, the ascended Jesus appeared in his cell with the Holy Grail. Its magical nourishment sustained Joseph for 42 years. The legend of the Grail quest, *Perceval, le Conte du Graal* by Chrestien de Troyes, was written during the same period.

In the Zoroastrian and Mithraic cults, the substance *haoma*, equivalent to the Sanskrit *soma*, from the roots *sav*, *su*, or *bu*, (squeeze or pound), is the name of a yellow plant whose juice is extracted for sacramental ceremonies.

The Nordic God Wotan, Woden, or Odin possesses a magic goat that fills the never-ending pitcher of "Poetic Mead" of inspiration—the most precious drink in the universe, which imparts secret wisdom and inspiration. The "Golden Apples of Immortality" bestow strength, health, and eternal youth to the Germanic and Norse Gods.

Philosopher's Stone

The vast writings of Hermes Trismegistus appeared in the Roman Empire in the 2nd century AD. In the Middle Ages and Renaissance, Hermeticism and the Hermetic Tradition became popular among alchemists. The Emerald Tablet, known as Smaragdine Table or The Secret of Hermes, was the bible of the alchemists' craft and was said to reveal the secret of the Philosopher's Stone.

The word *alchemy* has its roots in Arabic *al-kimia* (the art of transformation). Therefore, by definition, alchemists attempt to transmute one material into another, such as base metal into gold. In India and China, alchemists sought the Philosopher's Stone, the "Water Stone of the Wise," in the 4th century BC. Alchemists in Europe attempted to discover the stone for five centuries. This miraculous tincture or powder was believed to cure illness, reverse aging, grant eternal life, and bring spiritual realization.

The hundreds of names for the stone include the Sanskrit *soma rasa* (soma juice), *maha rasa* (great juice), *amrit rasa* (nectar of immortality juice) and *amrita* (nectar of immortality), and the Arabic *aab-i-hayat/aab-i-haiwan* (water of life), and *chashma-i-kausar* (fountain of beauty, located in Paradise).

> *And the next day, behold, a voice called me, saying, Esdras, open thy mouth, and drink that I give thee to drink. Then opened I my mouth, and, behold, he reached me a full cup, which was full as it were with water, but the color of it was like fire. And I took it, and drank: and when I had drunk of it, my heart uttered understanding, and wisdom grew in my breast, for my spirit strengthened my memory.*
> —Apocrypha: 2 Esdras 14:38–40

The Living Drops

Dr. Joanna Cherry of Mt. Shasta, California, believes that, due to humanity's universal belief in death, a "death hormone" is released from our pituitary gland, which programs the body for death. A biochemist formerly at Harvard, W. Donner Denckla theorizes that a substance called DECO, Decreasing Oxygen Consumption, is released by the pituitary gland from the time of puberty. Joanna Cherry has developed prayers and visualizations to reverse this process and stimulate production of a longevity-producing hormone.

There is such a chemical. In fact, an entire chapter of the most ancient scripture of India, Rig-Veda, is devoted to a mysterious substance called *soma* (also *Soma Pavamana* or *Indu*), which promises eternal life. From the Sanskrit root *sav-* (press or squeeze), soma is a drink of "living drops" produced by pressing stalks of the legendary soma plant.

Here are a few verses from the Rig-Veda, written by the seer Rishi Kashyapa, which invoke Soma Pavamana, and its properties of immortal life:

> Where light is perpetual, in the world in which the sun is placed, in that immortal imperishable world place me, Pavamana; flow, Indu, for Indra.

Where in the third heaven, in the third sphere, the sun wanders at will, where the regions are filled with light, there make me immortal; flow, Indu, for Indra.

Where there is happiness, pleasures, joy and enjoyment, where the wishes of the wisher are obtained, there make me immortal; flow, Indu, for Indra.[2]

Many legends are associated with soma. Some believe this chemical is existent in a rare Himalayan plant. It might be the potent antioxidant resveratrol, which is scientifically proven to slow aging and increase lifespan. The knotweed vine (*polygonum cuspidatum*), a natural source of resveratrol, is known in China as the anti-aging herbal remedy or elixir of life—*Fo Ti Tieng* roots *(Ho Shou Wu)* or Tiger Cane *(Hu Zhang)*—used as an herbal remedy in China for 1,500 years.

The tale of Ho Shou Wu began with an impotent Chinese man, age 58 years, who was trapped by a flood in the mountains for seven days. The only food he ate was the Fo-ti herb (Ho Shou Wu). As a result, he developed a strong sexual desire and fathered several offspring. One of these was Ho Ven Shiu, who lived to age 160. His son Ho Shou Wu had black hair until he died, at age 130. Li Ching Yuen, a legendary, famed Chinese herbalist, lived to age 256 by taking Ho Shou Wu, ginseng, goji berries, and other herbs daily. (Read about him on page 103 of this book.)

Many believe the legendary soma to be self-generated, in the pineal gland, where it programs the body to rejuvenate itself indefinitely. My personal experience is that soma juice trickles down the back of the throat and can be tasted as a sweet liquid. Yogic and Taoist practices stimulate the production and conservation of this precious immortal nectar. One of these is Khechari Mudra, described in *Hatha Yoga Pradipika* (the textbook of yoga practices, circa AD 1400). This dangerous technique should never be attempted without guidance from a yogic master. Otherwise, severe speech impairment will result:

The membrane under the tongue, *frenulum linguae*, which attaches the tongue to the floor of the mouth, is cut, only "a hair's breadth" daily, and treated with rock salt and herbs. The tongue is stretched and lengthened. After about six months, the membrane is completely cut away, and the tongue is curled up and thrust back toward the uvula at the back of the throat, to seal off the esophagus, windpipe, and palate. Hatha Yoga Pradipika states: "If the Yogi drinks *Somarasa* (soma juice) by sitting with the tongue turned backwards and mind concentrated, there is no doubt he conquers death within 15 days. As fire is inseparably connected with the wood and light is connected with the wick and oil, so does the soul not leave the body full of nectar exuding from the Soma."[3]

Secrets of Ojas

According to the science of Ayurveda (medicine in India), the treasured immortal nectar soma is derived from *ojas* ("vigor" in Sanskrit)—the fluid of life energy and storehouse of vital reserve. This subtle essence works ceaselessly, continually refreshing the body, mind, and senses, and integrating body, mind, and spirit. Ojas is responsible for bodily strength and immunity, and, when optimized, brings longevity. This vital fluid brings mental stability, calm, and contentment. Abundant ojas bestows physical, sexual, mental, and spiritual endurance.

Ojas is a product the genital fluids, which are a product of the marrow, which is a bone product, which is a fat product, which is a muscle product, which is a blood product, which is a lymph product, which is the product of food and oxygen.

Precious ojas substance flows copiously when your body and mind are in a state of purity. After spending a long time in deep silence and meditation, try rubbing your face just as you come out. A somewhat greasy substance with a sweet fragrance will transfer onto your hands. This is ojas, which cultures an emanation of radiance, effulgence, and charisma around the body. An individual replete with ojas has a highly energetic, magnetic, loving personality, lustrous eyes, a brilliant aura, and great intelligence.

Ojas can be developed through proper sleep, rest, relaxation, nourishment, digestion, meditation, and low-impact exercise, such as yoga *asanas*. For many secret practices that increase ojas in your body, see my books *Exploring Meditation*, *Exploring Chakras*, and *Exploring Auras*.

When the dweller in the body hath crossed over these three gunas,
whence all bodies have been produced, liberated from birth, death,
old age and sorrow, he drinketh amrita, the nectar of immortality.
—Bhagavad Gita 14:20

The Pot of Nectar of Immortality

Every 12 years, like clockwork, pilgrims and holy men and women from India meet at the extraordinary Maha Kumbh Mela ("great festival around the pot of nectar of immortality"). A staggering 100 million people attended the 2001 Kumbh Mela, estimated from satellite photographs—the "greatest recorded number of human beings assembled with a common purpose," according to the *Guinness Book of Records*.

The bathing event at the holy confluence of three sacred rivers at Allahabad, India is the central feature of the festival. The Kumbh Mela occurs during an auspicious planetary position believed to transmute the Ganges River into flowing nectar. Millions are purified through holy bathing rituals that wash away karmic consequences from past deeds.

Kumbh Mela celebrates a sacred legend: An ancient sage cursed the gods, and they became weak. In order to restore their strength, Lord Brahma advised them to retrieve the *kumbh* (pot) containing the *amrita* (nectar of immortality), which lay buried in the depths of the primeval ocean.

The gods made a pact with the demons to retrieve the nectar by churning the entire ocean. Mount Mandara was the churning rod. Vasuki, the serpent king, served as a rope. They churned the ocean for a thousand years. However, the first fruit of their labor was not the desired elixir, but a vial of poison so deadly that it threatened to annihilate the universe. Lord Shiva stepped in to save the universe by drinking the poison.

As the churning continued, 14 *ratnas* (gems or treasures) emerged from the ocean. One of these was Lakshmi, Goddess of wealth. Finally Dhanvantari, the divine healer, surfaced, bearing the coveted pot of nectar and the sacred book of Ayurveda.

Figure 14a. **Dhanvantari:** The divine physician and founder of Ayurvedic medicine, Dhanvantari emerged from the primordial ocean bearing the pot of nectar of immortality.

The Gods realized the demons would attain immortality by drinking the nectar. So they grabbed the pot of nectar. The demons gave chase, and a 12-year battle ensued between Gods and demons to wrest the pitcher. During the tug of war, a few drops of nectar fell to Earth in four sacred places.

Finally the demons seized the nectar. Lord Vishnu then incarnated as the most alluring woman, Mohini. Under her spell, the demons succumbed to her demand that they first purify themselves by bathing in the ocean before drinking the elixir. While they were thus distracted,

Mohini distributed the nectar to the gods, who drank all of it without delay.

Because the fight lasted 12 years, the Maha Kumbh Mela is celebrated every 12 years where the four drops of nectar fell: Allahabad, Haridwar, Ujjain, and Nasik. The festival takes place approximately every three years in rotation in the four sacred places.

I have personally led several tour groups to the Kumbh Mela. I can attest that bathing at that holy time and place, the river is like nectar, the experience is ambrosial, the result is blissful, and the transformation on mind, body, and spirit is dramatic and permanent. For information about how you can experience this blessing, visit our Kumbh Mela Website, *www.kumbhmela.net*.

Chapter 15

Building an Immortal Body

If you ask what is the sign of true liberation of body and spirit,
it is the physical body aglow with the fire of immortality.
—Siddha Roma Rishi

The great ancient sages perfected the art of inner alchemy. Through their secret practices, the physical body transmutes into the Christian "resurrection body" or "glorified body," the Sufi "most sacred body" or "supracelestial body," the Taoist "diamond body," the Buddhist "light body" or "rainbow body," the Indian siddha "body of bliss," or the Hermetic "immortal body."

Although the actual practices for achieving this state are closely guarded, in this chapter we will glimpse some experiences of those who have achieved the resplendent body of immortality.

Ramalinga Swami

The ocean of love and compassion, Ramalinga Swami (see page 74) described his transformation into an ascended body of light in 40,000 lines of verse. He mentions three stages of immortalizing the body:

In the first stage, the mortal human body becomes *suddha deham* (perfect body), a golden body of immeasurable brilliance. This is attained through reverence for life, devotional meditation, kindness, compassion, praying for grace, and universal love. When the heart melts in devotion to God, impure bodily elements transform into pure light by God's grace.

191

This purified body emits a golden hue and appears about 12 years old. There is no more eating, digestion, excretion, growth, or aging. Food, sleep, and sex are not required. The skin becomes soft and the muscles flexible. Immortal elixir flows through the body. The face shines with brilliance. The mind is pure, unlimited, and free from ego. The heart swells with love. The body is not limited by time, space, or other natural laws. Any miracle can be performed, including raising the dead and restoration of youth to the aged.

The second stage, *pranava deham* (body of grace and light), is a body that is visible but cannot be touched. It appears as a heavenly child of about 5 to 8 years of age with command over all the *siddhis* (miraculous powers).

In the third and final stage, *gnana deham* (body of bliss), the body merges with the body of supreme wisdom, and the individual transmutes into the Godhead. This body is omnipresent but imperceptible to the senses.

Kaya-Kalpa

In India, the ancient medical practice is called Ayurveda, "the science of life." One branch of Ayurveda deals with longevity, known as *kaya-kalpa*. *Kaya* means "body" and *kalpa* means "end or dissolution." The treatments for kaya-kalpa are described in *Siddha's Science of Longevity and Kalpa Medicine of India* by Dr. A. Shanmuga Velan. They are:

1. Preserving the vital energies by diverting the internal secretions of the body through pranayama (breathing exercises).
2. Transmuting the sexual energy and conserving the sperm by celibacy and Tantra Yoga practices.
3. Taking three consolidated mineral salts, known as *muppu,* which are elaborately prepared.
4. Taking calcined powders prepared from mercury, sulphur, mica, gold, copper, iron, and other minerals.
5. Using drugs prepared from rare Indian herbs, including Fo-ti Tieng and hydrocotyle asiatica.

Sushruta Samhita, an ancient Ayurvedic text, describes kaya-kalpa as a ritual of entering a chamber for seven days after detoxifying the system through purgatives, enemas, and sweat baths. The soma liquid (see page 185) is carefully prepared and administered by the physician. The patient then vomits blood, breaks out in swellings, and defecates worms. The muscles wither, and fingernails and hair fall out. The body expels all undesirable toxic matter accumulated through errors in diet and conduct. On the eighth day the rejuvenation process begins. The hair and nails grow back, muscles regain their vitality, skin assumes a new luster, and the body emerges new and youthful.

A famous actress who will remain anonymous went through the kaya-kalpa process at an Ayurvedic hospital in South India in 1991 at age 65. Her body had showed many signs of aging, including liver spots on the skin, non-elasticity of the skin, gray hair, a white ring around her iris, and folds of skin under her eyes. She spent six months at the hospital.

The first three months were devoted to detoxification processes, including laxatives, herbal oil massages, herbal oil head treatments, herbal sweat baths, enemas with herbs and oils, and nasal treatments. During her sweat baths, a goopy substance continually oozed from her eyes. She eliminated toxins from every orifice.

Then she entered a darkened room for three months. She was given secret practices, all her meals were brought to her, and she took drops that consisted of "mostly alcohol." During the three months, her skin became rough and scaly, and eventually shed. All her hair fell out.

When she returned to the United States, she had thick, beautiful auburn hair, bright, shining eyes with no white ring, and youthful elastic skin, without liver spots. She looked and felt years younger.

Boganath

Boganath (see page 83) describes his kaya-kalpa process in his poem "Boga Jnana Sutra." He prepared a tablet with 35 different herbs, including gold, cinnabar, and mercury ore, a deadly poison. Then he took his dog and three disciples to a mountaintop. First he gave a tablet to the dog, which immediately dropped dead. Then he gave a tablet to his main disciple, Yu, who fell over dead. His other disciples hid the tablets and pretended they had swallowed them. Boganath swallowed the remaining tablets and fell unconscious.

The grief-stricken disciples went down the mountain to get burial supplies. When they returned, they found a note, which stated that

the kaya-kalpa tablets had worked and Boganath had revived the faithful dog and Yu from their trance. He told them that they had missed
their chance for immortality. Boganath states: "With great care and
patience I made the (kaya-kalpa) tablet and then swallowed it, not
waiting for fools and skeptics who would not appreciate its hidden
meaning and importance. Steadily I lived in the land of the Parangis
(foreigners) for 12,000 years, my fellow! I lived for a long time and
fed on the vital ojas. With the *ojas vindhu* I received the name, Boga.
The body developed the golden color of the pill. Now I am living in a
world of gold."[1]

Boganath took this potion in China and was known there as Wei
Poyang, Taoist alchemist and author of one of the oldest known trea-
tises on immortality.

Saint Germain

The ascended master Saint Germain (see page 137) taught Count
Cagliostro the kaya-kalpa method. This rite of longevity consisted of a
40-day fast on distilled water. On the 17th day the patient drew blood
and took an elixir called "Master's White Drops" for the three following days. The patient then drew blood from his arm and took a grain
of the "philosopher's stone" for another three days. On the 33rd day,
the patient evacuated from all channels of the body. On the 35th day,
the hair and teeth fell out and the skin was shed. On the 37th day,
new skin and new teeth began to grow. By the 40th day, a complete
rejuvenation occurred.

By doing this process every 50 years, physical immortality was attained. This is the method by which Comte de Saint Germain arrested
his aging process.

Babaji

Swami Satyeswarananda of India claims that he witnessed an aged
saint, said to be Mahamuni Babaji, living in Sanyasgar, Bengal, dis-
card his body and trade it in for a new one. The old saint exhaled, and
a white thread-like substance came out of his mouth. The sage cut
this thread into three pieces and offered two pieces into a ritual fire as
he chanted mantras (power words). Then he ate the third piece. After
some time, his belly began to swell until it burst. A radiant, beautiful

young boy emerged from his belly and threw the old man's body into the fire.

Dzogchen Rainbow Body

Dzogchen ("great perfection") is said to be the natural, pure state of every living being. The all-encompassing, timeless, nameless, formless awareness, effulgence, or fullness, it is like a movie screen, reflecting images, but unaffected by those images. When you maintain the Dzogchen state continually, you are fully God-realized and enlightened.

The great sage Naropa (AD 1016–1100), also known as Naro Choe Druk, taught the "Six Yogas of Naropa," which help people quickly achieve Dzogchen. These six yogas, from the lineage of Tilopa (see page 98) to Naropa and Marpa, are known as:

1. Tummo (*candali*): yoga of inner or mystic heat.
2. Gyulu (*mayakaya*): yoga of the illusory body.
3. Osel (*prabhasvara*): yoga of the clear light or radiant light.
4. Milam (*svapnadarsana*): yoga of the dream state.
5. Bardo *(antarabhava)*: yoga of the intermediate state.
6. Phowa (*samkranti*): yoga of the transference of consciousness.

About a week before death, advanced Tibetan Buddhist Dzochen practitioners retreat into a walled-up cave or small tent. During the week after death, the physical body transforms into a light body. The corpse does not decompose, but starts to shrink until it disappears. Fingernails, toenails, and hair are left behind. However, those who have mastered *Phowa* never die. Their physical bodies gradually disappear.

To attain the rainbow body, the physical and subtle bodies merge with the truth body, *Dharmakaya*, the eternal, unmanifest, imperishable reality. The corporeal body de-densifies, or decreases its physicality.

Figure 15a. **Rainbow Body:** Tibetan letter "A," symbol of body of light.

It breaks down into its primary components, the "Five Pure Lights," which are the primordial essences of space, air, water, fire, and earth. (To learn more about these elements, read my books *Exploring Meditation* and *Exploring Chakras.*)

Consciousness is transferred into the Five Pure Lights, which are transmuted into the glorious bliss body, the *Sambhogakaya.* The rainbow body, the sign of complete realization of Dzogchen, becomes visible, and a brilliant rainbow of colors is seen above the Dzogchenpa's body, while the corpse becomes luminous, youthful, and fragrant.

In Kathog (Kathok) Monastery in Tibet, more than 100,000 people have attained the rainbow body since the 12th century. In nearby Dzogchen Monastery, more than 60,000 people have achieved it since the 17th century. Recent rainbow bodies include Khenpo A-Chos in September 1998, Khenchen Tsewang Rigdzin in September 1958, and Sonam Namgyal in 1952.

> *The realised Dzogchen practitioner, no longer deluded*
> *by apparent substantiality or dualism such as mind*
> *and matter, releases the energy of the elements that*
> *compose the physical body at the time of death.*
> —Tenzin Wangyal Rinpoche

Taoist Practices

Taoists are vitally interested in practicing longevity and physical immortality. Taoism is the only religion placing as much emphasis on the deathless body as other religions place on the deathless soul. Ko Hung (AD 288–343) wrote the original textbook on Taoist alchemy: *Pao P'u Tzu Nei P'ien* ("He who holds to simplicity," circa AD 320).

Since then, Taoists have sought immortality in two ways:

1. Wai-tan: transforming the transitory material of the body into indestructible matter through external alchemy by using breathing techniques, sexual practices, physical exercises, yoga, and medical skills.

2. Nei-tan: internal alchemy: transferring awareness, through sophisticated visualization processes, from the physical body into the subtle body, which, after death, continues indefinitely.

Taoist alchemy teaches aspirants to use their generative force, usually discharged to create offspring, to revitalize the body. When the force begins to find its usual outlet (ejaculation), it is turned back within the body into the "microcosmic orbit."

In the practice of internal alchemy, Taoists preserve and develop "Three Treasures": *ching* (original essence, primal energy, spark of life, sexual energy), *qi* or *chi* (life-force energy obtained from air and food), and *shen* (awareness, spiritual energy in the heart). The body relates to ching, breath relates to chi, and mind relates to shen.

Taoists believe that ching is finite. When it is used up, the individual dies. It can be conserved through conservation of sexual fluids. Chi, obtained from air and food, moves through the meridians (*nadis*), and is stored in *Dan Tien*, an energy center about 2 inches below the navel. The free flow of chi can be cultivated through Chi Gong, Tai Chi Chuan, and breathing exercises.

Taoist practitioners perceive themselves as energetic beings as they awaken their subtle bodies. Eventually, their yin or physical aspects get transmuted into the higher vibrational yang aspect—the immortal light body.

This process is facilitated by developing an immortal fetus. The seed of shen (soul or Spirit) impregnates ching (sexual energy) in a mystical internal union that results in a fetus built of congealed energy in the lower Dan Tien. By nurturing this fetus and gradually transferring consciousness into it, the physical body is transformed into a light body. Whatever portion of the body has been transformed can be taken with them at death.

This practice seems not entirely unique. Astonishingly, Annalee Skarin, an American Mormon who is said to have ascended in 1952 (see page 125 of this book), states in *Beyond Mortal Boundaries*:

> This holy, spiritual food, which is required for the complete formation and fulfilling of one's entire being, is drawn from the great love of God. One will be born of God when he has perfected the power of love. As one begins to exert the energies of his heart to draw love into himself he will soon discover that the fountains of Living Water are opened up within him to supply his every need. And this divine heart-center of Living Water or of great love is just behind the navel.
>
> And so the spiritual body is formed in like manner to the physical one, and the nourishment is drawn through the umbilical cord

connected to the very center of the soul. The spiritual food itself is drawn in through the high vibrations of released love and gladness and thanksgiving.... As one uses these laws of fulfillment he automatically advances into a stage beyond mortality.[2]

Secret Sexuality

Many spiritual systems profess that enlightenment and immortality cannot be achieved without celibacy. Conserved reproductive fluids provide the internal nourishment through which soma, the chemical that promises immortal life, is produced in the pineal gland. Internal genital secretions nourish endocrine glands and thereby conserve ojas and soma.

Taoist and Tantric sexual practices conserve and utilize the precious energy within the genital fluids. The vital force energies that sustain life are *ojas, tejas,* and *prana.* One particular type of prana is *kundalini* or *shakti.* The Taoist equivalent is *ching.* By nurturing this energy, life is enriched and preserved. By squandering it, health suffers and death results. Yogis believe kundalini energy is coiled up like a serpent at the base of the spine. By awakening this energy, raising it up the spine to the brain, enlightenment is attained.

The kundalini energy flows through the *chakras,* energy centers in your subtle body related to the endocrine glands. The endocrine glands are fed by your body's central heating system, the sexual center. If that center is weak, your entire system is weak. If that center is functioning optimally, the body can survive indefinitely.

Taoist and Tantric techniques strengthen the sexual chakra. Their methods conserve its precious fluids and also pump these nourishing fluids back into the body, directing them to the endocrine glands. These techniques stimulate the production of ojas and soma.

My only caution about Taoist and Tantric sexual practices is the following: Because of the tradition of patriarchal oppression, many of these practices are designed solely for the male to attain immortality, often at the expense of young, ignorant, inexperienced girls, whose vitality (*shakti*) is drained from their bodies.

The male is cautioned to never let semen leave his body, to practice *coitus reservatus,* stopping short of ejaculation. Yet he is advised to bring his partner to orgasm repeatedly. With his sperm held in check and his vital energy pumping back into his system continually, he invigorates and rejuvenates his body. Also pumping the energy and fluids of the female into his body at the time of her climax, he obtains her vitality as well. Practitioners are advised to engage in this female-draining activity a dozen or more times a day with several 14- to 19-year-old virgins. Innocent females are victims of this crime against their health, driving them to an early grave.

On the other hand, when both partners are fully knowledgeable and experienced in Taoist or Tantric sexual practices, a mutually beneficial, enriching, elevating relationship can grow. An exchange of energy can promote the production of soma in both partners. Such spiritual growth is only possible with mutual respect, love, honesty, commitment, and trust. When partners recognize and worship each other as divine beings, there can be an exchange of divine energy in both body and Spirit.

Chapter 16

The Incorruptibles

For this corruptible must put on incorruption,
and this mortal must put on immortality.
—1 Corinthians 15:53

A rare phenomenon often met with skepticism throughout the world is "incorruptibility." In such cases, after death, the human body does not undergo the normal decomposition process. Rather than succumbing to entropy, which disintegrates an average corpse, the body is instead mysteriously preserved to a remarkable degree.

For a body to be deemed "incorruptible" in the Roman Catholic or Orthodox churches, it has never been mummified, embalmed, or otherwise treated for preservation, yet it remains flexible, with few signs of decay—sometimes for centuries. In fact, despite the burial method, temperature, or moisture content, the body can have lifelike, moist, flexible skin, and exude an "Odor of Sanctity"—a sweet, pleasant fragrance.

Such incorruptible beings have something in common—a life of extraordinary sanctity, fervent faith, and love for God. In Roman Catholicism, a person whose body remains incorruptible after death is usually considered a saint. However, sainthood is not exclusively reserved for incorruptibles.

Although incorruptible bodies have been examined regularly, no one has yet discovered the physical cause for this phenomenon. The wonder of these well-preserved bodies is magnified by miracles or supernatural experiences that people have undergone in their presence.

I believe one explanation for this occurrence might be that divine Spirit, which gives rise to and maintains life, can transform a body into a spiritualized entity and thereby slow the entropic process that, under normal circumstances, returns matter to the primal elements of nature. So the body is preserved beyond its average time of decomposition.

Bodhisattva in Flesh

Although the cause of incorruptibility remains a mystery, this phenomenon is not exclusively Christian. For centuries, many intact corpses have dotted the monastic landscape of China, Taiwan, and Thailand, where incorruptibility is a sign of higher consciousness. The corporeal remains of Buddhist spiritual masters are called *shari-ra*, (the Sanskrit term for "body"). There are two kinds of sharira: a "full-body sharira" and a "broken-body sharira."

A full-body sharira is an entire incorrupt corpse, sometimes gilded or painted black. These "Bodhisattvas in Flesh" are venerated as deities. The decision to attempt this is voluntarily chosen before the master's demise. A large terracotta container, called a *Gone,* houses the untreated, seated corpse, which has not been drained of fluids or eviscerated. The container is filled with lime, incense ash, sawdust, tea leaves, spices, charcoal, and sandalwood. Another Gone acts as a lid, and the opening is sealed for three to six years.

If the Gone begins to emit the stench of decomposing flesh, then the body is removed from the Gone and cremated. Otherwise, the corpse remains in the Gone for the length of time specified in the will of the deceased. Amidst pomp and ceremony of "Kai-Gone," the Gone is then opened, and, if successful, the body remains intact, with elastic muscles and movable joints.

A broken-body sharira is a pearl-, crystal-, gem-, or bead-like relic found among the cremated ashes of a spiritual master. Buddhists believe that the spiritual essence of an enlightened being lives on as a remnant, called a sharira or *ringsel*, after the body is cremated. These remains are said to embody the spiritual knowledge, teachings, and realizations of the master.

One of the earliest full-body shariras is the sixth and last Chinese Buddhist Patriarch, Hui Neng (AD 638–713), often credited as the true father of Zen Buddhism. In the Nan Hua Shan Monastery near

Shaozhou, his corpse, exuding a sweet fragrance, remains seated and robed to this day. His chest maintains its natural position, and skin appears glossy and flexible. In AD 1236 the Mongol troops violated Hui Neng's tomb and slashed the abdomen of the 500-year old corpse with a sword. When they saw the heart and liver in a perfect state of preservation, they fled.

The corpse of the monk Shih Tzu-kung, also called Wu Chi Ta Shih, known as the "Stone Monk," was shipped to Taiwan in May 1975. The preserved body of emaciated skin and bones, seated cross-legged, had rested in Japan since World War II, when a Japanese military dentist secretly shipped it there. The Stone Monk was a T'ang Buddhist leader born about AD 700 in Guangdong, China, into a family named Ch'en. He has now been returned to his monastery in Taiwan.

Some recent famed incidents of full-body sharira include:

- Ci Hang (1893–1954), the first person from Taiwan to attain full-body sharira.
- Chin Yen (1924–1970), a Buddhist master who became famous in Taiwan after successful full-body sharira. He is housed in Sindian.
- Miao Zhe (1888–2003), who was named the healthiest senior citizen in China.
- Mrs. Song, who lived in the 20th century, a vegetarian for 60 years. Her full-body sharira is said to indicate extraordinary spiritual prowess, because, unlike other masters, only a thin layer of sand was placed in her Gone.

Paramahansa Yogananda

Author of *Autobiography of a Yogi,* Paramahansa Yogananda (1893–1952) was founder of the Self-Realization Fellowship. For 30 years, the famed Hindu saint spread teachings of yoga and self-liberation in America during the early 20th century. Beginning in November 1951, he indicated that he would be leaving the world soon. He finished his writings and became silent. On March 7, 1952, many of his special guests attended a banquet at the Biltmore Hotel in Los Angeles, in honor of the new Ambassador of India, Binay Ranjan Sen, and his wife.

Figure 16a. **Paramahansa Yogananda:** Great saint from India and inspiration to millions of seekers of truth, Yogananda lived and died in grace, integrity, and perfection, filled with the light of God.

After ingesting a modest meal, Yogananda spoke about "spiritual India," and ended by reciting his own poem: "Where Ganges, woods, Himalayan caves, and men dream God—I am hallowed; my body touched that sod." Just then, Yogananda entered *mahasamadhi* (a saint's final departure from the body). His eyes lifted, his body turned slightly to the right, and he dropped to the floor.[1]

Twenty days later, on March 27, Mortuary Director Harry T. Rowe of Forest Lawn cemetery in Los Angeles wrote a notarized letter indicating his astonishment at the preservation of Yogananda's body as "the most extraordinary case in our experience." There were no visual signs of bodily decay, odor, mold on the skin, nor desiccation of bodily tissues. Mr. Rowe stated, "This state of perfect preservation of a body is, so far as we know from mortuary annals, an unparalleled one.... Yogananda's body was apparently in a phenomenal state of immutability.... The physical appearance of Yogananda on March 27th...was the same as it had been on March 7th."[2]

Incorruptible Christian Saints

When a person is a candidate for canonization in the Catholic Church, the body is disinterred. Many such corpses are found completely or partially intact. The first incorrupt Christian saint ever discovered was Saint Cecilia, a Roman Christian martyred in AD 177. Partially decapitated by an incompetent executioner whose sword stopped halfway through her neck, she lay bleeding for three days, with her face toward the floor and hands in prayer. Fourteen centuries later, in 1599, the Church of St. Cecilia in Rome was restored, and her original coffin, discovered inside a marble sarcophagus, was opened. Her body was found in the same position, free from corruption, soft and pliable, with her neck wound still visible.

In this chapter it would be impossible to relate the many miraculous stories of more than 100 incorruptible Christian saints who were canonized. Here we will explore a handful.

Saint Anthony of Padua (1195–1231) was a Franciscan preacher canonized a year after his death. He was well known, not only for his godly nature, but also for his eloquence, oratorical skills, and powers of persuasion. In 1263 his coffin was disinterred, and his remains inspected. His corpse had been reduced to gray dust. However, miraculously, among the dust was a soft, pink, fresh, perfectly formed tongue that looked like one of a living human. His incorrupt larynx cartilages, jaw, and tongue are still intact, 780 years later, in the Basilica of Saint Anthony.

Saint Bernadette Soubirous (1844–1879) was the visionary at Lourdes, France. A lady in white, standing in a niche in a rock, appeared to Bernadette and directed her to dig up a spring of healing waters, which have effected countless miraculous cures since that time. (Read about her visions on page 143 of this book.)

Bernadette died at age 35; 30 years later, in 1909, and again in 1919, her body was exhumed. Although the crucifix in her hand and the rosary had oxidized, her body was incorrupt and free from odor. In 1925, when Bernadette was disinterred again, the skeleton was perfectly preserved, the fibrous muscle tissues were supple and firm, the ligaments and skin were in good condition, and the liver was soft with nearly normal consistency. Her body has rested in the Church of St. Gildard in Nevers, France, in a crystal coffin, covered with a wax mask of face and hands, since 1925.

Saint Catherine of Bologna (1413–1463), a talented artist and author, became a Franciscan tertiary at age 14. In 1431 she founded a Monastery of the Order of Poor Clares. Her writings describe many visions of Jesus, one of which occurred on Christmas day. Catherine died at age 50. Inexplicable miraculous cures occurred at the grave site, and a sweet scent exuded from her grave. Eighteen days later, her body was exhumed and found incorrupt. Several years after her death, Catherine appeared to a nun at the convent, asking that her body be placed in seated position. Her extraordinary, well-formed body remains intact, 550 years later, seated in the Chapel of the Poor Clares in Bologna today.

Saint Catherine Labouré (1806–1876) experienced a visitation from Mother Mary, who charged her with creating the Miraculous Medal, worn by millions of people today. This medal, if worn with faith and devotion, is believed to bring special graces through Mary's intercession. The design of the medal is an exact replica of how Mary appeared to Catherine in her vision.

Catherine's incorrupt body was exhumed 57 years after her death. Her eyes remained blue, and her limbs were as supple as if she were asleep. Today her body remains in the chapel where she experienced her visions, at the Daughters of Charity in Paris. Her hands have been amputated and placed in a separate reliquary. These were replaced with wax figures on her body.

Saint Rita of Cascia (1381–1457) joined the Augustinian monastery of Saint Mary Magdalene at Cascia, Italy, at age 36. Beginning at age 12, she suffered an abusive marriage. After her husband was murdered, her two sons vowed to exact revenge on the murderers. She prayed that this crime be prevented, and her sons died of natural causes one year later. Strangely, at age 60, as she prayed before a crucifix, a small puncture appeared on her forehead, as though wounded from the crown of thorns endured by Jesus. This bleeding wound remained until she died at age 76.

Her body has stayed incorrupt for more than 550 years in the Basilica of St. Rita in Cascia, Italy, and at times exudes a sweet fragrance. Amazingly, the wound is seen on her forehead, and her body is said to sometimes assume different positions in the glass case, with her eyes opening and closing. Recently part of her face was covered in wax.

Saint Teresa of Avila (1515–1582) entered the Carmelite Monastery of the Incarnation at Avila, Spain, at age 20. She suffered a severe illness, coma for several days, and leg paralysis for three years. At age 39 she began to have mystical experiences, including transverberation (mystical piercing of the heart). She authored several books: *Life Written by Herself*, *Meditations on the Canticle*, *The Way of Perfection*, *Book of Foundations*, and *Interior Castle*.

Her mystical visions led her to reform her order by first reforming herself. Her autobiography speaks of four stages of the soul's ascent, which culminate in "devotion of ecstasy or rapture." Several times Teresa was observed levitating during mass. At age 47, she founded the convent of Discalced (Barefoot) Carmelites, with a strict, ascetic lifestyle. She died at age 67.

Nine months after her burial, the sisters noticed the scent of roses around Teresa's tomb. They dug up her grave and found the coffin damp, collapsed, rotten, stinking, and molding. Teresa's clothing had disintegrated. Dirt had fallen onto her body. But her body appeared as though buried the night before. The nuns clothed and interred her again. A fragrance of roses wafted throughout the monastery.

Three years after her death, her incorruptibility was declared a miracle. Without embalming, her body was in a state of perfect preservation, with a wonderful scent. Relic hunters removed body parts and distributed them throughout the world. Her heart, marked with the transverberation, is in the Carmelite Convent in Alba de Tormes, Spain.

Saint Zita (c. 1218–1272) became a servant for a wealthy family at age 12. Every day she awoke many hours early for prayer. Though viciously abused by her employers and coworkers, she never complained. By the time of her death, at age 60, the entire family venerated her. The church verified 150 miracles wrought by her intercession. Her body, found incorrupt in 1580, 300 years after her death, is still remarkably preserved, nearly 750 years later. It is enshrined in the Basilica di San Frediano in Lucca, Italy, with her face and hands exposed to view through a crystal glass.

Nectar Flowing From Corpses

Not only do deceased saints exhibit incorruptibility, but some of them also exude fragrant, curative oils from their bodies that might be related to soma or ojas (see Chapter 14). A few examples of incorruptible saints who apparently exhibited this manifestation of soma in their corpses are as follows:

Charbel Makhlouf (1828–1898), a monk from St. Maroun monastery in Annaya, Lebanon, was buried in 1898. Bright lights were seen around his grave and continued 45 days afterward. Later the body was disinterred, washed, and placed in a wooden coffin in the chapel of the monastery. No signs of decay were found. Soon an oily, blood-like liquid soaked the body and overflowed so prolifically that his clothing had to be changed twice a week. The soaked clothing displayed miraculous healing properties.

In 1927, 29 years after his death, doctors reexamined his body and declared it free from decay. It was sealed in a zinc-lined coffin and placed in the monastery wall. In 1950 the oily liquid began to seep through the brick that walled in the coffin. Again the body was exhumed and no decay was found, as though he were merely asleep. The oily substance emitted by the body is still removed from the coffin periodically and used for its curative properties.

Saint Nicholas of Bari (280–342), Roman Catholic Bishop of Myra (now Lycia, Turkey) was known as Defender of Orthodoxy and Nicholas the Wonderworker. He was a secret, generous gift-giver, using his family inheritance. Thus he became the model for Sankt Niklaus or Santa Claus. One legend says that he resurrected three bodies that had been slaughtered by a butcher. In another legend, Saint Nicholas dropped bags of gold through the window or down the chimney of a father who could not afford the dowry for his three unwed daughters. One of the daughters was drying a stocking over the fire, and one bag of gold landed in her stocking.

In the church in Myra, the incorrupt remains of Saint Nicholas flowed with fragrant curative myrrh. Many people received healing from this balm. In 1087 his relics were transferred to Bari, Italy, where they still flow with copious healing liquid—1,700 years later! Vials of this ointment are available from the Saint Nicholas church in Bari.

Chapter 17

Perpetuating Life

*Our Creator would never have made such lovely days, and
have given us the deep hearts to enjoy them, above and
beyond all thought, unless we were meant to be immortal.*
—Nathaniel Hawthorne

There is no scientific reason why the human body ages or dies.
If people were to believe that they could live eternally, they would.
Wellness and longevity are more about the mind than the body. Modern
medicine has discovered amazing secrets that attest to the body's ability to renew itself continually and perpetuate itself indefinitely.

How Life Renews Itself

In Oak Ridge laboratories in California, it was proven by radioiso-
tope studies that 98 percent of the atoms of your body are replaced every year. The time is takes to replace your stomach lining is five days,
your skin takes five weeks, and your fat cells take three weeks. Your
skeleton is completely renewed every three months. The DNA mol-
ecule, the blueprint of all life, has maintained its perfect integrity for
billions of years.

The cells of every species, which replicate themselves indefinitely
to form the body of every living thing, have the property of unlimited
youth. Some species, called "non-senescent," simply do not age. They
live perpetually and only die by accident or by some outside force, such
as a predator, fire, or flood. No natural law of decay or old age exists
within these species to create any abnormality within their cells.

Bristlecone pine trees, creosote bushes, rockfish, some paramecia, and certain social insect queens have this uncanny property of non-senescence. One bristlecone pine tree in the Sierra Nevada in south-western United States has survived 4,600 years, adding new cells during rainy periods and shutting down during droughts. Creosote bushes in southern California are 10,000 years old. Scientists believe that non-senescence was the original way of life, since those species are less complex, and evolved earlier.

The buds of the giant, long-lived banyan tree appear every spring, just as youthful and vital as the first sprout on the first seedling that later became a full-grown tree. Just as the banyan's new leaves are as youthful as its original seed, each new cell replicated within your body should be as vital as its original ovum. Your body is an ever-changing river with a rhythm of continual renewal. It is only due to the break-down of this cycle of renewal that it begins to age.

Secrets of Longevity

The intelligence within your body's cells creates perpetual self-healing and regeneration. Aging is the loss of the body's ability to continually repair itself. To age means to forget how to fix things when they go wrong. It is only due to the body functioning at a level far less than optimum that it begins to deteriorate.

The cells of newborn babies and those of the elderly are extremely different from each other. A baby's cells are fresh and perfect, without anomalies or irregularities. Aged cells are scarred, battered, and appear depleted. The tissues are fibrous and there is debris and dark, patchy spots with numerous abnormalities. But DNA has the ability to maintain the body indefinitely, replicating cells perfectly.

The genes of DNA keep their integrity perfectly throughout your life. However, some of them are active and some are switched off. On the end of each gene is a cap that tends to deteriorate with age. Researchers have discovered that certain genes, called maintenance and repair genes, are responsible for maintaining the integrity of these caps. The maintenance and repair genes tend to switch off their functioning as humans age.

I met a man who has been visualizing his maintenance and repair genes to be switched back on. Well beyond 80 years old, he has made tremendous progress in youthing his body. As a youngster, he used to sprint to his mailbox quickly each day. Then, as he aged, he became increasingly slower, until he could barely walk to his mailbox. Now he is jogging to the mailbox every day. His hair is reverting from white to black. His sexual desire and virility is returning.

There is a reason for the gulf between what DNA should be doing and what the physical body actually does. It is because your bodily cells are made not only of atoms and molecules but also of intelligence and awareness. The intelligence within your body, in the form of conscious and subconscious beliefs, creates and re-creates your physical body daily.

Thoughts of fear, guilt, hatred, and unworthiness, of sickness and death, create the phenomenon of aging. Joyous thoughts of youth, love, happiness, and fulfillment maintain youthfulness. You can revitalize your body daily by visualizing a divine child within you.

Annalee Skarin repeatedly gives the following advice for attaining eternal life in her book *Beyond Mortal Boundaries*: "Think only the most beautiful things possible."

During the past 30 years, Dean Ornish, MD, and his colleagues at The Preventive Medicine Research Institute have conducted scientific studies demonstrating that even severe coronary heart disease can be reversed through changes in diet and lifestyle. These research findings are published in leading peer-reviewed medical journals. Dr. Ornish's findings prove that the body can be transformed. The innate intelligence within the body just needs to be pointed into a new direction—toward health.

Deepak Chopra, MD, states in his book *Perfect Health* that with every breath you add 11,000,000,000,000,000,000,000 new atoms to your body. These atoms are delivered via your circulatory system throughout your body to create new cells. The infusion of atoms you receive with each breath should be sufficient to perpetuate your body indefinitely.

You can build new tissues, bones, arteries, and muscles in a matter of weeks or months. There is no reason, in the realm of science, why your body should decay at all. It is only your belief system, thoughts, and habits that create degeneration. Dr. Chopra states that death is a cultural belief and not an absolute fact: "The human body has no definite beginning or end. It is constantly creating itself, again and again, every day.... If we are creating ourselves all the time, then it is never too late to begin creating the bodies we want instead of the ones we mistakenly assume we are stuck with."[1]

Lifespans Extraordinaire

Many people in the Bible lived extraordinarily long lives. For example, Genesis, Chapter 5, states that Adam lived 930 years. His son Seth lived 912 years. Enos, the son of Seth, lived 905 years. The son of Enos, Cainan, lived to 910. His son, Mahalaleel, lived 895 years. Jared, his son, lived 962 years. Enoch attained immortality and disappeared in his ascended body at age 365. Methuselah, his son, lived 969 years. Lamech, his son, lived 777 years. His son Noah lived 950 years.

In India, the ancient scriptures speak of inconceivably long cycles of time during which there is greater or lesser longevity. During the Golden Age, people commonly lived for many thousands of years.

Maintaining youthful, radiant health is possible, and many cultures today prove it with citizens who live extraordinarily long lives. Here are some places that have more centenarians than anywhere else:

- Georgia, in the Caucasus region of Eurasia.
- Bama County, in southern China.
- Hunza, Pakistan, in a remote valley in the Karakoram Range.
- Vilcabamba Valley, near Loja, in southern Ecuador.
- Nicoya Peninsula, on the Pacific coast of Costa Rica.
- Okinawa Island, Japan, the largest island in Okinawa Prefecture.
- Loma Linda, in San Bernardino County, California.
- Ikaria, Greece, a Greek Island in the Eastern Aegean Sea.
- Sardinia, Italy, a large island in the Mediterranean Sea.

In all of these remarkable cultures, the elderly possess the keys to longevity—purposefulness, belonging, and happiness. They continue to work, contribute to society, and exercise vigorously. Living in extended families brings security and love. Family and social interactions is their first priority. Their religious faith, sense of humor, and positivism is strong. They have a life plan and therefore a reason to get up in the morning to live another day.

They maintain a low-fat diet with high complex carbohydrates, are moderate in alcohol consumption, drink plenty of pristine water high in mineral content, get plenty of sunshine, and have an easygoing lifestyle. Their food is grown in their own backyard. They eat more at breakfast and less at dinner. Their calorie intake is small. They recognize a sacred energy in food and respect the land that produces it.

Telos: The Underground City of Longevity

Some people believe that a city exists right now where people live for thousands of years. It is called Telos. Joanna Cherry interviewed Princess Sharula Dux, who claims to come from this highly advanced Lemurian underground city. Sharula attests that she has come to the surface to share her culture with ours, so that we might mutually benefit. Joanna has known Sharula for many years and finds her unassuming, with a good sense of humor, and radiating a lot of love.

The information shared by Sharula is highly controversial. But the Agartha underground cities are an ancient traditional belief in Tibet and China. So let us come to this information with an open mind. Here is what Sharula tells us:

Telos was built as a result of a thermonuclear war that occurred 25,000 years ago, between two major civilizations. One was the continent of Lemuria, or Mu, including much of the Pacific Ocean, the western United States, and parts of Asia. The other was Atlantis, over much of the Atlantic Ocean and parts of Africa and Europe. Eventually, both of these continents sank.

After the war, the Lemurian priests and priestesses of the Order of Melchizedek foretold the sinking of the continent. So they built an underground city underneath sacred Mount Shasta, in the eastern part of Lemuria. During the coming cataclysm, this location would be safe from the sinking of the two continents, and from harmful ultraviolet rays resulting from the loss of Earth's atmospheric mantle. The southwestern United States was called Telos ("union with spirit") at that time, so that name was chosen.

The Atlanteans also built an underground city under the Mato Grosso plateau of Brazil. The Agartha Network contains a total of 120 subterranean cities. (See page 105.)

A great domed cavern within Mount Shasta, several square miles in area and hundreds of feet high, became the top level of Telos. Four more levels were built below that, with the lowest level about one mile beneath ground level. The city was built to house up to two million people. About 12,000 years ago, 100 years before Lemuria sank, 25,000 people moved into Telos. Few others survived the earthquakes, tidal waves, and volcanic activity.

Telos is a temple society. In the center of the top level, a temple was built to hold 10,000 people. It is white and pyramid-shaped, with a capstone made of "livingstone," a substance from Venus. It looks crystalline, and emanates all rays of the color spectrum. The temple is dedicated to the Order of Melchizedek, a cosmic priesthood.

The high priest is Adama, a blue-ray ascended master working directly under the archangel Michael, assisting humanity with ascension. The high priestess, Terra Ra, also an ascended master, teaches the students in the temple and is much loved by them.

The hydroponics gardens feed the 1,500,000 people now living in Telos, from just a few square miles of land. None of the Telosians' supplies come from the surface; they trade with other Agartha cities. They have created lakes, grown tall trees, and live in harmony with many animals that are extinct on the surface. The inhabitants of Telos enjoy a peaceful life without crime, disease, war, or other ills.

To create light underground, stones with a high crystalline content are fused with an electromagnetic force field of energy. The stones can absorb invisible rays and re-emit them as visible, full-spectrum light. Oxygen comes from an ecosystem of plants and trees, though some vents go to the surface. In some areas water moves at high speeds, circulating air and negative ions.

Sharula Dux says:

> Telosians are about a foot taller than surface folks, on average. Telosians are genetically the same as humans. However, we know that we do not age, so we do not.... My age is 269. Most Telosians are between a few hundred and a few thousand years old. One man has been in his body for 30,000 years. We jokingly nicknamed him "Longest." There is death in Telos, but it is rare. Sometimes a person dies in an accident. We have pets in Telos, and pets do die.

> When people are ready to leave Telos, a large portion of them ascend—take their body into light and move into a lighter dimension.

Others may not be ready to ascend, so they learn how to leave their body, and then dematerialize it.

When people know they will live and stay young as long as they want, there is a completely different feeling about life than on the earth's surface. There is no "You are only young once" wildness, as in your society, with reckless behavior and maybe drugs or alcohol. Also, since we live for hundreds or thousands of years, we take care of the environment. We are more responsible.

The most wonderful thing about living without aging or dying is that you get to do all the things you want. Up here [on the surface of earth], just about the time you get enough wisdom and knowledge to start really living, you are too old to do much with it.

Part V

How to Ascend Now

Chapter 18

Achieving Ascension

*And they shall see his face; and his name shall be in their
foreheads. And there shall be no night there; and they need
no candle, neither light of the sun; for the Lord God giveth
them light: and they shall reign for ever and ever.*
—Revelation 22:4-5

In this chapter you will learn some practical ways to begin your
own ascension process. You will learn an awesome ascension meditation and some powerful ascension affirmations.

Meditating Your Way to Ascension

Dr. Joanna Cherry has studied, practiced, and taught the ascension process for decades. The precious meditation practice her fortunate students have learned is now available to every one of you.

Before you begin this meditation technique, it is best to read the
words that guide you into meditation in your own soft, slow, soothing
voice, onto a recording device, such as a computer or tape recorder.
Then you can burn a CD, make a tape, create a digital file, or use another device. When you are ready to meditate, simply get comfortable,
play back your recording, and follow the instructions.

What follows are Joanna's instructions for this method.

Preparation

First, here are some things you may experience that could frighten you, if not understood. In the meditation you may see a light—it could blaze incredibly—in your third eye. You are this light; you cannot disappear within it. You may feel great heat in your body, or cold. Your heartbeat may speed up or slow down, slightly or dramatically. You may feel or even see your body, or part of it, disappear.

Whatever happens, because we are giving the meditation into the hands of your divine presence, you are safe. You cannot go too high, and you will always go "high enough"—as far into your God Light as is optimum for this time. You can relax and let things happen. Also, if you notice nothing dramatic, you are still doing it perfectly—we each experience ascension in our own way.

I challenge you to experience your chakras in a whole new way. Although chakra opening is common now, seldom do we really understand what it can be. Your "I AM Presence" encompasses the universe. Thus a true opening of your chakras can give the knowing of being fully alive and present everywhere, in every dimension of the eternal now. This realization came to me after years of chakra-opening.

Meditation Part 1: Elevating Awareness Into Spirit

Sit comfortably. Close your eyes and begin to breathe deeply and gently. Feel grounded from your root chakra area and from your feet. Imagine cords of energy going into the center of the earth. Invite love energy to flow up from Mother Earth, or down from the top of your head, as you choose.

Continue to breathe gently and freely as you allow the release of tension from all body parts to go deeper and deeper. When you feel as relaxed as you possibly can, send love into all of your body and bless it.

Now say the following statements aloud:

God's love and will run this body. This is God's heartbeat. This is God's breath. These are God's organs, God's glands, God's bones. Every particle of this body is God. All the space of this body is God. This body is God Light, God love, God joy!

Being immortal, young, and beautiful follows God energy naturally, and it also obeys my beliefs. I now think unlimited God-thoughts about this body. This body is the everlasting and expanding life of God. It is the resurrection and the life. This body lives forever. When I am ready to leave the earth plane, I take it up into light and ascend. SO BE IT.

Turn more deeply now, away from the awareness of your body, and into awareness of mind. Unify with any thoughts you notice, and relax your thinking mind. Love and bless your thoughts. Unenlightened thoughts and feelings are like our children; we created them, and they are here to be loved. As we do, they lift into lighter and more joyous expression.

Say something like this aloud:

This mind moves now into unlimited thoughts of God. I AM the love of God. I AM the light of God. I AM the joy of God. I AM the freedom of God. I AM the majestic power of God's pure, Divine Love. I AM everywhere present and know all things. I AM the beloved of God. I AM That I AM.

Turn still more deeply, away from the awareness of mind, into the awareness of feeling. Send love to any feelings you notice, no matter what they may be. Bless your feeling nature.

Say something like this:

My feelings are becoming the natural feelings of God: love, joy, peace, abundance, wholeness, well-being.

Turn still more deeply now, into the awareness of your Spirit. If you are already in touch with your inner Self, or have a favorite master(s) you know and love, you may call upon these now, or simply ask God to assist you in your ascension process. Tune in to the inner love, light, and wisdom—it is being poured out to you right now. Feel as deeply connected and one with it as you can.

Say something like this aloud:

I give this meditation fully into the hands of my divine I AM Presence, the love and light of God, to guide me to the optimum levels of my own God Light. So be it.

Meditation Part 2: Opening Your Chakras

When you feel ready, begin a chakra opening. To help you open each one maximally, here are several suggestions:

1. Awaken in each chakra its beautiful light, like the sun, and allow it to be any color you see there, or white, gold, or white-gold. Let this sun blaze out to fill your body, your room, your area, your world, this universe.

2. Use your in-breaths to expand each chakra more and more, keeping your breath free and alive.

3. Think of a chakra as a camera aperture that opens to infinity, or some other vision that produces the same affect.

4. Use your hands to touch the chakra area and sweep outward in an expanding energy.

5. Feel openness, a relaxation, a vulnerability there; aliveness; emotion.

Now open each chakra separately:

First Chakra: at the base of your spine. Feel your groundedness even more clearly through this. *I AM safe on Earth. I AM abundantly provided for by God and the universe. The Earth is a pleasurable place for me to be.*

Second Chakra: in your abdomen. *I AM centered. I AM safe and loved in expressing my creativity, which is welcomed in the world. My sexuality is divine energy and God approves of it.*

Third Chakra: in your solar plexus. *I AM safe and loved in expressing my power. My power and my love are one.*

Fourth Chakra: heart chakra, in the center of your chest. *I AM safe to love and be loved without limit. I AM full of love and compassion for myself and all others. My love blesses all life.*

Fifth Chakra: in your throat. *I AM safe and loved in expressing my truth, my joy, my power, my creativity, and my passion. I AM full and free-giving and receiving. I AM abundance.*

Sixth Chakra: the third eye between your eyebrows and back in your head a bit. *I AM safe and loved to BE the Light I AM, and to know everything.*

Seventh Chakra: the crown chakra at the top of your head. *I AM safe and loved to BE God I AM. I AM unlimited Being, everywhere present in all universes.*

Eighth Chakra: can be pictured above the head. *I AM safe and loved to step through the dimensions.*

Ninth through Twelfth Chakras: open if and as you feel to.

Now create a column of golden light from the highest chakra you opened to below the bottom of your feet, gently reopening any chakras that may have closed again.

Begin to spin this column. (I see this going around to the right, horizontal to the floor, but you should follow any direction that feels correct for you.) Let it move slowly at first, and gradually pick up speed. As it spins, it is spinning your chakras, your cells, your atoms, your aura—everything!

Here are some statements you can say aloud:

I AM quickening the vibrational frequencies of my body, mind, and feelings now. I AM merging with my inner God Self. I AM quickening, I AM lifting! I AM ascending! Ascending is easy, ascending is natural. I am safe. I lift higher and higher, faster and faster. I AM merging with Light. I AM becoming transparent now! (Add any other statements you choose here.)

Go back and forth between increasing the speed of the light column—finally to whirlwind speed—and proclaiming your ascension, until you feel you are about as high as you can go. Next, to make sure you reach present optimum levels, give your I AM presence (your master friend, etc.) three opportunities to take you higher, one third of any remaining distance each time. You do not have to do it yourself or even think about it; simply trust your spirit to take you up.

Say "One, two, three, Lift—Lift—!" and let yourself go! Do this twice more, and you will probably be at your optimum light, optimum frequency, for now.

Now you can say:

I AM the Light of God I AM. I AM all that God Is. I AM ascended now. I AM an ascended master now! I AM That I AM.

Now you can sit in the great silence and be that which you are. You may travel somewhere. Besides receiving the great gifts of your Being, you might receive specific messages, crystals implanted in your etheric body to help your ascension, healing of some kind, and so on. Be and receive everything given.

When you feel finished, begin to come back gently, bringing back your awareness of feeling and mind, body and environment, breathing deeply and energetically. Stay in love, stay high, and know that you are already combining this wonderful state more and more with your everyday life.

Open your eyes and see only God around you, see the beauty of everything. Come all the way back to full alertness and objectivity. Look in the mirror and see God. Give love as best you can to all your daily tasks, and follow any guidance you may have received in the meditation (if you feel it came from your highest love and joy).

Do this meditation as often as you like. You can quicken more every time you do it, and although you still fluctuate around a median, the lifting is permanent.

Every blessing to you in your ascension process!

(You may order Joanna's CD set, "Steps in Your Ascension," which has this meditation in it, at *www.divinerevelation.org*.)

Following are some affirmations that might be helpful in developing your ascension. Use them anytime you want to lift your vibration and invite greater light into your energy field.

Immortality Affirmation

I AM the resurrection and the life. I AM the ascension now.
I AM perfection everywhere now. I AM perfection here now.
I AM filled with the light of God. I AM a beauteous being of light.
I AM the perfection of being. I AM the light of life.
I AM the imperishable. I AM the diamond body now.
I AM the immortal body now. I AM the rainbow body now.
I AM the body of bliss now. I AM That I AM, now and always.
Thank you, God, and SO IT IS.

Invocation of Lights of the Ascended Masters

Let there be light.
The holy light of God fills and encompasses me now.
With light of immeasurable beauty and glory.
Jesus Christ now fills and surrounds me
With a radiant golden sphere of protective light.
Archangel Michael now stands sentry
Above, below, and on every side of this sphere,
Waving his blue flame sword of truth and protection.
The mystic white fire of the Holy Spirit
Lifts my vibration now and brings perfect peace.

The violet, cleansing flame of Saint Germain
Swirls through me now, purifying my energy field.
Mother Mary's pink light of unconditional love
Now touches me with gentleness.
Mahavatar Babaji's clear light of enlightenment
Now illumines my mind and purifies my soul.
I AM now lovingly lifted, healed, and cleansed
By the pure light of God's love,
Under grace, in God's own wise and perfect ways.
Thank you, God, and SO IT IS.

Violet Flame Invocation

I call forth beloved Saint Germain and Archangel Zadkiel
And the mighty Elohim Arcturus and Victoria
To bring forth the violet, cleansing flame of transmutation.
The beauteous violet flame now fills my body of light
And the space in the environment around me
With the powerful, purifying light of the violet fire.
I AM now purified, healed, and cleansed by the action
Of this all-consuming fire of transmutation now,
Which brings peace, love, prosperity, creativity, and joy
Into this situation and all situations, right here and now.
Thank you, God, and SO IT IS.

Saint Francis of Assisi's Simple Prayer
(Preghiera Semplice)

Lord, make me an instrument of your peace.
Where there is hatred, let me sow love.
Where there is injury, let me sow pardon.
Where there is friction, let me sow union.
Where there is error, let me sow truth.
Where there is doubt, let me sow faith.
Where there is despair, let me sow hope.
Where there is darkness, let me sow light.

Where there is sadness, let me sow joy.
O Divine Master, grant that I may not so much seek
To be consoled as to console,
To be understood as to understand,
To be loved as to love.
For it is in giving that we receive.
It is in pardoning that we are pardoned.
It is in dying that we are born to eternal life.

Chapter 19

Practicing "The Easy Way"

When prayer is at its highest we wait in silence for God's voice to us; we linger in His presence for His peace and His power to flow over us and around us; we lean back in His everlasting arms and feel the serenity of perfect security in Him.
—William Barclay

In October 2001, I met a young man who has discovered something very precious. I will call him Joseph. He believes it is more important to focus on the message than the messenger, and prefers to remain anonymous. In his words: "The message is from God, and God doesn't really like it when you get between one of his children and Him."

Joseph spent several years in seclusion and introspection, speaking to no one, struggling to attain ascension. Finally he came to the conclusion that there is only one way to achieve his goal: He had to make the decision to ascend and then simply step into that state of awareness. That is exactly what he did. The rest of this chapter is Joseph's story and his teachings.

How My Mother Guided Me

I was born in 1968, outside the United States. My mom was the main influence that led me into a spiritual life. She tried to live what I would call "true." Mom had been studying Annalee Skarin's books and introduced me to them. So I had a huge head start.

My father lived in another country. So from Mom I learned to behave, what to expect of myself, and what to expect of God, which is probably more important. My brother and I lived with Mom's parents and were raised by the three of them.

Ignoring the Voice of God

I do not remember the first time I heard God speaking to me in my head. In my memory, I have always had it. As a child, when the voice told me not to do something, I would probably get hurt if I ignored it. The voice was not punishing me. It was just warning me: "Don't do that. There is trouble ahead if you do."

Sometimes I listened, but usually I did not. One time, the voice told me not to attend a particular party, but I went anyway, and rode my bike there. On the way, I was hit by a car. So, by disobeying the voice repeatedly, and reaping the consequences, I learned to trust it and know God was really speaking to me.

What helped me obey that voice over time was realizing the voice was not restricting me or imposing rules. It did not say, "You must do this." It said, "If you do this, your life will be better." The voice was protecting me.

As a teenager, I had a number of jobs—as a fireman, in the Army, at a bank—and I graduated from college. In 1990, at age 21, I went skiing in Colorado. It was my first time in America. I had just bought new skis, rented an apartment, and got a job. That same afternoon, God's voice spoke inside my head, asking me to move to a house in California where friends of my grandparents lived. But I said no, because I was having fun skiing.

Then, a couple of months later, my friend and I decided to drive half an hour west, and move to a new ski resort. There was a right-hand turn, but, for some reason, we never turned. Three days later we ended up in California. We drove to the place where God had told me to go. We cannot explain why or how.

How *Ye Are Gods* Changed My Life

When I arrived in California, God's voice asked me to read a certain book, *Ye Are Gods* by Annalee Skarin. One citation in that book quoted the biblical Book of Revelation. As I read that passage, it made me cry. An energy and a prayer came down from heaven, like a pillar that knocked me down. It was a prayer I had prayed long ago—a powerful desire that no one should experience anything like Revelation.

From then on, I tried to find the way to help people avoid suffering. I realized the only way to help someone else was to do it myself. So I started looking, by asking basic questions. I asked people around me, and ministers in churches. But I did not get much satisfaction. I wanted experiential knowledge. If someone told me something was true, it was just hearsay. I wanted to know for myself.

Finally, I made the decision to ask God within to teach me and show me the truth, because there were so many "truths" out there. The voice of God, which had been speaking to me most of my life, told me to stop asking questions or listening to others.

So I affirmed, "I'm going to find the voice within first and do what it says and believe what it says, because that will be the truth. That will be the way."

Seeking and Struggling

How I resolved to find the truth was to lie down on my bed and look, listen, and wait for God to appear and say, "This is what you do." My theory was, the best way to get answers was from the horse's mouth. That was my way. Other ways may be different.

Because I did not know how to find God, I tried everything. I knew that, to reach the kingdom of heaven, I would have to give up everything. So I gave everything away or threw it out, and denied myself certain things. This was what I did, and not meant as advice for anyone else. I do not advocate any of it.

I wanted to make sure I was not being vain, so, during one period, I never looked in a mirror, combed my hair, or cleaned my room. I rarely bathed and never shaved. I wore everything until it fell to pieces. Then there was a phase of not speaking unless God spoke through me. Since I never heard God's voice in those days, I remained silent. Most things I tried were self-denial, which I now know is not the way.

Eventually I did see God. I must have been inching closer without knowing it. But I never felt huge leaps and bounds of growth. It was a daily struggle, spending time alone, trying to see God's face. I wanted to see his lips move and see the words come out. Then I would be sure of what he said, and know it was true.

So I did that for years. It was a length of time, but more importantly it was a length of effort and struggle. Nearly all the struggles were internal—like giving up fear of being alone or abandoned. We all have secret fears. With God's help, I burned all these out of me, at least those I am aware of. This cleansing process did not feel great. Part of me was clinging and did not want them to go. Another part was trying to rip them out. This caused inner conflict. But because I kept going, God helped me, and I finally got done.

Overcoming Fear and Doubt

My main challenge was fear. There was nothing to be afraid of. I was just lying in my bed. But I felt very afraid. It was like poison being forced out to the surface. As it came out, something was replacing it—a kind of steel. Even though I was still afraid, and it was still as intense, the amount of fear began to lessen and the steel increased.

Perhaps my greatest fear was of disappearing and becoming nothing. I felt that, if I surrendered my will totally to God, then part of me would not survive. I wanted to stop that battle against God, but I could not stop trying to survive.

Another struggle I had was with doubt. I did not doubt the concept of God, but I doubted whether I could meet God—the real deal. A person can have an amazing experience. But in a few days, he will typically revert to doubting again. Once in a while there is a life-changer, such as Saul on the road to Damascus. But in general we tend to forget quickly. Over the years, what helped me with doubt, and still does, are enough little experiences that proved true. That builds up a level of confidence.

The Book of Life

When I got near the end of that phase of struggle, I had a vision of a huge book, like a big old leather tome, about a foot thick. The pages were two or three feet tall. The book was open in the middle. Half of it was blank, and half was full.

The pages were turning over backwards, and the words were getting erased. It was in a strange language, made of lines and symbols, so I could not read it. It was my "Book of Life," and the writing was all the things out of alignment with God's will.

As I lay there, staring into God's eyes as best I could, those things were being erased. I did not have to know what the things were. In fact, it was best if I did not know. The universe was purifying me, as a river flows through, automatically removing these things. My job was to stay in one place, be willing, and get myself out of the way. Then all that stuff would be wiped free from me. I would be clean again.

For me, staring into the eyes of God was real. He cared about the process, and he made sure it was all going okay, so I did not have to. The feeling was safety, trust, assurance, and a level of power. It was like being rocked like a baby, but all your life, carried like a baby everywhere through everything.

The Turning Point

I was on this path for about four years. I had changed houses and countries a couple of times. But all the while, I had one purpose—the desire to know God.

Then I was holed up in an attic in California for a few months. I stayed with great people, but I am pretty sure they thought I was crazy at the time. I was in my room in the attic most of the time. When people came, I never went down to see them.

As I lay on my bed, for about eight hours a day, sometimes nothing would happen. Sometimes I would just lie there, trying and failing. Other times, the room would disappear, the world would disappear, and I would just be there. Lots of amazing things happened, all good experiences.

I was looking for God, waiting for God. Eventually, God did begin to appear in my room, as a cloud of light, while I lay on my bed. I remember thinking, "Man, holy crap, God is going to appear. I've got to get out of here!" And I got up and ran out of my room. God tried to appear to me twice during that four-year period. Both those times, I physically ran out of the room.

I was definitely afraid. I believe that, even for those who really want to know, a part of them does not want to know, mainly because, once you know, a responsibility or obligation comes along with it. [Then] I finally found what I call "The Easy Way," [which] has a built-in way to counter that resistance.

So I was in the attic, lying on the floor. I had just given a friend some spiritual advice that I felt God had given me for him. It was about him giving up something. My friend came back later and said, "Joseph, I have prayed and thought about this, and I really feel this advice is not for me, but for you."

When he said that, I felt bad, because I felt the advice would be of benefit for him. Also, I felt I had given up every single thing. I had nothing. I was lying on a board in an attic with millions of flies around me. I had to sleep under the sheets and cover everything so the dead flies would not fall into my mouth. I had a backpack with a couple of things, my pillow, a board, and a sleeping bag.

So that night I went upstairs in emotional agony. I had never experienced that much of having nothing. I had to give up something else, and I had nothing else to give up. Which meant I was not going to make it.

So I lay there in distress, when a moth came—a tiny, thin one with white on its wings. He lay on my backpack, right beside my face. I knew that the moth was God, and he had come to be with me. I went to sleep with that little moth. When I woke up, he was gone.

The next night, a three-foot man lay down beside me on the board, floating three inches above the floor. He was my company for the night. I did not feel he was God. He was a stand-in, a trusted, faithful servant or foster parent, someone who was sent for that night to comfort and supervise.

The next night I started to see a curtain of light. It seemed to be a foot thick and about 12 feet wide. I stared at that curtain continually until I went to sleep. When I woke up, it was there again. I stared at it for days. It was getting thinner and more transparent, and I could make out something behind the curtain. It was a throne. A young man sat on the throne, and another man stood beside it.

I kept staring at it every night for seven nights. Then one night the curtain, the throne, everything disappeared. Instead, the giant face of that young man appeared in the room and said, "Now go down and do what you've got to do."

I took that to be the face of God. It felt like peace, and it looked like love—whatever love can look like. I never questioned it. The lips never did move, but the feeling of assurance, power, and confidence was there.

I did not ask any questions about what I had to do. I just went downstairs. A spiritual meeting happened to be going on. So I sat down in the middle of it and listened. I did that for a few weeks, just sat and listened.

Then people started asking me questions. I told them what I thought was the answer. After some time they asked me more questions. That is how I began to teach "The Easy Way."

What Ascension Is

Ascension is usually defined as leaving the earth in this body before death, disappearing from this realm, and taking your body to another realm, what you might call heaven. After that, you can come back as you choose, move your body at will, and display a number of other abilities.

However, I personally believe that a more helpful and true way to look at ascension is as a state of being one with God. It does not matter whether you are here, there, or anywhere else, whether you have a big flash of light, or disappear and come back. What matters is that you are at one with God.

This does not mean that physical ascension will not happen. The best way to make it happen is to not worry or get hung up on it. Instead, concentrate on uniting with God. Physical ascension is a byproduct of being one with God, when your will and God's will are one. In that state, whatever you think, desire, and feel is the same as God, just naturally—not because you have to. You just do.

A major part of being one with God is the desire for it to be so. You are one with God, in word and deed, because you know it is the best thing. Then you obey God, from that moment on.

When Peter walked on the water, Jesus said, "Come," and Peter did it automatically. It was a miraculous event, but obedience was what made it happen. Once Peter started doubting it, he started to sink. The single-minded obedience allowed him to perform a miracle.

God has no limits. If God says "Walk on the water," then you walk on the water. If God tells you to ascend, then you ascend. However, if God says physical ascension is not for you, then you have to let go of it. You might have to give up any spiritual desires, aside from oneness with God. Obedience is the key to everything you want. But it is a double-edged sword, because God's will might be different from what you expect.

The Secret to Ascension

I like to draw a diagram to explain the process of ascension. Figure 19a shows the stick-figure "Fred." To the right of Fred is a line, like the centerline in a road. I call that line "the veil of unbelief." Susan Shumsky calls it the "façade barrier" or "false belief of separation from God."

On the left side of the line is Fred in his current reality. The arrows above Fred's head represent him moving forward in spiritual growth. The box with an X symbolizes his goal, whether it be enlightenment, ascension, or another achievement. Ascension or God has always been viewed as near the top of that lane, represented by the box with the X.

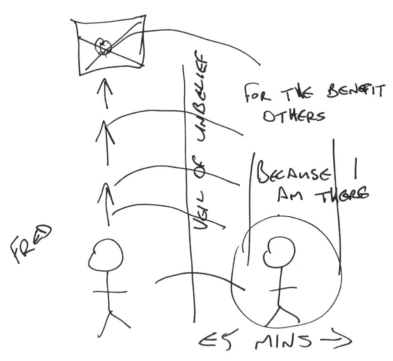

Figure 19a. The Easy Way to Ascension.

In actual fact, ascension, or oneness with God, is not in that box with the X. It is, instead, just one single step sideways to the right, across the veil of unbelief that runs down the middle of the page, into the other lane, or the other truth. It is one step of faith only—even for those that get all the way up to the top, where the box is. What happens to everyone is eventually a voice within says, "Look, just take one step to the right." The truth is that you can take that step anywhere along that lane of spiritual growth.

The stick figure on the right side of the line represents Fred as a faith person or ascended person. There is a circle around Fred and lines coming out from the circle, as if a road is coming out from the circle. Those lines represent a beam of light that I call "The Beam." However, the "beam" energy actually flows out from Fred in all directions.

When you cross over the veil of unbelief, it is not enough to say, "Okay, I believe I am done." And it is not enough to say, "Okay, I'm done," or to say to someone, "You're it, you're done." Once you are at that point of faith, just briefly, you need to then exercise your new truth by acting from that place.

It is a good idea, as a seeker, to work toward your goal. So continue seeking, just as Fred moves up the lane towards the box with the X. But then, take a moment to decide you have already reached your goal. Step across the veil of unbelief and experience your goal for as long as you can, right now. In this way you are practicing faith.

How to Practice "The Beam"

The only thing stopping you from ascension or oneness with God is unbelief. Nothing else. You do not need to be more loving, or to learn more spiritual things. You are already good enough. All you need is to make a habit of believing. Because unbelief is the only thing stopping you, belief is the only thing that can help you.

The way I suggest, "The Easy Way" to practice your faith, is what I call "The Beam." The best way to get started is to sit down for about five minutes, with the intention to experience God. You may close your eyes or not. Step across the veil of unbelief, and choose to believe you are there. Or stop disbelieving. Then, because you are already there, act from there. Let the fullness of God's energy and power flow through you, as that full being, with intention, for the benefit of others.

With the alert awareness and focused concentration of a laser, imagine a beam of energy, about the size of a soccer ball, leaving from your being and heading towards the center of the universe, knowing that at some point it will veer off to where it is needed. You do not need to know where. Your only responsibility is to focus on the energy of God going out for the benefit of others. You are a conduit for that energy. It is passing through you anyway. You just need to give it attention.

You can practice this several periods each day. I always tell people three times a day, five minutes per time. Then it becomes habitual and begins to take a life of its own. You naturally begin to live from that place. Your goal is accomplished, whatever that may be. Including ascension.

In my mind, The Beam is a circuit or circle of energy that originates from the center of the universe, which flows through us and back, guided by divine intelligence, so it is allocated to wherever that intelligence feels the need is greatest. It has been there since the universe was created. Its source is God, and it is self-propagating. In fact, everything is made from it. You might call it the "Christ light." It is God's energy.

As you get more experienced, you can become aware that the energy is coming in from that infinite source. As you push it out, a little more comes in. For example, if you push out 10 grams, 11 grams comes in, so the next time you can do more.

Even though a part of us wants to move toward God and be one with God, a part of us does not. That is what we might call the ego or mortal self, with its survival instinct. It is hard to overcome this primal human impulse. So I suggest you take short periods of practicing The Beam.

Choose to be done, or free of ego, for just five minutes, giving yourself permission to be less than perfect again in a few minutes. That makes your ego feel safer and less afraid. By doing this enough times, your ego learns it is not so bad on the other side. A habit of letting go begins to grow. You unclench your fingers from your weaknesses and limitations, and are drawn to God's presence, like a magnet. There is no more struggle—or at least a manageable struggle.

How The Beam Came to Me

The Beam started as an energy built up inside me that I could not get rid of. It was like bees or another flying, buzzing insect inside my chest, trying to escape. It built up to such a degree that I had to get it out to survive. So, by instinct, I started pushing it out from my heart. I expelled it from my being, in a laser-like beam.

That helped me, and I felt relief. So I stopped. Then, over the next few days, that energy built up again, so I had to do it again. After a while, I figured out that if I did The Beam before the energy built up, then I would feel more enlivened. That energy would not drive me crazy. I started doing it as a form of maintenance, a survival mechanism, to stay comfortable within my own skin. Then I continued doing it because it felt good, and I felt progress. I felt closer to God.

How I would define The Beam is letting the flow of the universe, or the river of life, pass through my body and clear away all the stuff. Every moment I am not focused on God I am adding lines to my big book of life. For a moment, I may not recognize when someone needs my help. That is unacceptable to me. In my mind that is a line in my book.

When I spend time sending out that energy, I am erasing all those lines I have added to the book in the last few hours, plus some extra things. If I keep doing that often enough, then my book will be completely clean, with no entries. In my mind, that has a lot to do with being one with God.

How The Beam Purifies Us

One time I was in the energy of The Beam, and I looked down. The beam of light was passing through my body, as wide as my body. I could see the cells of my body, and between the cells. The cells were golden and perfect. I believe that everyone's cells are perfect—not just someone who has been doing The Beam, but every single person.

I noticed that where the energy was flowing, tiny black flecks, like ash, were being washed away from between the cells by this river. Those little black flecks were all the negative things I had collected in my lifetime, such as fears, doubts, worries, unbelief, and other untrue things.

This taught me that I do not need to deal with that negative stuff. All I need to do is fulfill that first commandment: "Love the Lord your God with all of your heart, all of your mind and all of your strength."[1] Then everything else will be taken care of. Those other things I thought I needed to work on will be washed away, because I am fulfilling the one law. That experience helped me, because I could just do my job, which is to be that energy, and let the other stuff be taken care of.

Giving Up

My main spiritual practice has been choosing to be one with God at the expense of something else—giving up the world for God. This is analogous to holding a pen: Imagine you have only one hand, and you are grasping that pen with your fist. But you want to pick up a banana. In order to pick it up, you have to put down that pen. You cannot pick up the banana at the same time you are clutching that pen.

Now I know how to do this without giving up the world entirely. That is why I really believe in this one way, "The Easy Way," because you only have to put down that pen, or give up everything and be one with God, for a short time. Five minutes later, you can pick up the world again and resume your life for the rest of the day. Cross the line again whenever you are ready. In this way you can live a regular life and still experience God. You should have that option. It is too hard, too scary, and too essentially crappy to put down the pen right now, forever.

If You Want to Attain Ascension

What I would say to people who aspire to attain ascension is that it is possible. You can do it easily. One thing that holds you back is trying to do it. Trying is the very opposite of doing it. It takes faith, so you need to just do it. Just be there now and come to that place. Just keep putting in effort, with faith.

You do not have to do it all at once. A misconception about ascension is that there is a big bang, and then you are done. In actual fact it is a lot of little bangs. The fact is that the first time you do it, you have accomplished a huge thing.

I choose ascension. I accept it for myself and for others. What I really believe is it is in God's time. Ascension is not up to the individual. It happens when you have done what you are supposed to do, and when are ready. Ascension is almost nothing in comparison to knowing God.

At one time, I was planting all the pits from the avocados I was eating. One avocado seemed overripe and rotten. So I took it outside to the veggie garden and started chopping on it. When you cut a ripe avocado, the pit just falls out. But it turned out this avocado was no-where near ripe, and the pit was stuck. So to get that pit out, I had to destroy the avocado. I hacked it to pieces.

As I was doing that, God was teaching me, "This is what it is like if God takes someone before they are ready." If someone were to go through ascension or another spiritual experience before they are ready, even if they look or feel ready, it destroys that individual. God knows when things should happen, so you do not have to worry about it. All you have to do is be that energy, and the rest will take care of itself.

Part VI

Greeting Your Inner Teachers

Chapter 20

The Mighty "I AM" Presence

The living word of pure consciousness—you are That.
The reflection of the King's Face—you are That.
There is nothing outside of yourself, Look within,
Everything you want is there—you are That.
—Jalal Al-Din Rumi

The mighty "I AM" presence is your true nature of being. It is God within you. At the core of your being, in the deepest recesses of your heart, there God dwells as "God I AM." It is your higher self. It is who you really are. And it is beckoning for you to come and experience the glory of its radiance.

Allow your heart to open to that brilliant light of your beingness. All that is required is a sincere willingness to experience it. You have all that you need within you, and God's love fills your heart with peace, blessings, and grace. Now it is time for you to open the door to this magnificence and discover that you are this "God I AM." In this chapter, you will prepare for that opening.

What Is the Mighty "I AM"?

If you recall the story in the Bible about Moses and the burning bush, God spoke to Moses directly as the mighty "I AM." Here is what transpired:

Moses was a shepherd. One day, he led his father-in-law's flock to the "mountain of God," Horeb, where an angel appeared in the midst of a bush as fire. As Moses turned to see why the bush was not being consumed by the flames, suddenly God spoke, "Moses, Moses, Here am I."

Then God reminded Moses that the Israelites were living in slavery, sorrow, and oppression in Egypt. He instructed Moses to go to Pharaoh, and to deliver the children of Israel "out of the hand of the Egyptians, and to bring them up out of that land unto a good land and a large, unto a land flowing with milk and honey."

Moses objected, thinking himself unworthy of this monumental task. But God reassured him. Moses then asked God, "Behold, when I come unto the children of Israel, and shall say unto them, The God of your fathers hath sent me unto you; and they shall say to me, What is his name? What shall I say unto them?" God then answered, "I AM THAT I AM.... Thus shalt thou say unto the children of Israel, I AM hath sent me unto you."

This mighty "I AM" presence, the presence of God, is the nature of God within you and within this entire creation. This inner being is unlimited, absolute, pure, whole, beauteous, and filled with wisdom. It is your inner teacher, your divine guidance, and it is who you really are.

There are many aspects to this inner divinity. The teaching of Divine Revelation helps you discover these aspects yourself. Unlike many ascended master teachings that place a particular channeler or medium on a pedestal and proclaim that medium to be the only conduit or one accredited spokesperson for the ascended masters, Divine Revelation helps you discover the mighty "I AM" yourself. It helps you directly experience the many radiant light-beings that we have met in this book—and so much more.

In this section of the book, you are about to embark on the amazing journey of inner discovery so that you may begin your own personal relationship with the mighty "I AM" at the center of your being.

How Is This Possible?

I have helped thousands of people to open to this holy divine presence. Somehow, and I do not know how or why, I have been given this amazing blessing and special gift to help people contact God directly and experience their mighty "I AM" and their inner divinity, divine beings, deities, and inner teachers.

Happily and luckily, you found this book and this precious teaching of Divine Revelation, because this is what you have been seeking for many lifetimes. It is a rare individual who consciously desires to know God. But it is even more rare to aspire to surrender your life to God and follow inner guidance.

Many people want to serve humanity and to do their part in making this a better world. With the best of intentions, they hang on to what they perceive as their so-called ideals, independence, and integrity. The trouble is that, if they were to surrender to God and follow God's will, their ego and their worldview would be dismantled. Their ideals might change. Therefore, they are not willing to do that.

> *We spend a great deal of time telling God what we*
> *think should be done, and not enough time waiting*
> *in the stillness for God to tell us what to do.*
> —Peace Pilgrim

In other cases, people are not ready to take the responsibility of receiving their own inner guidance. It is easier to follow a guru, psychic, channeler, priest, or another proxy, and just stand on the sidelines. These proxies are more than happy to take this role, because it feeds their egos, and their pocketbooks as well.

That is why it is highly unusual for anyone to want to contact the "I AM" and divine teachers within. Few people are even willing to hear about it. Fewer are ready to believe it is possible. But those who are prepared to have this direct mystical experience, these precious, uncommon individuals, struggle for lifetimes to achieve what this rare teaching helps them attain in just a few minutes.

Are you one of these people? If so, you will begin to learn how right now.

Aspects of Your Inner Identity

In the next chapter is a Breakthrough Meditation. This meditation will help you break through the barriers that have prevented you from experiencing your mighty "I AM" presence. During your breakthrough, you will travel through various levels of awareness into your higher self.

The Breakthrough Meditation does not add anything new. Instead it peels back layers of beliefs, habits, and conditions that are not who you really are. In this way, this process helps you realize who you really are. In other words, during your breakthrough, you will not practice anything. You will instead do what I call the "do-nothing program." You will do nothing, nothing, and less than nothing.

You are a multidimensional being with many facets. Your physical body is just one of these. You also have a subtle body with many layers and a divine body with more layers. In fact, you have countless aspects of your lower and higher self. During the Divine Revelation Breakthrough, you will begin to recognize some of these. And ultimately, you will experience your true nature of oneness, wholeness, and unity. That oneness is "God I AM."

During the meditation in the next chapter, you will travel from the outer world into the inner world. You will move from awareness of your environment to awareness of your physical body. Then you will experience your conscious mind and subconscious mind. You will then pass through the seeming barrier or veil, called the façade barrier, which has separated you from your mighty "I AM" presence. And you will begin to experience higher aspects of yourself.

At that point, the meditation will help you to contact aspects of your higher self or master-teachers you wish to meet. You may choose what aspects of inner divinity you feel attuned to and comfortable with.

Goals of Your Breakthrough

You will accomplish four goals during the Breakthrough Meditation. These are called the Inner Divine Contact, Inner Divine Name, Inner Divine Signal, and Inner Divine Message. Let us now elaborate on these.

Inner Divine Contact

Your inner contact is the experience of the mighty "I AM" presence within. It is the direct mystical connection with "God I AM," which brings love, peace, acceptance, and contentment. When you are in contact with God, you experience expansion, inner peace, unconditional love, inner strength, harmony, oneness, and wholeness. You feel loved, safe, secure, assured, confident, centered, balanced, and fulfilled. That holy presence brings grace, blessings, and wisdom. You no longer feel alone. You know that God is with you, comforting you and bringing you peace.

Inner Divine Name

You have many facets of your higher self, which have inner names. Some of these are familiar names, such as Holy Spirit. Others you may have never heard of. A few examples might be God, Mother-Father God, Jesus Christ, Mother Mary, Kwan Yin, Buddha, Krishna, Durga, Allah, Babaji, Hashem, or Saint Germain.

In this book you have already met many masters and deities. During your Breakthrough Meditation, you may call upon one or more inner teachers and begin to communicate with those divine beings.

Figure 20a. **Etheric Soul Self of a Divine Revelation Student:** This soul self is an innocent, guileless, graceful being. The immortal nature of being, beyond all façades and masks, the soul-self body of pure light is ever-youthful, about age 20, with perfect symmetry and divine radiance. Flawless, vibrant, luminous, and beautiful, the soul body is the same sex as the physical body during each particular incarnation.

Inner Divine Signal

One very unique aspect of Divine Revelation is the inner signal or vibrational signal. This signal is a sign indicating which particular aspect of your higher self is present. A signal is God's way of saying, "Hello. Wake up and pay attention. I am here." Let us describe a signal further now.

At some time in your life, you have felt inspired, elevated, or elated. Perhaps you were watching an especially magnificent sunrise. Maybe you were moved by poetry that was achingly beautiful. Or you were thrilled by exquisite music at a concert. Perhaps a minister gave a message at church that really moved you. Maybe a piece of artwork at a museum touched your soul. Or, you helped someone in need, and when your eyes met, magic happened.

At the very peak point of such an experience, something occured. You got goose bumps, your hair stood on end, or electricity went through your body. That experience is one of your signals. It is God saying, "Hi."

Each of your inner names has a signal associated with it. Each signal is separate, unique, and personal. In other words, your signal for Jesus will be different from your signal for Mother Mary. My signal for Jesus will be different from yours. Everyone has his or her own signals that are specific and special.

Whatever signals you identify will not change. In other words, the signal that you identify for Holy Spirit will always be your Holy Spirit signal, throughout your life. It might become subtler with time, but it will still be the same signal.

Signals come to you in one of six ways: seeing, hearing, tasting, smelling, feeling, or getting an involuntary body movement. Let us elaborate further:

Seeing: You might see an inner light of a particular color in a particular place—in your field of vision, in an energy center in your body, or somewhere within or around you. With your inner eye, you might see a symbol, such as a rose, a tree, a mountain, the Star of David, a cross, a sunrise, a geometric pattern, or something else. You may see the face of a saint or deity, or a beautiful, shimmering angel.

Hearing: Perhaps you hear music in your inner ear. Maybe you hear bells, chimes, harps, angelic choirs, violins, concertos, music of the spheres, humming, an "OM" sound, rustling leaves, rushing water, birds singing, or something else.

Tasting: Maybe you taste something sweet or pleasant in your mouth or throat, though you have not eaten anything. Perhaps you taste peach, pear, strawberries, orange, apricot, apple, milk, rosewater, or another agreeable taste. It might be familiar or unfamiliar.

Smelling: Maybe a sweet-smelling, ambrosial fragrance wafts into your inner sensing, such as lilac, jasmine, sandalwood, gardenia, rose, strawberry, orange, peach, or another, unidentifiable perfume.

Feeling: Maybe you feel heat somewhere in your body, or a cool breeze. Perhaps electricity moves through your body, or a rush or current of energy. Or you feel tingling or an odd sensation. Maybe your body seems to change size or shape. Or it disappears or becomes numb. Perhaps you feel a strong, pleasant sensation somewhere. Or you feel something touching, cloaking, or surrounding you. Maybe a spiraling sensation or another geometric configuration seems to be moving within or around your body.

Involuntary Movements: Maybe your body moves involuntarily. Perhaps your head or body rocks. Or your head moves in a particular direction. Maybe your head goes back, sideways, or forward. Perhaps your eyes roll back in your head, or your eyelashes flutter. Maybe your body shakes or quakes, or an extremity moves, shakes, or taps.

These are six possible ways you might receive a signal. Each signal will fall into one of these categories. Each inner contact will give you one of these signals. So, if you are in contact with Lord Buddha, he will give you a specific signal. If you are in contact with Kwan Yin, she will give you a different signal. Whenever you contact Kwan Yin, you will recognize her by her signal. A signal is a sign that the particular inner teacher is present.

Figure 20b. **Contacting Your Inner Teacher:** Practicing the Divine Revelation meditation technique brings you in contact with your divine self, who may appear as an inner teacher radiating love and light. This experience lifts your awareness into God-consciousness.

Inner Divine Message

The fourth goal of your Breakthrough Meditation is to receive a message from your higher self or inner teacher. The message will have meaning, and it will often answer a question or give you inspiration. In Chapter 22 of this book, you will read examples of divinely revealed messages from some light-beings. The message will come in one of three ways: seeing, hearing, or feeling. Here is how:

Seeing: You might see the message, with eyes closed, just like a motion picture playing in your inner eye. A possible example might be seeing an open doorway with light streaming through it.

Hearing: You might hear the message as words in your inner ear, just as other thoughts occur to you in your mind. For example, you might hear the words, "I love you. I am always with you."

Feeling: You might get the message as a deep feeling, such as a deep, abiding feeling of love, peace, or joy.

Do not confuse the signal with the message:

The signal is a sign. It is like a signature or an identity badge that identifies a particular divine being. It never changes. It stays the same for the rest of your life.

The message is inspirational and answers a question or bestows special wisdom or knowledge. It is specific to a particular time, circumstance, or situation. It is usually different from previous messages.

In the next chapter, you will learn a powerful meditation that will help you experience all these four goals of your own personal Divine Revelation Breakthrough: The inner divine contact, inner divine name, inner divine signal, and inner divine message. Let us begin that process now.

Chapter 21

Opening to the Divine Beings

Before embarking on important undertakings, sit quietly,
calm your senses and thoughts, and meditate deeply. You
will then be guided by the great creative power of Spirit.
—Paramahansa Yogananda

Many ascended masters are assisting in the teaching of Divine Revelation. Those who are learning to hear the "still small voice" of God within their heart can receive messages, guidance, and healing from the ascended masters and other divine teachers.

The Divine Revelation Breakthrough is a key to unlock the door to the world of the immortal masters and beings of light. They are beckoning you to awaken your heart to their teachings. These divine beings are the teachers of Divine Revelation and of the teachings of ascension.

Is it possible to directly experience the wondrous beings of light that have been described in this book? Yes, you can. In this chapter, you will learn how. Here you will practice a simple, step-by-step meditation to open your heart and mind to your inner divinity, spiritual guidance, and higher self. This practice of meditation is based upon one easy principle: "Ask, and it shall be given you."[1] Simplicity is the key. All you need to do is ask for it.

Figure 21a. **Divine Revelation:** The Divine Revelation Breakthrough experience is a way to open to ecstatic union with God. When you are bathed in the light of God, you bask in God's divine radiance and glory. When God's love pervades your heart, you are filled with God's joy and beauty. When you are blessed by God's holy presence, you live in divine grace.

You Can Do it Now

Whether or not you have meditated before, you can directly experience your "I AM" presence and inner teachers right now. You need no special preparation, experience, training, belief, or talent. By practicing the simple method in this chapter, you can attain what you seek. All that is required is sufficient openness to attempt the experiment.

By practicing the simple meditation offered here, you can contact your inner divinity, beginning today. With repeated practice, you can attain greater clarity and intimacy with your inner communications. Depending on your personality, physical make-up, and heartfelt desires, you will experience your inner teachers in a way that is perfect for you. Because everyone is different, experiences vary widely. Know and trust that your experiences are exactly right. Therefore, there is no need to compare yourself to anyone else.

Are you ready to begin? Let us get started now.

Your Breakthrough Experience

The meditation in this chapter will help you break through the façade barrier and experience your higher self, deep within your soul. Once you pass through the barrier, you can begin to contact your inner teachers. These beauteous beings of light are aspects of your own inner divinity. They are ready to welcome you with open arms whenever you ask them to come forth.

This meditation can be practiced easily by reading the following words into an audio recorder, computer, or other recording device, and then making a tape, CD, or file. Then you can play it back when you are ready to experience your breakthrough.

You only need to record the words that are in quotation marks. When you see three dots (...), then pause. Do not record words in brackets: [ ]. Read slowly, consciously, and with feeling. You may notice that some of the sentences are constructed awkwardly, ungrammatically, or redundantly. There is a reason these words are placed in this sequence, so just read it as written and practice the meditation as suggested.

If you do not like the word *God*, then replace it with *Spirit, Holy Spirit, Mother-Father God, God/Goddess, creator, divine light, source, divine, divinity, higher self, Lord Buddha, Jesus Christ, Lord Krishna, Allah,* or any other divine name with which you feel comfortable.

This particular meditation will help you contact the female aspect of the Holy Spirit. However, in the context of this meditation, you may substitute the name "Holy Spirit" for another name and call on any divine being that you want to contact at this time.

What follows is the Breakthrough Meditation, specifically designed to help you experience your inner teachers. Let us get started now.

The Breakthrough Meditation

"Let us now get comfortable in our chair, and let us now close our eyes. Let us take a big, deep breath to unite with each other. Breathe in... and out... Let us take a deep breath of divine love. Breathe in... and out... Let us take a deep breath of inner peace. Breathe in... and out... Let us take a deep breath of relaxation. Breathe in... and out... Peace, peace, be still. Be still and be at peace. Peace, peace, be at peace. Be still and be at peace...

"We recognize that there is one power and one presence at work in the universe and in our lives, God the good, omnipotent. We recognize that God is the one truth, the one light, the one divine intelligence, the one perfection of being. God is the source of unconditional love, the source of peace, of joy, of light, of fulfillment. God is the light of life, the light of truth, perfection everywhere now, perfection here now.

"I AM one with this source of light in the universe. I AM one with divine light, divine truth, and divine wisdom. I AM one with the truth of being, the light of God's love. I AM one with my higher self, divine beings, deities, guardian angels, and master-teachers now. I AM the love that God is. I AM the power that God is. I AM the holy presence that God is. I AM the light that God is. I AM the truth of being, the light of life. I AM perfection everywhere now.

"I therefore claim for myself, [state your full name aloud here], my perfect breakthrough to Spirit, my perfect experience of my own higher self and of all the divine beings, deities, guardian angels, and master-teachers who come in the name of God, whom it is highest wisdom for me to contact today.

"I release from my mind all negations, limitations, and blockages that do not reflect the truth of my being and that prevent me from clearly experiencing my beautiful inner teachers who come in the name of God. I let go of all these negative thoughts and emotions now. I now call upon the Holy Spirit to eliminate all thoughts of... [say aloud whatever negative thoughts and emotions come up for you] and any other limiting thoughts, whether known or unknown, conscious or unconscious. These thoughts are now lovingly lifted, healed, released, dissolved, and completely let go. They are now lifted into the light of God's love and truth.

"I now lovingly accept and welcome positive, life-supporting, energizing thoughts and emotions. I open my heart to receive thoughts of... [say aloud positive thoughts and emotions that replace the previously stated negative ones]. These thoughts are permanently established in my consciousness now.

"I AM in balance. I AM in control. I AM the only authority in my life. I AM divinely protected by the light of my being. I close off my aura and body of light to the lower astral levels of mind, and I open to the spiritual world and to my own God Self and consciousness. Thank you God, and SO IT IS.

"Let us now take a deep breath and go deeper. Breathe in... and out...

"The light of God surrounds me. The love of God enfolds me. The power of God protects me. The presence of God watches over me. Wherever I AM, God is, and all is well.

"Let us now take a deep breath and go deeper. Breathe in... and out...

"I now call upon the Holy Spirit to lovingly heal any and all dear ones whom it is highest wisdom to heal at this time. Dear ones, you are now lovingly healed and forgiven. You are healed and forgiven, healed and forgiven, healed and forgiven. You are unified in love with the truth of your being. God's love and light fill and surround you now. The vibration of the earth no longer binds you. You are bless-ed, forgiven, and released, into the love, light, and wholeness, of the eternal divine presence. You are bless-ed, forgiven, and released, into the love, light, and wholeness of the eternal divine presence. You are bless-ed, forgiven, and released, into the love, light, and wholeness of the eternal divine presence. You are lifted into the light of God, lifted into the light of God, lifted into the light of God, lifted into the light of God. You are now free to go into your perfect place of expression. Go now in peace and love. Thank you, God, and SO IT IS.

"Let us now take a deep breath and go deeper. Breathe in... and out...

"I now let go of all psychic ties, karmic bonds, emotions, resentments, addictions, attachments, and repulsions between myself and anyone or anything that does not reflect the truth of my being and that prevents me from experiencing my own higher self and divine inner teachers who come in the name of God. I call upon the Holy Spirit to cut these psychic ties and karmic bonds now. They are now lovingly and permanently cut, cut, cut, cut, cut, cut, cut, lifted, loved, healed, released, dissolved, and completely let go. Thank you God, and SO IT IS.

"Let us now take a deep breath and go deeper. Breathe in... and out...

"I AM a God/Goddess of divine love and light. I AM ready to receive my perfect experience of God consciousness now, in the form of direct contact and communication with my own inner teachers, divine beings, master-teachers, and deities, according to my own spiritual beliefs and understandings.

"I thank God for manifesting this good in my life now, under grace, in God's own wise and perfect ways. Thank you, God, and SO IT IS.

"Let us now take a deep breath and go deeper. Breathe in... and out...

"Let us go deeper now as we let go of all cares and concerns of the day... We let go of our environment and all influences around us as we take our awareness deep, deep within to the depth of our being, our inner nature, our own higher self... We turn our awareness from the outer world and go deep within to experience our true nature.

"Let us now take a deep breath and go deeper. Breathe in... and out...

"Let us now become aware of our physical body... We now become aware of any place within our physical body that is now drawing our attention... As we easily and comfortably place our attention on our physical body, we notice any sensations or feelings anywhere in the body... We now allow these feelings to let go and dissipate as we place our attention in that place or places within the body that need healing...

"Let us now become aware of each part of our physical body, as we now relax our physical body. Let us now place our attention on our eyes. Breathe and let go as we relax our eyes now... Let us now let go of our eyebrows as we breathe and relax our eyebrows now... Let go of the space between our eyebrows... Let go of our temples... Let go of our jaw as we breathe now... Let go of our chin... Our neck... Let the neck go as we relax and breathe into the neck...

"Let us now relax our shoulders as we breathe and let go... Now relax our shoulders completely as we let them drop and relax... Now become aware of our chest as we let go and relax our chest... Breathe in and out of the chest and let go... Now become aware of our stomach... Let the stomach go and relax... Let the stomach drop... Now become aware of our pelvic area... Relax the pelvis and let it go...

"Let us now become aware of our upper back... Relax and let go of our upper back now… We now let go of our lower back... Our waist... Our sides... Our buttocks. We relax our buttocks now...

"Let us now become aware of our shoulders as we breathe… Place our attention on our upper arms... Our elbows... Our lower arms... Our wrists... Hands and fingers... We now relax our arms and hands completely as we breathe...

"Let us now become aware of our thighs as we breathe deeply... Our knees... Let our knees relax and let go completely... Relax our lower legs... Our calves... Our ankles... Our feet... The soles of our feet... We now relax our legs and feet completely as we breathe...

"Let us now become aware of our forehead... Our eyebrows... The space between our eyebrows... Our eyes... Our jaw... Breathe deeply as we relax our entire body...

"Let us now take a big deep breath and go deeper, deeper, deeper, into the wells of Spirit... Deeper, deeper, deeper, into the silence of our being... Peace, peace, be still. Be still and be at peace...

"Let us now become aware that our entire body is relaxing and becoming quiet and still... As our body settles down, our body becomes quiet and still, our heart rate becomes quiet, our breathing is still. Breathing becomes quiet, still, subtle, and refined. Our body is serene, still, and relaxed...

"We now become aware that as our body settles down to deep relaxation, our mind is also quiet, still, and relaxed, like a still pond without a ripple... Our mind is becoming silent, still, and deep, like the water at the bottom of the ocean... We are deep, serene, tranquil, and at rest in the depth of that ocean of mind...

"Let us now take a big deep breath and go deeper... Deeper, deeper, deeper, into the wells of Spirit, into the silence of being... Peace, peace, be at peace... Be at peace and one with God...

"We now become aware of our subconscious mind, knowing that we now quietly pass through the subconscious mind, letting it rest quietly and easily. We know that divine light now shines on the subconscious mind, bringing peace, comfort, and relaxation...

"Let us now take a big deep breath and go even deeper... Deeper, deeper, deeper into silence, peace, and relaxation... Peace, be at peace... We let go and let God as we surrender to Spirit...

"Now we walk through the seeming façade barrier that has prevented us from experiencing the true nature of our being. As we walk through the gate into Spirit, we easily glide into the spiritual realm, the divine nature of our being, deep within our soul...

"Let us now take a big deep breath... And go even deeper as we let go of all ego façades and now experience our own higher self... We walk through the gate into Spirit and turn our face to the almighty presence, the glory and splendor of God consciousness...

"Let us now take a deep breath and go deeper... As we now become aware of the streams of God's light showering into our being, lifting our vibration and opening us to its radiance and glory... We open our heart and mind as we bask in the radiance and warmth of God's love, the waves of God's love filling us with peace and blessings... We open to the altar of the living God... The tabernacle of the living presence of the most high, the holy of holies, the almighty creator...

"We bathe in the holy presence of God's love and light with gratitude in our hearts and joy in our souls... Let us now take a deep breath and go deeper... Deeper, deeper, deeper, into the wells of Spirit, into the silence of being... Peace, peace, be at peace. Be still and be at peace. Peace, peace, be at peace. Be still and be at peace. Be still and know that I AM God...

"Let us now go even deeper as we move beyond even this celestial world into the realm of the nameless, formless absolute... The perfection of being. The absolute transcendental pure consciousness... The one without a second... Beyond all forms and phenomena of this universe... Pure awareness, the place of perfect peace and silence within... Let us now dwell in this perfect place of silence and deep relaxation for a few moments... [Pause for one minute.]

"Let us now take a deep breath and go even deeper... Deeper, deeper. deeper, into the silence of being... Peace, peace, be at peace... Peace, peace, be at peace. Be still and be at peace...

"Let us now call upon the beautiful inner teachers, guardian angels, archangels, deities, ascended masters, light-beings, and aspects of our higher self to come forth now to help us contact and communicate with them.

"Let us call on the beautiful female aspect of the Holy Spirit to come forth now... [Or, throughout the meditation, substitute the words *Holy Spirit* for another inner teacher you want to contact.]

"We ask the Holy Spirit in the female form [or substitute the name of your chosen inner teacher] to come now and give us a beautiful inner signal, a sign that we are in contact and communication with her. We know that this signal comes as a vision, feeling, sound, taste, smell, or a body movement. In whatever way is of highest wisdom for the Holy Spirit to give us her signal, she now gives it.

"Let us now take a big deep breath. As we let go of this deep breath, we pretend that we sink out of our head and into our heart. Let us now breathe in... And out... Sink out of our head and into our heart as we let go... Again, breathe in... And out... Sink out of our head and into our heart as we let go completely... Once again, breathe in... And out... Sink out of our head and into our heart as we let go......

"Now we do the do-nothing program. That means we do nothing, nothing, and less than nothing, as we ask the Holy Spirit to come forth now and give us a signal... We now let go and give up completely. Do nothing, nothing, and less than nothing...

"As we completely let go, we allow the Holy Spirit to come forth with her beautiful signal that is personal to us. We receive our own unique signal of the Holy Spirit, whether it be a vision, feeling, sound, taste, smell, or body movement. We now ask the Holy Spirit to give her signal clearly and precisely, so we can recognize it easily...

"Let us take a big deep breath and then let go as we let the Holy Spirit give us her signal... Breathe in... And out...

"Holy Spirit, feed us your signal... Feed it stronger... Feed it stronger... Feed it stronger... Feed it stronger... Feed it stronger. Holy Spirit, feed your signal strong and clear so we can recognize our own inner signal...

"We now take a deep breath and then completely give up and let go... Breathe in... And out... [Pause for one minute to give time to receive and recognize the signal.]

"Let us now take a deep breath. Breathe in... And out...

"Once we have recognized the signal, let us now ask the beautiful Holy Spirit to give us a message. We now ask the beautiful Holy Spirit to feed us a beautiful, clear message.

"Let us take a big deep breath and then let go as we let the Holy Spirit give us her message... Breathe in... And out...

"Holy Spirit, feed us your message... Feed it stronger... Feed it stronger... Feed it stronger... Feed it stronger... Feed it stronger. Holy Spirit, feed your message strong and clear so we can recognize the message clearly... We now take a deep breath and then completely give up and let go... Breathe in... And out...

"Now say the message out loud. The message may be in words; if so, say the words out loud. It may be one word, two words, or a whole sentence. The message may be a vision; if so, describe the vision. Describe it out loud now. The message may be a feeling; if so, describe the feeling. Describe the message aloud now...

"We now take a deep breath and then completely give up and let go... Breathe in... And out... [Pause for one minute so there is time to receive and describe the message.]

"If we feel we are not yet getting a message, take another deep breath, and as we exhale, sink out of our head and into our heart. Then do nothing, nothing, and less than nothing...

"Please, Holy Spirit, feed your message now.

"Breathe in... And out... Relax, let go, and do nothing, nothing, and less than nothing... Say the message aloud now... [Pause for one minute so there is time to receive and describe the message.]

"If we still have not received a message, then now is the time to ask our higher self a question. We may ask about any problem or concern that is bothering us now. Or we may ask for direction or guidance. Now ask the question inwardly now... [Pause for one minute so there is time to ask the question.]

"Once we have asked our question, now take a deep breath. Breathe in... And out... As we breathe out, pretend that we are sinking out of our head and into our heart. Again, breathe in... And out... Sink into our heart.

"Now completely let go and give up... Do nothing, nothing, and less than nothing as we allow the answer to occur to us on this deep level... [Pause for a few minutes and receive the answer.]

"Thank you, Spirit, for your beautiful message. Thank you for the beautiful experiences we have received today in this meditation. Now it is time to come out of meditation.

"We thank God for all the beautiful experiences we have received today. Thank you for our clear connection with Spirit, for our beautiful inner signals, inner messages, and inner contact with the holy presence of our inner teachers today.

"We now begin to come forth from this meditation, bringing with us all the love, light, and energy we have received. We keep our eyes closed until we are ready to open them. We now take a deep breath to come forth from the level of divine Spirit as we pretend that we are blowing out a candle. Breathe in and out, as we pretend to blow out a candle...

"We now come forth to the level of subconscious mind, knowing that our subconscious mind is transformed and lifted by this meditation. Our subconscious mind is filled with the light of Spirit. God's love and light fill the subconscious mind with enlightenment.

"Let us now pretend we are blowing out another candle. Breathe in and out...

"We now come forth to the level of conscious mind, knowing that our conscious mind is now one with the mind of God, one with divine mind. Our conscious mind is in continual communication with God, and every thought we think is a divine revelation.

"Let us now blow out another candle. Breathe in and out...

"We now come forth to the level of physical body, knowing that our body is now transformed and healed by this meditation. It is filled with divine health, well-being, energy, and vitality. Our physical body is one with divine Spirit, and if we choose ascension, our body is now transforming into a light body of pure radiance, love, and glory. We are now the ascended masters of light, powerful spiritual beings of magnificent luminescence.

"Let us now blow out another candle. Breathe in and out...

"Still keeping our eyes closed, we now come forth to the level of environment, becoming aware of the room and environment around us. With our feet flat on the floor, we are one with the earth and, at the same time, one with heaven. We know now that we bring with us all the love, light, power, and energy from this meditation into our environment now. We are the walking, talking, breathing vessels of Spirit. We are the mouthpieces of God. We are the divine ambassadors of Spirit, the messengers of God.

"We now take four deep, vigorous breaths and pretend to blow out four candles as we come all the way out to inward and outward balance... Then we open our eyes slowly when we are ready...

"Now that our eyes are open, let us repeat the following affirmation aloud, in a strong and clear voice: 'I AM alert. I AM awake. I AM subjectively and objectively balanced. I AM in control. I AM the only authority in my life. I AM divinely protected by the light of my being. Thank you God, and SO IT IS.'"

After Your Breakthrough

Once you have had your breakthrough experience, you have begun a powerful process of transformation. Now your life is on track for discovering and fulfilling your true life plan and purpose, by working with your inner divine guidance.

In this book, there is not adequate space to cover the vast subject of how to receive divine messages clearly, how to heal what blocks you from receiving them, and how to discern and test whether the messages are coming from inner divinity and not from your mind, your ego, wishful thinking, or some other voice.

Therefore, to learn how to develop, use, clarify, and test your inner contact, I strongly urge you to study two of my other books, *Divine Revelation* and *How to Hear the Voice of God*. The latter includes a 70-minute CD, bound into the book, which guides you through a meditation similar to the one printed here. Also, I recommend using the 42-minute "Divine Revelation Guided Meditation CD" every day. It is available at *www.divinerevelation.org*.

For a profound experience of inner divinity, attend one of our live classes or Ascended Master retreats. There are many opportunities at *www.ascensionretreats.com* and *www.divinetravels.com*.

Chapter 22

Messages From the Masters

And Moses said unto him, Enviest thou for my sake?
would God that all the Lord's people were prophets,
and that the Lord would put his spirit upon them!
—Numbers 11:29

In this, our last chapter, you will experience the holy presence of some of the ascended masters through the vibration carried in their simple words of wisdom. It is easy to receive such inspiring messages. All you have to do is ask. The entire principle of Divine Revelation is one thing: "Ask, and it shall be given you."[1]

By asking God to show you the way, you take steps toward your goal, which brings freedom, joy, and love. God is always there, within you, ready to answer any question, solve any problem, and heal any discomfort. Show your faith by asking and receiving. The rest of this chapter consists of simple messages from our beautiful inner teachers.

Holy Spirit

My beloved ones, you are filled with the light of God. Trust in God to be your guide. You have all that you need within you. You are blessed, and you are a blessing. We love you now and always, with immeasurable love and glory. Trust in God. You are never alone. We are always here to guide you. You hold a special place in our heart. You are loved with infinite love and peace. Be at peace.

Open to receive our blessings. Open to your good. You deserve to have all that God has in store for you. You deserve prosperity. You deserve the fulfillment of your cherished desires. You deserve to be happy and to be at peace. Let go of all your fears and come to me, for I will guide you. I will bring you to glory. I will hold you in my loving arms and bring you peace. Call upon me to be your guide.

Beloved ones, you are filled with truth. You are the embodiment of truth. You have an invincible body of truth, which can never be harmed. Your truth body goes with you wherever you go, even after death. Nothing can harm this invincible body. Your truth body is immortal, and you are an immortal being of light. Trust in this truth, and be at peace.

Jesus

Open, open, open to our love. Be caressed in the loving embrace of our comfort. Be held in our loving arms. You are never alone, nor have you ever been. You are with us now and always. There is nothing to fear. Allow us to soothe your aching, broken heart, to touch you with our love, to fill you with our light. We are here with you, and we will never leave you. Trust in our love, and be at peace.

My blessed and beloved, love of my heart. Embrace me. Allow my arms to surround you. I rock you in my arms, like a little baby. I soothe you and comfort you. I breathe life into you and keep you safe and warm. I will never leave you. I will not abandon you. I will always be by your side, comforting you and bringing you peace. You can call upon me anytime to guide you and to heal you. Be at peace in my love and live in my light.

Saint Germain

Open to receive the light of God's love. Open to the majesty of God's presence. Open to God's grace. You are the ascension now! You are the ascension now! You are the ascension now! You are filled with the light of God.

Are you ready to step into your light body and experience ascension now? Are you ready to be cloaked in immutable fabric? Are you willing to let go of everything, to hand your life over to God, and serve at the feet of glory? Are you willing to make ascension your pathway? Let go of all your fears, and know that when you let go, all this and much greater will be added unto you. You are blessed and you are a blessing. Be at peace.

Babaji

Blessed and beloved beings of light, I love you. I am with you now and always. You have come to me through this book, which is an expression of God's love. You are magnetized to this teaching, which I have brought to this planet. That is because it is the pathway to glory, the way that you have chosen to bring you home again.

God is waiting with loving arms to welcome you, the prodigal son and daughter. God has not abandoned you. God has not cast you out of the Garden of Eden. You can return at any time, whenever you are ready to open to God's holy presence, the light of life, the immortal beingness within you.

That sacred tabernacle, within your heart, is the altar of God. There God dwells in glory. All you need do is open to its magnificent radiance. You have all that you need within you, right now, to accomplish this goal. Just open to God.

Allow God's grace to pour over you with waters of living substance, which heal and refresh you. The fount of living waters is right here, within your heart. It is not far off, impossible to reach. It is right here, right now. Open to those waters of eternal life. Open to the everflowing stream of magnetic substance, which is eternally refreshing, vivifying, and sustaining. That rich sustenance, the substance of eternal, immortal life is right here. Just dip your pitcher into the waters and drink deeply of immortality.

My promise to all living beings is to remain here with you and assist you in your ascension and in your realization of God consciousness. My role is your inner guru, and I will never leave you. You belong to me, and I belong to you. Trust in me to be your guide. For I will be with you, always and always, unto the end of the world.

Be at peace and live in the light of God's love.

Figure 22a. Etching by Gustav Doré.

Notes

Chapter 1
1. Matthew 13:46.
2. Job 28:15–18.

Chapter 2
1. Matthew 7:7.

Chapter 3
1. John 20:17.
2. Luke 24:51.
3. John 1.1.
4. Nirmalananda Giri, Swami, "Glory of Om."
5. John 21:23.
6. Book of Mormon: 3 Nephi 28:7.
7. Smith, Joseph, *The Doctrine and Covenants* 7:3.
8. Butler, 23.
9. Genesis 5:24.
10. Hebrews 11:5.
11. Genesis 14:18.
12. Psalms 110:4.
13. II Kings 2:8
14. II Kings 2:9–11.
15. II Kings 2:14.
16. II Kings 2:15.
17. Exodus 23:20–21.
18. Scribd, "The Third Book of Enoch," 4:1–2.
19. Genesis 6:2.

Chapter 4
1. Lippard, George, 394.

Chapter 5
1. Hallstrom, 39.
2. Srinivasan, 29. *Thiruvarutpa*, Canto 6, Chapter 13, verse 59.
3. Thirumoolar, Verse 80.

Chapter 6
1. Mahesh Yogi, *Bhagavad Gita* 4:8–9.

Chapter 7
1. "Li Ching-Yun Dead."

Chapter 9
1. Ascension Mastery International.

Chapter 10
1. Stevens, Luke.

Chapter 11
1. *www.craigwebb.ca.*
2. *www.marissabracke.com.*
3. *www.seandavidmorton.com.*

Chapter 12
1. Nirmalananda Giri, Chandogya Upanishad 3:6.2.2–3.
2. Deuteronomy 6:4.
3. Holmes, Ernest, 1926 edition, 256.
4. Hosea 13:14.
5. Isaiah 25:8.
6. Isaiah 35:8.
7. Skarin, *Beyond Mortal*, 5.

Chapter 13
1. Matthew 19:2.
2. Deuteronomy 6:4–5.
3. Matthew 22:39, Leviticus 19:18.

4. Luke 10:28.
5. John 3:5–8.

Chapter 14
1. John 4:14.
2. Scribd, "Mandala 9." *Rig-Veda* 9.113.07, 9.113.09, 9.113.10.
3. "Hatha Yoga Pradipika," 3.43,45.

Chapter 15
1. Govindan, 115.
2. Skarin, *Beyond Mortal*, 43.

Chapter 16
1. "Guru's Exit."
2. Edwards, Harry.

Chapter 17
1. Chopra, "Infinite Possibilities."

Chapter 19
1. Deuteronomy 6:5.

Chapter 21
1. Matthew 7:7.

Chapter 22
1. Matthew 7:7.

Bibliography

Books

Anandamayi, Sri Sri Anandamyi Sangha. *Ananda Varta*. Varanasi, India: Sri Sri Anandamayi Ceritebala Sosati, 1977.

Besant, Annie. *The Bhagavad-Gita*. Adyar. Madras, India: Theosophical Publishing House, 1973.

Besant, Annie Wood. *Theosophist Magazine September 1930–December 1930*. Whitefish, Mont.: Kessinger Publishing, 2003.

Blavatsky, Helena Petrovna. *The Secret Doctrine (3 Volume Set)*. Wheaton, Ill.: Theosophical Publishing House, 1980.

Bonaventure, Saint, Cardinal, and Ewert Cousins. *Bonaventure: The Soul's Journey Into God/The Tree of Life/The Life of St. Francis*. Mahwah, N.J.: Paulist Press, 1978.

Butler, Alban, Herbert Thurston, and Donald Attwater, ed. *Butler's Lives of the Saints*. Notre Dame, Ind.: Ave Maria Press, 1956.

Chang, Stephen T. *The Tao of Sexology: The Book of Infinite Wisdom*. San Francisco, Calif.: Tao Publishing, 1988.

Cherry, Joanna. *Living Mastery: The Expression of Your Divinity*. Port Washington, N.Y.: Oughten House International, 1997.

———. *Self Initiations: A Manual for Spiritual Breakthrough*. Mt. Shasta, Calif.: AMI Publishing, 1999.

Chopra, Deepak, MD. *Perfect Health*. New York: Harmony Books, 1991.

Crockett, Arthur, and Timothy Green Beckley. *Count Saint Germain: The New Age Prophet who Lives Forever.* New Brunswick, N.J.: Inner Light Publications, 1990.

Cruz, Joan Carroll, OCDS. *The Incorruptibles: A Study of the Incorruption of the Bodies of Various Catholic Saints and Beati.* Charlotte, N.C.: Tan Books, 1977.

Dowman, Keith. *Masters of Enchantment: The Lives and Legends of the Mahasiddhas.* Rochester, Vt.: Inner Traditions International, 1988.

————. *Masters of Mahamudra: Songs and Histories of the Eighty-Four Buddhist Siddhas.* Albany, N.Y.: State University of New York Press, 1985.

Fuller, Jean Overton. *Blavatsky and Her Teachers.* London: East West Publications, 1988.

Goswami, C.L., and M.A. Sastri. *Srimad Bhagavata Mahapurana.* Gorakhpur, U.P., India: Motilal Jalan, Gita Press, 1982.

Govindan, Marshall. *Babaji and the 18 Siddha Kriya Yoga Tradition.* Montreal, Canada: Kriya Yoga Publications, 1991.

Hallstrom, Lisa Lassell. *Mother of Bliss: Anandamayi Ma (1896–1982).* Cary, N.C.: Oxford University Press, 1999.

Ho, Kwok Man, and Joanne O'Brien. *The Eight Immortals of Taoism.* New York: Meridian, 1991.

Holmes, Ernest. *The Science of Mind.* California: Ancient Wisdom Publications (reprint of 1926 edition), 2006.

Holy Bible, The. Iowa Falls, Iowa: World Bible Publishers.

Jones, Charles W. *Saint Nicholas of Myra, Bari, and Manhattan: Biography of a Legend.* Chicago: University of Chicago Press, 1978.

Karyalaya, Gobind Bhawan. *The Bhagavadgita.* Gorakhpur, India: Gita Press, 1984.

King, Godfre Ray. *The "I AM" Discourses.* Schaumburg, Ill.: Saint Germain Press, 1940.

————. *The Magic Presence.* Schaumburg, Ill.: Saint Germain Press, 1982.

————. *Unveiled Mysteries (Original).* Schaumburg, Ill.: Saint Germain Press, 1982.

Leadbeater, C.W. *The Masters and the Path*. Madras, India: Theosophical Publishing House, Adyar, 1988.

Lippard, George. *Washington and His Generals "1776": The Legends of the American Revolution*. University Park, Penn.: Pennsylvania State University Press, 2008.

Liu, Da. *Taoist Health Exercise Book*. New York: Putnam Publishing Group, 1983.

Luk, A.D.K. *Law of Life: Book I & Book II*. Pueblo, Colo.: A.D.K. Luk Publications, 1989.

Mahesh Yogi, Maharishi. *Bhagavad Gita: A New Translation and Commentary With Sanskrit Text*. London: International SRM Publications, 1967.

Mavromataki, Maria. *Greek Mythology and Religion*. Athens, Greece: Haitalis, 1997.

Meyer, Ann P., and Peter V. Meyer. *Being a Christ!* Lemon Grove, Calif.: Dawning Publications, 1988.

Orr, Leonard. *Breaking the Death Habit: The Science of Everlasting Life*. Berkeley, Calif.: North Atlantic Books, Frog Ltd., 1998.

Remy, A.F.J. *The Catholic Encyclopedia*. New York: Robert Appleton Company, 1909. New Advent. *www.newadvent.org*.

Rinpoche, Tenzin Wangyal. *Healing With Form, Energy, and Light*. Ithaca, N.Y.: Snow Lion Publications, 2002.

Satyeswarananda Giri, Swami. *Babaji: The Divine Himalayan Yogi*. San Diego: Swami Satyeswarandanda Giri, 1984.

———. *Lahiri Mahasay: The Father of Kriya Yoga*. San Diego: Swami Satyeswarandanda Giri, 1983.

Skarin, Annalee. *Beyond Mortal Boundaries*. Marina del Rey, Calif.: DeVorss & Company, 1969.

———. *Ye Are Gods*. Marina del Rey, Calif.: DeVorss & Company, 1952.

Smith, Joseph. *The Book of Mormon, the Doctrine and Covenants, the Pearl of Great Price*. Salt Lake City: The Church of Jesus Christ of Latter-Day Saints, 1981.

Srinivasan, Comaraswamy. *An Introduction to the Philosophy of Ramalinga Swami*. Tiruchi, India: Ilakkia Nilayam, 1968.

Star, Jonathan. *Rumi: In the Arms of the Beloved.* New York: Tarcher Putnam, 1997. *www.lightandlife.com/lighthouse4.htm.*

Teresa of Avila. Trans. by E. Allison Peers. *The Life of Teresa of Jesus: The Autobiography of Teresa of Avila.* New York: Doubleday, 1991, Chapters 10–22.

Thirumoolar, Siddhar. Trans. by Dr. B. Natarajan. *Thirumandiram: A Classic of Yoga and Tantra.* Montreal, Canada: Kriya Yoga Publications, 1993.

Trochu, Abbé François. *Saint Bernadette Soubirous.* Charlotte, N.C.: Tan Books, 1985.

Tsu, Lao. Gia-Fu Feng and Jane English, trans. *Tao Te Ching.* London: Wildwood House, 1991.

Welch, Holmes. *Taoism: The Parting of the Way.* Boston: Beacon Press, 1971.

White, David Gordon. *The Alchemical Body: Siddha Traditions in Medieval India.* Chicago: University of Chicago Press, 1998.

Yogananda, Paramahansa. *Autobiography of a Yogi.* Los Angeles: Self-Realization Fellowship, 1981.

Yu, Lu K'uan. *Taoist Yoga, Alchemy & Immortality.* York Beach, Maine: Samuel Weiser, 1973.

Yudelove, Eric Steven. *100 Days to Better Health, Good Sex & Long Life: A Guide to Taoist Yoga & Chi Kung.* Woodbury, Minn.: Llewellyn Publications, 2002.

Zubko, Andy, ed. *Treasury of Spiritual Wisdom.* San Diego: Blue Dove Press, 1996.

Zvelebil, Kamil. *The Smile of Murugan on Tamil Literature of South India.* Leiden, Netherlands: E.J. Brill, 1973.

Newspaper and Magazine Articles

Bradshaw, Wesley. *The National Review* 4, No. 12, December 1880.

Brooke, Anthony. "Where is Annalee Skarin?" *Fate Magazine* 20, No. 5, May 1967.

"Guru's Exit," *Time,* Aug. 4, 1952. *www.time.com/time/magazine/article/0,9171,822420,00.html*

"Li Ching-Yun Dead; Gave His Age as 197," *New York Times* May 6, 1933, p. 13.

Siddhanath, Yogiraj Gurunath. "Cosmic Rebirth, My First Meeting with the Immortal Mahavatar Babaji." *Awareness Magazine*, July/August 2008, p. 14.

Websites*

Ambrosia Society, The. *www.ambrosiasociety.org.*

Association of the Miraculous Medal. *www.amm.org/catherine.asp.*

Ascension Mastery International. *www.ascensionmastery.com.*

AyurBalance, "What is my dosha?" *www.ayurbalance.com/explore_articlethreedoshas.htm.*

Bartleby.com. Great Books Online. *www.bartleby.com/100/216.html.*

Basilica of St. Anthony, The. *www.basilicadelsanto.org/ing/visita/storia .asp.*

Beyond Well Being. *www.beyondwellbeing.com/herbs/resveratrol.shtml.*

Body of St. Bernadette, The. *www.catholicpilgrims.com/lourdes/ bb_bernadette_body.htm.*

Bradshaw, Wesley, *The National Review* 4, No. 12, December 1880. *www.geocities.com/athens/aegean/2444/gwvision.html.*

Brainy Quote. *www.brainyquote.com/quotes/quotes/n/nathanielh153019 .html.*

Cherry, Joanna. "Annalee Skarin Taught on Earth After Her Ascension." Ascension Mastery International. *www.ascensionmastery .com/AnnaleeSkarin.html.*

"Chinese Preserved Monks." *http://sunzi1.lib.hku.hk/hkjo/ view/44/4401346.pdf.*

Chopra, Deepak. "Infinite Possibilities for Body, Mind and Soul." Monthly Newsletter, November 1998. *www.geocities.com/ ~spiritwalk/chopra.htm.*

Edwards, Harry. "Incorruptibility: Miracle or Myth?" *http://users .adam.com.au/bstett/PaIncorruptibility.htm.*

Elohim Arcturus Dictation of July 4, 1932. *http://janrice.tripod.com/ index-97.html.*

"Hatha Yoga Pradipika." *www.yogavidya.com/Yoga/ HathaYogaPradipika.pdf*.

"Ho-shou-wu, What's in an herb name?" *www.itmonline.org/arts/ hoshouwu.htm*.

Hughes, Marilynn. "The Mysterious Incorruptibles." *http:// catholic-saints.suite101.com/article.cfm/incorruptibles*.

"I Am Liberty: One Mind's Journey Through Ascension." *www .iamliberty.us*.

In Defense of the Cross. *www.indefenseofthecross.com*.

Internet Sacred Text Archive, The. "Apocrypha: 2 Esdras." *www .sacred-texts.com/bib/apo/es2.htm*.

"Man of Miracles." *www.mcn.org/1/Miracles/Charbel.html*.

Medieval Sourcebook: The Translation of Saint Nicholas. Fordham University Center. *www.fordham.edu/halsall/basis/nicholas-bari .html*.

My Yoga Online, Ojas-Ayurvedic Medicine and Energy. *www .myyogaonline.com/healthy_living_198_Ojas-Ayurvedic_Medicine_ and_Energy.html*.

Nirmalananda Giri, Swami. "Commentary on the Chandogya Upanishad: The Glory of Om." Atma Jyoti Ashram. *www .atmajyoti.org/up_chandogya_upanishad_1.asp*.

Reluctant Messenger, The: *The Life of Saint Issa, Best of the Sons of Men*, Translation by Notovitch. *www.reluctant-messenger.com/issa1.htm*.

Remy, A.F.J. *The Catholic Encyclopedia*. New York: Robert Appleton Company, 1909. New Advent. *www.newadvent.org*.

Root of the Matter, The. *www.therootofthematter.ca*.

Sacred Journeys. Andean Connection. *www.andes007.com*.

Sacred Text Archive. *The Garuda Purana. www.sacred-texts.com/hin/ gpu/index.htm*.

———. *The Sayings of Ramakrishna. www.sacred-texts.com/hin/rls/ rls25.htm*.

———. *The Upanishads, Part I*, translated by Max Muller: *www .sacred-texts.com/hin/sbe01/index.htm*.

———. *The Upanishads, Part II*, translated by Max Muller. *www .sacred-texts.com/hin/sbe15/sbe15076.htm*.

"Saint Rita of Cascia: Saint of the Impossible." *www.catholictradition .org/Cascia/rita.htm.*

"St. Teresa of Avila, Doctor of Prayer 1515–1582." *http:// catholic-saints.suite101.com/article.cfm/st_teresa_of_ avila#ixzzODNxNcHyP&A.*

"St. Zita, Virgin." Global Catholic Network. *www.ewtn.com/library/ mary/zita.htm.*

"Sariras, Ringsels and Mummies." *http://philosophy.dude.googlepages .com/sariras.html.*

Scribd. "Mandala 9." *www.scribd.com/doc/7781880/Mandala-9.*

———. "The Third Book of Enoch." *www.scribd.com/ doc/16741079/3a-the-Third-Book-of-Enoch.*

Star, Jonathan. *Rumi: In the Arms of the Beloved.* New York: Tarcher Putnam, 1997. *www.lightandlife.com/lighthouse4.htm.*

Stevens, Luke. *www.geocities.com/athens/aegean/2444/gwvision.html.*

Sufi Movement International. *www.sufimovement.net/path.htm.*

"Story of Saint Cecilia, The." *www.pureinsight.org/node/3099.*

Swami Sivananda's Page. Yoga Vidya. *www.my.yoga-vidya.org/profile/ Sivananda.*

"White Buffalo Calf Woman." *www.kstrom.net/isk/arvol/buffpipe.html.*

"Wish-Fulfilling Jewel Mirror." *www.zhaxizhuoma.net.*

*All Websites accessed July 2009.

Index

About the Author

Dr. Susan Shumsky is a foremost spirituality expert, a pioneer in the self-development field, and a highly acclaimed and greatly respected professional speaker, New Thought minister, and Doctor of Divinity. She has authored *Divine Revelation*, in continuous print with Simon & Schuster since 1996, as well as her three award-winning books *Miracle Prayer*, published by Random House, *Exploring Chakras*, and *How to Hear the Voice of God*, plus the books *Exploring Meditation* and *Exploring Auras*. Her books have been published in several languages worldwide.

Dr. Shumsky has practiced self-development disciplines since 1967. For 22 of those years she lived in the Himalayas, the Swiss Alps, and other secluded areas, under the personal guidance of enlightened master from India Maharishi Mahesh Yogi, founder of Transcendental Meditation and guru of the Beatles and Deepak Chopra. She was on Maharishi's personal staff for seven of those years. She then studied New Thought and metaphysics for another 20 years and became a Doctor of Divinity.

Dr. Shumsky has taught yoga, meditation, prayer, and intuition to thousands of students all over the world since 1970 as a true New Thought pioneer. She has been featured in *Woman's World*, *GQ*, *Cosmopolitan*, nationally syndicated network TV, and "Coast to Coast AM" with George Noory.

She is founder of Divine Revelation®, a complete technology for contacting the divine presence and listening to the inner voice. She now travels extensively, facilitating workshops, seminars, spiritual retreats, as well as tours to India, Peru, and other sacred destinations worldwide. Dr. Shumsky also offers spiritual coaching, prayer therapy sessions, and breakthrough sessions.

On our Website, *www.divinerevelation.org*, you can:

- Join our mailing list.
- See Dr. Shumsky's itinerary.
- Invite Dr. Shumsky to speak to your group.
- Find Divine Revelation teachers in your area.
- See the Divine Revelation curriculum.
- Register for Divine Revelation retreats and Teacher Training Courses.
- Order books, audio and video products, or home study courses.
- Order beautiful, full-color prints of the illustrations in this book.
- Register for telephone sessions and teleconferences with Dr. Shumsky.
- Register for spiritual tours to sacred destinations worldwide.

When you join our mailing list at *www.divinerevelation.org*, you will receive a free, downloadable, guided mini-meditation, plus access to our free weekly teleconference prayer circle, our free online community group forum, and free teleseminars.

As a gift for reading this book, please use the following special discount code when you register for one of our ascended master retreats, divine revelation retreats, or tours at *www.divinetravels.com*: ASCENSION108.

We want to hear from you. Please write about your personal experiences of ascension, of visitations, and of inner contact with the divine beings and your higher self:

Teaching of Intuitional Metaphysics
P.O. Box 7185
New York, NY 10116
212-946-5132
divinerev@aol.com

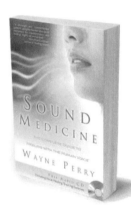

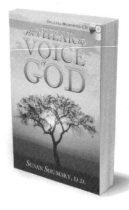

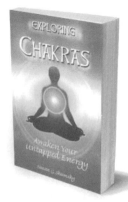